The Natural World in Latin American Literatures

The Natural World in Latin American Literatures

Ecocritical Essays on Twentieth Century Writings

Edited by
ADRIAN TAYLOR KANE

McFarland & Company, Inc., Publishers

Jefferson, North Carolina, and London

LIBRARY OF CONGRESS CATALOGUING-IN-PUBLICATION DATA

The natural world in Latin American literatures : ecocritical essays
    on twentieth century writings / edited by Adrian Taylor Kane.
        p.   cm.
    Includes bibliographical references and index.

    ISBN 978-0-7864-4287-4
    softcover : 50# alkaline paper

    1. Spanish American fiction — 20th century — History and
criticism.   2. Latin American fiction — 20th century — History
and criticism.   3. Ecology in literature.   4. Human ecology in
literature.   5. Ecocriticism.   I. Kane, Adrian Taylor, 1976–
PQ7082.N7N28 2010
860.9'36 — dc22

                                                2010008149

British Library cataloguing data are available

Front cover ©2010 Shutterstock

Manufactured in the United States of America

*McFarland & Company, Inc., Publishers
    Box 611, Jefferson, North Carolina 28640
    www.mcfarlandpub.com*

"La liberación no sólo la ansiaban los humanos.
Toda la ecología gemía. La revolución
es también de lagos, ríos, árboles, animales."
[Not only humans desired liberation.
The whole of ecology cried for it. The revolution
is also of lakes, rivers, trees, animals.]
— *Ernesto Cardenal*

Table of Contents

III. ECOLOGY AND THE SUBALTERN

Preface

From the *Popol Vuh* to postmodernism, imagery of the natural world has played varied and important roles in Latin American literature.[1] The imperial gaze in Christopher Columbus's letters to the Spanish monarchs, Andres Bello's call for cultural independence through agrarianism in "La agricultura de la zona tórrida" (Agriculture of the Torrid Zone) and Ernesto Cardenal's Sandinista poem "Ecología" (Ecology) are but a few examples of the many ways in which nature has remained embedded in cultural discourses and historical projects throughout the centuries in Latin America.[2] In comparison with the burgeoning quantity of ecocritical[3] scholarship seen in Anglophone literary and cultural studies, however, and despite what Scott Slovic describes as "a rapidly expanding international movement in this field," environmental criticism of Latin American cultural production has been slower to take root, as other theoretical discourses have continued to dominate during the last fifteen years.[4] The present volume is thus intended to help advance the discussion of ecocriticism among Latin Americanists, and to afford ecocritics further insight into the cultural discourses that have informed perceptions of the relation between humans and their environments in Latin America.

Perhaps the body of Latin American literature in which the analysis of the nonhuman natural world has received the most critical attention has been the Spanish American regional novel of the 1920s and 30s. In 1933 Alfred Coester observed in his article "Maelstroms, Green Hells, and Sentimental Jungles," that "a decidedly new use of the landscape has come into vogue. It is no longer a mere setting or decoration. It has become a character in the story, or, if not precisely a character, at least a maleficent influence which neither human beings nor animals can escape."[5] Six years later, Arturo Torres Rioseco asserted that the rural setting of such novels made them "authentically American," and grouped them together in his study as "La novela de la tierra" (the novel of the land/earth or telluric novel).[6] Although neither Coester nor Torres Rioseco expounded a theory of the regional or telluric novel, in recent decades critics have returned to these texts[7] through the lens of contemporary literary theories. Carlos Alonso, for example, posits that the regionalist attempt to create an autochthonous literature through imagery of the

1

natural world is the result of a perceived crisis of identity in the face of external modernizing forces and the threat of United States imperialism.[8] Sharon
Magnarelli, arguing from a feminist perspective, calls attention to the misog-
ynistic portrayal of women and nature as threatening "others" in certain
regional novels.[9] Jorge Marcone has proposed that, in particular, the *novela
de la selva*, or romance of the jungle, embodies a form of thought that anticipates and illuminates contemporary environmental debates.[10] Most recently,
Jennifer French has argued that the regional narratives from this period belong
to the international literature on colonialism, as they reflect "the global struggle for access to land and control of natural resources" in the context of the
"invisible" British economic empire in Latin America.[11] She observes that several of the issues at stake in these texts, such as economic and environmental justice, are far from resolved today and calls for increased critical attention
to what she views as "one of the most neglected bodies of texts in the Spanish American canon."[12]

Beyond criticism dedicated to Spanish American regionalism, special
editions of *Hispanic Journal* (Fall 1998) and *Anales de literatura hispanoamericana* (2004) are significant early contributions to environmental criticism of
Latin American literature. Janet Pérez and Wendell Aycock's *Climate and Literature: Reflections of Environment* (1995) contains several essays that focus on
the role of climate in Spanish American fiction, and Patrick Murphy's *Literature of Nature: An International Sourcebook* (1998) contains a brief section
on Latin America. *Teaching North American Environmental Literature* also
includes chapters on Mexican and Chicana/o literature as well as a thorough
list of resources related to environmental issues on both sides of the border.
A modest quantity of ecocritical articles on Latin American cultural production has also appeared in *Interdisciplinary Studies in Literature and Environment*, the flagship journal for the Association for the Study of Literature and
Environment (ASLE) as well as other journals such as *Hispania*. For readers
interested in environmentally oriented poetry from Spanish America, Niall
Binns's *Callejón sin salida: La crisis ecológica en la poesía hispanoamericana* is
a valuable introduction.[13] And finally, *Caribbean Literature and the Environment: Between Nature and Culture* is an important anthology whose essays
highlight the inexorable relationship between landscape and the region's history of colonization.

The present volume is intended to contribute to the discussion initiated
by this early ecocritical work in the field of Latin American studies. The first
section, "Nature, Modernity and Technology in Twentieth-Century Latin
American Fiction," is based on the premise that an historical approach to literature through the lens of ecocriticism offers a more profound understanding of the complex nature/culture relationship that inevitably shifts with

historical circumstances. As environmental historian Shawn Miller observes, "The human relationship with nature is never static. Cultures change, or are changed, sometimes for the ecological better, sometimes for the worse. And nature itself changes, sometimes handing out new, substantial benefits to humans, sometimes painful liabilities, and in a few cases, utter destruction."[14] Since the primary focus of this volume is twentieth-century narrative, the first section explores how nature is incorporated into Latin American fiction at different moments throughout the century (including brief glances into the nineteenth century and a glimpse of the twenty-first), and how authors from different generations negotiate the relationship between the natural environment and concepts such as modernity and technology.

Jonathan Tittler's essay "Ecological Criticism and Spanish American Fiction: An Overview" begins with a brief introduction to the concept of ecocriticism, locates it within the tradition of Western thought and provides a broad view of the possibilities of this form of criticism for Spanish American fiction. He offers re-readings of regional narratives of the 1920s and compares these texts to novels by Mario Vargas Llosa from the 1980s. He suggests that if the regional *novela de la tierra* is a novel of the land, *El hablador* (*The Storyteller*) by Vargas Llosa moves toward a *novela de la Tierra*, or novel of the Earth, in its environmental consciousness. My essay "Nature and the Discourse of Modernity in Spanish American Avant-Garde Fiction" attempts to demonstrate the ways in which the discourse of modernity affected representations of the environment in this often overlooked body of works from the 1920s. The first half of my essay examines the ways in which avant-garde fiction moves away from nineteenth-century realist and naturalist traditions, while the second part is dedicated to the relation between nature and urban spaces as represented in texts from this period. The third essay, "Nature in the Twentieth-Century Latin American Novel (1900–1967) and in *Cien años de soledad* of García Márquez" by Raymond L. Williams, provides an overview of several canonical texts by authors such as Carlos Fuentes, João Guimarães Rosa, Jorge Isaacs, José Eustacio Rivera, Vargas Llosa, and Gabriel García Márquez. He begins by foregrounding the importance of land in Latin American fiction and continues his discussion by demonstrating how representations of nature and technology ranging from neoclassicism to modernism filter into García Márquez's masterpiece *Cien años de soledad*. In the final essay of the first section, "The Long and Winding Road of Technology from *María* to *Cien años de soledad* to *Mantra*: An Ecocritical Reading," Gustavo Llarull places three seemingly disparate novels into fruitful dialogue by analyzing the representation of the nature/technology relationship in Jorge Isaacs's *María* (1867), García Márquez's *Cien años de soledad* (1967; One Hundred Years of Solitude), and Rodrigo Fresán's *Mantra* (2001). In doing so, Llarull illuminates changes in perspective with regard to the complex nature/technology relationship from the romantic era to the millennium. By examining texts from the periods represented in these four essays, the first section of this anthology seeks a more profound understanding of the rhetoric that has shaped cultural attitudes toward nature and guided historical projects that have ultimately led to today's environmental crises.

Rooted in the notion that the edifice of Latin American history is underpinned by the continual creation and collapse of utopian projects, section II of the current volume, "Environmental Utopias and Dystopias," is dedicated to the intersections between the environment and discourses of utopia. The first essay, "Caribbean Utopias and Dystopias: The Emergence of the Environmental Writer and Artist," is an analysis of Caribbean culture in which Lizabeth Paravisini-Gebert provides several examples of how writers, artists, and musicians across the region have engaged with environmental issues (such as U.S. test bombings in Vieques, Puerto Rico, rampant development in Martinique and deforestation in Haiti) both as activists and in their own creative endeavors. She identifies in their rhetoric a common theme of "a return to an often-imagined prior sense of national identity rooted in an agrarian economy that is the pre-requisite for an environmentally sustainable national wholeness." In the following essay, "Paradise Lost: A Reading of *Waslala* from the Perspectives of Feminist Utopianism and Ecofeminism," Marisa Pereyra suggests that in Gioconda Belli's 1996 novel environmentalist and feminist discourses converge to subvert the patriarchal power structure and create a common utopian project for a society in which women and nature are liberated from oppression. In the final essay of this section, "Barbarian Civilization: Travel and Landscape in *Don Segundo Sombra* and the Contemporary Argentinean Novel," Martín Camps compares the representation of the pampas in *Don Segundo Sombra* with the varied Argentinean landscapes in novels by contemporary writers Héctor Tizón, Juan José Saer, Osvaldo Soriano, and Mempo Giardinelli. He argues that the meat industry's quest to modernize Argentina through capitalist expansion and domination of the pampas is an ironic inversion of the utopian discourse of progress implied in Sarmiento's notion of civilization vs. barbarism. That is, the so-called project of civilization marks the beginning of a barbaric process that has led to an ecological imbalance. He ultimately suggests that the prevalent use of provincial landscapes in contemporary Argentine fiction might indicate a return to a form of regionalism as a reaction to the forces of globalization, which seek to erase heterogeneity.

The third and final section, "Ecology and the Subaltern," explores the relation between the environment and marginalized groups in Latin America and the Southwestern United States. Dora Ramírez-Dhoore, in "Dissecting

Environmental Racism: Redirecting the 'Toxic' in Alicia Gaspar de Alba's *Desert Blood* and Helena María Viramontes's *Under the Feet of Jesus*," examines how the 2005 Gaspar de Alba novel and the 1995 Viramontes novel function as resistance narratives to forms of racism and environmental injustice with regard to migrant and immigrant workers in the U.S.-Mexico border region. Specifically, she analyzes the uses of myth in contrasting the rhetoric of difference that often leads to toxic environmental conditions (such as water contaminated by pesticides) in marginalized communities. Traci Roberts-Camps's essay, "Nature as Articulate and Inspired in *Oficio de tinieblas* by Rosario Castellanos," compares the human-nature relationship in two texts regarding indigenous groups that have been systematically oppressed throughout the histories of Mexico and Guatemala. In her reading of Castellanos's 1962 novel (translated as *The Book of Lamentations*) she finds commonalities with the Mayan book of advice, the *Popol Vuh*, particularly with respect to these works' non–Western representations of nature as articulate and inspirited. Finally, Mark D. Anderson, in "National Nature and Ecologies of Abjection in Brazilian Literature at the Turn of the Twentieth Century," provides an overview of the uses of Paradise throughout the history of Brazilian literature, arguing that the foundational discourse of Brazil's nationhood was based on the trope of abundant nature. He subsequently analyzes the creation of a Brazilian literature of ecological otherness that frequently represents environmental and cultural difference not only as abjection, but also as a threat to the modern nation. He ends by addressing counter-discourses that have formed, often locally, to challenge the exclusion of inhabitants of marginalized regions from Brazilian concepts of cultural citizenship. In different ways, the three essays in this final section move toward what T.V. Reed calls for as a form of environmental justice ecocriticism that addresses questions of race and class.[15] Ramírez-Dhoore confronts issues of environmental racism,[16] Roberts-Camps examines the representation of nature outside of the hegemonic *mestizo* culture in Latin America, and Anderson explores the racialization of pseudo-scientific discourse in the Brazilian cultural tradition.

The content of this volume furthermore address two previous charges against ecocriticism. Elizabeth M. DeLoughrey, Renée K. Gosson, and George B. Handley, lamenting the lack of ecocritical focus on the Caribbean and Latin America in "American" studies, assert in the introduction to *Caribbean Literature and the Environment* that "Ironically, a field that upholds the environment as the predominant spatial focus of analysis has quite rigidly adhered to that which is most inimical to ecology itself: a bounded national frame."[17] The current anthology transcends national boundaries by presenting analyses of literary and cultural production ranging from Patagonia to Amazonia to the Chihuahua Desert, and in doing so attempts to convey a sense of the ecological, cultural and linguistic diversity of Latin America. It also seeks to address the problem observed by Ursula K. Heise that "monolingualism is currently one of ecocriticism's most serious intellectual limitations."[18] While the majority of the following essays focus on Spanish American literature, others analyze texts originally written in English, French, Portuguese and Classical Quiché. The decision to include an essay on Chicana literature is based on the notion that although Mexican and Chicana/o literatures emerge from "a distinct vantage point on either side of the United States — Mexico border, [...] they remain linked by common bioregions, immigration exchanges, and some shared narrative traditions."[19]

In addition to the multiplicity of texts and cultures analyzed in this volume, the authors of these essays employ a range of methodologies that reflect the diversity and continued evolution of ecocriticism. As Slovic observes, "There is no single, dominant worldview guiding ecocritical practice — no single strategy at work from example to example of ecocritical writing or teaching."[20] Although none of the following essays focus exclusively on analysis of the city, several of them include sections on representations of the relation between nature and urban spaces, and thus acknowledge the expansion of the concept of ecocriticism over the last ten years beyond the study of texts that are imbued with imagery and contemplation of the natural world to include urban environments, suburbs and rural areas.[21] The forms of environmental criticism practiced in this anthology converge at various moments with literary history, aesthetic theory, postcolonialism, feminism, Marxism, and cultural studies. What binds these essays together is the common conviction that the scrutiny of the diverse roles and representations of the environment in literary and cultural production affords a more profound understanding of unique cultures and the human-nature relations within them.

NOTES

1. See José Ramón Naranjo's "La ecología profunda y el *Popol Vuh*" for a reading of the *Popol Vuh* in relation to deep ecology.

2. See page 126 of Mary Louise Pratt's *Imperial Eyes: Travel Writing and Transculturation* for a discussion of how the writings of Columbus and other early "inventors of America" influenced Alexander von Humboldt's vision of nature. See pages 172–78 of Pratt's study and pages 2–8 of Jennifer French's *Nature, Neo-Colonialism and the Spanish American Regional Writers*, for analysis of Bello's poem.

3. Jonathan Tittler discusses definitions of ecocriticism (ecological criticism) in the first essay of the current anthology. Scott Slovic's description of ecocriticism is also particularly useful: "the study of explicitly environmental texts by way of any scholarly approach or, conversely, the scrutiny of ecological implications and human-nature relations in any literary text, even texts that seem, at first glance, oblivious of the nonhuman world." Arnold, et al., "Forum on Literatures of the Environment," 1102. Lawrence Buell has sug-

gested that "environmental criticism" might be a more appropriate term given that ecocriticism "implies a non-existent methodological holism." *The Future of Environmental Criticism*, 12. I use the terms ecocriticism and environmental criticism interchangeably in this preface and have allowed individual contributors to establish their own terminology in their essays. For summaries of the emergence of ecocriticism see Chapter 1 of Buell's *The Future of Environmental Criticism*, Ursula K. Heise's "The Hitchhiker's Guide to Ecocriticism," Fred Waage's "Introduction: Teaching Environmental Literature — A Trek through the Field," and chapter 1 of Greg Garrard's *Ecocriticism*.

4. Slovic points to the increasing amount of international submissions to the journal *Interdisciplinary Studies in Literature and Environment* as evidence that "the notion that environmental literature is an exclusively Americanist subject holds little water." Arnold, et al., "Forum on Literatures of the Environment," 1102.

5. Coester, "Maelstroms, Green Hells, and Sentimental Jungles," 43.

6. Torres Rioseco, *Novelistas contemporáneos de América*, 5.

7. Among the major regional narratives are: Horacio Quiroga's *Cuentos de amor, de locura, y de muerte* (1917; Stories of love, madness, and death) and *Los desterrados* (1926; *The Exiles and Other Stories*) José Eustasio Rivera's *La vorágine* (1924; *The Vortex*), Ricardo Güiraldes's *Don Segundo Sombra* (1926), Rómulo Gallegos's *Doña Bárbara* (1929) and *Canaima* (1935), and Ciro Alegría's *La serpiente de oro* (1935; *The Golden Serpent*).

8. Alonso, *The Spanish American Regional Novel*, 50.

9. See "Women and Nature," chapter 2 of Magnarelli's study *The Lost Rib*.

10. Marcone, "De retorno a lo natural: *La serpiente de oro*, la 'novela de la selva' y la crítica ecológica," 299.

11. French, *Nature, Neo-Colonialism, and the Spanish American Regional Writers* 29.

12. Ibid., 37, 8.

13. See also Forns-Broggi, "Ecology and Latin American Poetry."

14. Miller, *An Environmental History of Latin America*, 45.

15. T.V. Reed, "Toward an Environmental Justice Ecocriticism," 145–62.

16. The Reverend Benjamin Chavis defines environmental racism as "racial discrimination in environmental policy-making and the enforcement of regulations and laws, the deliberate targeting of people of color communities for toxic waste facilities, the official sanctioning of the life-threatening presence of poisons and pollutants in our communities, and the history of excluding people of color from leadership in the environmental movement." Qtd. in Adamson, Evans, and Stein, *The Environmental Justice Reader*, 4.

17. DeLoughrey, Gosson, and Handley, *Caribbean Literature and the Environment*, 27. Slovic disputes this assertion. See note 4.

18. Heise, "The Hitchhiker's Guide to Ecocriticism," 513. She acknowledges that "Critics such as Patrick Murphy and [Scott] Slovic have also made sustained efforts to spread ecocritical analysis to the study of other cultures and languages, though their success has been limited." Andrea Parra notes that Chicano and Chicana critics have also "been rather slow to take up the literary ecocritical cause," suggesting that "perhaps ecocriticism has been constituted as primarily an Anglo domain." Arnold et al., "Forum on Literatures of the Environment," 1100.

19. Marcone and Solis Ybarra, "Mexican and Chicana/o Environmental Writing," 93.

20. Arnold et al., "Forum on Literatures of the Environment," 1102.

21. In *Beyond Nature Writing*, Wallace and Armbuster contend that "If ecocriticism is to have any real force as a theoretical and pedagogical approach, ecocritics need to attend to the landscapes in which most people live — cities, suburbs, and rural areas" (6). See also Bennett and Teague, *The Nature of Cities*. The essays in their anthology "explore the theoretical issues that arise when one attempts to adopt and adapt an environmental perspective to analyze urban life" (10).

WORKS CITED

Adamson, Joni, Evans, Mei Mei, and Rachel Stein, eds. *The Environmental Justice Reader: Politics Poetics and Pedagogy.* Tucson: University of Arizona Press, 2002.

Alonso, Carlos J. *The Spanish American Regional Novel: Modernity and Autochthony.* Cambridge: Cambridge University Press, 1990.

Arnold, Jean, et al. "Forum on Literatures of the Environment." *PMLA* 114.5 (Oct. 1999): 1089–1104.

Bennet, Michael, and David W. Teague, eds. *The Nature of Cities: Ecocriticism and Urban Environments.* Tucson: University of Arizona Press, 1999.

Binns, Niall. *¿Callejón sin salida? La crisis ecológica en la poesía hispanoamericana.* Zaragoza: Prensas Universitarias de Zaragoza, 2004.

Buell, Lawrence. *The Future of Environmental Criticism: Environmental Crisis and Literary Imagination.* Blackwell Manifestos. Malden, MA: Blackwell, 2005.

Christensen, Laird, Long, Mark C., and Fred Waage, eds. *Teaching North American Environmental Literature.* Options for Teaching. New York: MLA of America, 2008.

Coester, Alfred. "Maelstroms, Green Hells, and Sentimental Jungles," *Hispania* 16.1 (Feb.-Mar. 1933): 43–50.

DeLoughrey, Elizabeth M., Gosson, Renée K., and George B. Handley, eds. *Caribbean Literature and the Environment: Between Nature and Culture.* New World Studies. Charlottesville: University Press of Virginia, 2005.

French, Jennifer. *Nature, Neo-Colonialism and the Spanish American Regional Writers.* Reencounters with Colonialism: New Perspectives on the Americas. Hanover: Dartmouth College Press, 2005.

Forns-Broggi, Roberto. "Ecology and Latin American Poetry." In Murphy et al., *Literature of Nature,* 374–84.

Heise, Ursula K. "The Hitchhiker's Guide to Ecocriticism." *PMLA* 121.2 (March 2006): 503–16.

Magnarelli, Sharon. *The Lost Rib: Female Characters in the Spanish-American Novel.* Lewisburg: Bucknell University Press, 1985.

Marcone, Jorge. "De retorno a lo natural: *La serpiente de oro,* la 'novela de la selva' y la crítica ecológica." *Hispania* 81.2 (May 1998): 299–308.

_____ and Priscilla Solis Ybarra. "Mexican and Chicana/o Environmental Writing: Unearthing and Inhabiting." In Christensen et al., *Teaching North American Environmental Literature,* 93–111.

Miller, Shawn William. *An Environmental History of Latin America.* New Approaches to the Americas. Cambridge: Cambridge University Press, 2007.

Murphy, Patrick, Terry Gifford and Katsunori Yamazato, eds. *Literature of Nature: An International Sourcebook.* Chicago: Fitzroy Dearborn Publishers, 1998.

Naranjo, José Ramón. "La ecología profunda y el *Popol Vuh.*" *Anales de literatura hispanoamericana* 33 (2004): 85–100.

Pérez, Janet and Wendell Aycock, eds. *Climate and Literature: Reflections of Environment.* Studies in Comparative Literature 25. Lubbock: Texas Tech University Press, 1995.

Pratt, Mary Louise. *Imperial Eyes: Travel Writing and Transculturation.* London: Routledge, 1992.

Reed, T.V. "Toward an Environmental Justice Ecocriticism." In Adamson et al., *The Environmental Justice Reader,* 145–62.

Torres Rioseco, Arturo. *Novelistas contemporáneos de América.* Santiago, Chile: Nascimento, 1939.

Waage, Fred. "Introduction: Teaching Environmental Literature — A Trek through the Field." In Christensen et al., *Teaching North American Environmental Literature,* 9–23.

Wallace, Kathleen R., and Karla Armbuster, eds. *Beyond Nature Writing: Expanding the Boundaries of Ecocriticism.* Under the Sign of Nature: Explorations in Ecocriticism. Charlottesville: University Press of Virginia, 2001.

I. Nature, Modernity and Technology in Twentieth-Century Latin American Fiction

Ecological Criticism and Spanish American Fiction: An Overview

Jonathan Tittler

Although ecological criticism has gained notable traction among literary and cultural scholars in the U.S. and western Europe over the past dozen or so years, it is still a minority school of thought and political movement. Ecocriticism is composed of two discrete parts, which also belong to separate disciplines: ecology and criticism. Ecology is a relatively young science, having appeared in the scientific literature for the first time in the 1860s, when its parent disciplines, biology and chemistry, had matured sufficiently so as to allow researchers to study the relationship between the one and the other. Ecology studies the systems of interrelationship between organisms and the environments that support them.

Ecology could study, for example, the way in which certain mollusks (let's say, oysters) depend upon certain levels of salinity or other chemicals in the water so that the micro-organisms on which they feed can live in sufficient number. It would study the variations that occur with seasonal changes, with different temperatures and hours of sunlight. It would take into account the necessary migrations of vertebrates (perhaps lizards, fish, or mammals) that depend upon the mollusks as a food source. And those displacements could be connected to birds of prey or human beings that, in turn, consider those organisms a tasty meal. These animals, of course, would — while alive — create solid and liquid waste that fertilizes or otherwise affects the surrounding ground and water, feeding, sickening, or killing other organisms in those environs. What I am sketching is not just a food chain or habitat but an entire ecosystem, where elements both living and inorganic enter into a series of relations that constitute a dynamic and sustainable equilibrium. Remove or change one element and everything else must adjust, if it can. If it can't, it dies.

As always, etymologies help explain the basis of a concept. "Ecology" consists of two parts, both from the ancient Greek: *oikos* means "house" or "home," and *logos* can mean "word," "logic," or "order." In common parlance, ecology studies the "order of the house," with "house" given the sense of our natural surroundings: the Earth or that part of our planet that sustains life, the biosphere. What mankind seems not to want to learn, in practice at least, is that sullying our house or subjecting it to disorder threatens our well-being and even our survival. Exhausting our natural resources at an ever accelerating pace has put us into a crisis, one in which we are committing gradual suicide as a species (that the earth itself would rebound and survive the lifespan of our species goes without saying). Understanding these principles is the *sine qua non* of ecological literacy. It is hardly an overstatement to declare that extending ecological literacy throughout society should be among the highest priorities for educators and thinkers who believe thriving, rather than merely surviving, is crucial to mankind.

These comments help clarify the label "ecology," but what is ecological *criticism*? For that explanation I shall cite Cheryll Glotfelty, editor of *The Ecocriticism Reader: Landmarks in Literary Ecology*, an anthology that has become seminal for the movement. In her introduction to the collection, Glotfelty says:

> ecocriticism is the study of the relationship between literature and the physical environment. Just as feminist criticism examines language and literature from a gender-conscious perspective, and Marxist criticism brings an awareness of modes of production and economic class to its reading of texts, ecocriticism takes an earth-centered approach to literary studies.[1]

One question ecocritics might ask, she adds, is how environmental crises seep into literature. The list of crises would be interminable, but to mention a few outstanding examples of the grave ecological problems that daily confront the Americas and the world, consider the following: the lead and asbestos in many of the homes in which we and our children live; the increasing demand and consumption of petroleum (doubtless a major cause of the current war in Iraq); the greenhouse gases spewed constantly from the exhaust pipes of our cars and the chimneys of our factories; the resulting "climate change" (euphemism for global warming) that threatens to melt the global ice caps and inundate many of the world's coastal cities (former Vice-president Al Gore's Academy Award-winning documentary movie *An Inconvenient Truth*[2] has been uniquely effective in bringing this aspect to the attention of a broad audience); world population growth in general, and in relation to diminishing potable water supplies in particular; the relentless clearing of the Amazon jungle, the "lungs of the world," by the lumber, sugar cane, soy bean, and cattle industries; the hunting to near-extinction of certain species of whales in the oceans of the Antarctic; radiation leaks from atomic plants at

Three Mile Island and Chernobyl; the environmental ravages of continuing wars in the Middle East, etc. *ad nauseum.*

The manifestations of the current crisis may be ubiquitous, but the origins are not always obvious. Although it may sound like heresy, one of the most powerful sources of our present attitude of indifference toward nature is the Judeo-Christian tradition, i.e., the Bible. In the book of Genesis, Adam — made in the image of God — names all the other creatures of Creation, exercising thereby his superiority over those things. On the basis of that story, known to all, values are expressed and perpetuated that give license to the pitiless exploitation of the non-human world.[3] Quite a bit later (some two thousand years, in fact), at the dawn of the modern era, in what is called the European Renaissance, that anthropocentrism is taken to new heights. Having managed to separate itself from the Christian church, humanism took as a worthy object of study the human being, not as a symbol of God's grandeur but as a valuable entity in itself. If with the Bible Western civilization generated a human-centered worldview, humanism took that system of values and extended it to unsuspected proportions.

At this point the plot thickens considerably. Two additional forces enter: science and technology. We tend to equate the two nowadays, but according to historians of science they have separate trajectories.[4] Science, originally an offspring of natural philosophy, was always urban, aristocratic, and abstract. Technology, in contrast, has its roots in the countryside, where it was the domain of humble practitioners. It is not until the middle of the nineteenth century that the spread of democracy permits these two currents to flow together. But once the coalescence of science and technology takes place there is no stopping it. Their combined force, buoyed by the supportive attitudes of both the church and secular society, wages an assault on nature's bounty. These cultural conditions create the possibility of today's unrestrained industrial, communicational, and consumerist development, as well as the precarious state of the environment it is our purpose to remedy.

According to Newton's second law of physics, every force in the universe generates a contrary force of the same magnitude. To resist the titanic forces of science and technology two theories have emerged whose vectors point in the opposite direction. The first is of common knowledge although not universal acceptance: natural selection. Fruit of the naturalist Charles Darwin's empirical sense and imagination, natural selection proposes that the diverse life forms in the world are the result of an impersonal and mechanical process that moves chronologically in one lone direction — from the simple and generic toward the complex and specialized. The most important aspect of Darwinism is not the complex and specialized nature of the species *Homo sapiens* but rather the process that has produced the species. Although traditional

Western vision would like to see there proof of mankind's supremacy in the world hierarchy, science tells us that the most successful species, in terms of the number of individual specimens, is the cockroach. Similarly, the species with the most families and classes are the fungi. We always see what we want or need to see, not necessarily what existence presents us.

Another theory opposed to the dominant Western paradigm is what has come to be called "Deep Ecology."[5] This relatively young movement (its naming dates back no farther than the 1970s) begins by negating anthropocentrism and goes from there to mount an alternative scale of values in favor of bio-centrism or eco-centrism. In lieu of the instant gratification of consumerism and profits, it advocates a balance between unavoidable consumption for the maintenance of wellbeing and the restoration of natural resources (or the use of renewable resources, such as trees, wind, or sun). It emphasizes the diversity of species of certain ecological zones in order to ensure the sustainability of the entire system, not just certain, more aggressive or self-concerned individuals. It considers mankind to be the earth's shepherd rather than its proprietor. And — perhaps most fundamental of all — it projects a vision of the world that is not partial or atomistic but rather holistic and interwoven. In the words of Barry Commoner, a leading biologist and one of the founders of the ecological movement in the United States, "Everything is connected to everything else."[6] When there is a violation or rift, every part of the system is impacted by the force of the blow. The interconnectedness at the base of ecocritical thinking is what has earned it the sobriquet of the "subversive science." Its subversiveness goes so far as to question the subject/object relation that empowers empirical science. Well considered, there is no way to measure any natural phenomenon (let's say the temperature of water), without affecting or changing that very phenomenon. Our thermometer is always at a certain temperature or another, and when we dip it we cannot help but inflect our object of study. Just as we cannot get outside the biosphere in order to analyze it dispassionately, there is nowhere for us to run when we ruin it.

Now, let's consider how some of the aspects of an ecocritical discourse apply to the reading of Spanish American narrative texts. Later I hope to demonstrate in considerable detail its potential for producing significant insights: new readings of both classical and newer texts.[7] For the moment I only wish to illustrate with brief samples its capacity to surprise and illuminate, leaving us with a more comprehensive appreciation, both of the literary work and of the relation between mankind and our physical surroundings.

My first example is a fragment of the story "El hombre muerto" ("The Dead Man") by the Uruguayan Horacio Quiroga (1870–1937), who is widely regarded as one of the masters of the short story as well as a respected practitioner of regionalist or *criollista* literature. This lengthy excerpt comes from the final lines of the tale. The plot traces a routine morning in the life of a settler, a man who tills the soil: a splendidly sunny day; the man's pride upon seeing himself surrounded by the fields that he himself has cleared, planted, and weeded; his casual decision to go through the fence to take a nap; and the fateful accident when he slips on a banana leaf, causing his machete, which he had kept in his belt, to penetrate his abdomen. The rest of the story is a mixture, narrated in *tempo lento*, of his impressions of disbelief at his mortal dilemma and the serene constancy of the natural medium that surrounds him:

> Nada, nada ha cambiado. Sólo él es distinto. Desde hace dos minutos su persona, su personalidad viviente, nada tiene ya que ver ni con el potrero, que formó él mismo a azada, durante cinco meses consecutivos; ni con el bananal, obra de sus solas manos. Ni con su familia. Ha sido arrancado bruscamente, naturalmente, por obra de una cáscara lustrosa y un machete en el vientre. Hace dos minutos: se muere [....]
>
> ¿La prueba...? Pero esa gramilla que entra ahora por la comisura de su boca la plantó él mismo, en panes de tierra distantes un metro uno de otro! ¡Y ése es su bananal y ése es su malacara, resoplando cauteloso ante las púas del alambre! [....]
>
> Pero el caballo rayado de sudor, e inmóvil de cautela ante el esquinado del alambrado, ve también al hombre en el suelo y no se atreve a costear el bananal, como desearía. Ante las voces que ya están próximas —¡Piapiá!—, vuelve un largo, largo rato las orejas inmóviles al bulto: y tranquizado al fin, se decide a pasar entre el poste y el hombre tendido — que ya ha descansado.[8]

> [Nothing, nothing has changed. Only he is different. For two minutes now his person, his living personality, has had no connection with the cleared land he himself spaded up during five consecutive months, nor with the grove, work of his hands alone. Nor with his family. He has been uprooted, brusquely, naturally, because of a slippery piece of bark and a machete in the belly. Two minutes: he is dying (...)
>
> The proof? But he himself planted this grama grass that is poking between his lips in squares of land a meter apart! And that is his banana grove and that his starred mare snorting cautiously by the barbed wire!
>
> (...)
>
> But the horse, striped with sweat, cautiously motionless at a corner of the fence, also sees the man on the ground and doesn't dare enter the banana grove, as she would like to. With the voices nearby now — "Pah-pah" — for a long, long while, the mare turns her motionless ears toward the heap on the ground and finally, quieted, decides to pass between the post and the fallen man — who has rested now.][9]

How can everything circumstantial remain the same, when the mortally wounded man's situation has changed so drastically? The familiar and the known, all of a sudden, acquire a strange, defamiliarized tone. The former landowner now finds himself lying on the ground, his ground, prostrate, literally eating soil and figuratively turning back into clay. Without declaring or preaching it, the story shows that existence is a process,[10] inexorable and incomprehensible, *from the perspective of the individual.* What bears all the signs of tragedy for the man, however, is no more than a routine day for the cosmos, which continues its cycles of life and death, creation and destruction, with absolute impassivity.

Mankind seeks to dominate nature and almost convinces himself that he succeeds. But it is nature that has the last word: mankind carries nature within himself and, no matter how hard he tries to postpone the moment of truth, his connection with the natural world always returns to the fore. In the quoted passage, when the horse finally dares to walk past the man's corpse, what emerges is the impermanence of cultural achievement. The horse obeys its master's commands, but not those of a mere object. That is the order of things. Thanks to Quiroga — whose experiences homesteading in the jungle of northern Argentina anticipate those of the modern green movement by some fifty years — we can access these precious glimpses of eco-wisdom.

A passage that is much more contemporary and urban (as much of Spanish American literature has become) comes from *Historia de Mayta* (translated as *The Real Life of Alejandro Mayta*), a novel by the outstanding Peruvian writer Mario Vargas Llosa (1936 —). It portrays the efforts of one zealous individual to mount a popular guerrilla uprising against the corrupt and sclerotic regime of the dictator President Manuel Odría. Set, at the level of the enunciation, in the same country and the same time period as the infamous *Sendero Luminoso* (Shining Path), the book was a phenomenal success, with both the critical establishment and the general public. As one might imagine, given Vargas Llosa's pro-establishment politics (he later ran for the presidency of Peru on a conservative platform), the story recounts the colossal failure of the uprising. In this case, however, the cause of the uprising's failure is almost laughable: upon arriving at the 11,000 foot-high plateau of Cuzco from coastal Lima, Mayta suffers from *soroche* (altitude sickness) and is incapable of carrying out the heroic action he had contemplated. The great international revolution predicted by Marx, Engels, Lenin, and Mao fails because the leader has a headache, feels dizzy, and can't think straight (not every exotic species prospers in alien climes!). With that tragicomic trajectory in mind, let us look at the opening and concluding paragraphs of the novel — descriptions of Lima —, which set the scene and powerfully embody the human drama. The novel commences with the following description:

> Correr en las mañanas por el Malecón de Barranco, cuando la humedad de la noche todavía impregna el aire y tiene a las veredas resbaladizas y brillosas, es una buena manera de comenzar el día. El cielo está gris, aun en el verano, pues

el sol jamás aparece sobre el barrio antes de las diez, y la neblina imprecisa la frontera de las cosas, el perfil de las gaviotas, el alcatraz que cruza volando la quebradiza línea del acantilado. El mar se ve plomizo, verde oscuro, humeante, encabritado, con manchas de espuma y olas que avanzan guardando la misma distancia hacia la playa. A veces, una barquita de pescadores zangolotea entre los tumbos; a veces, un golpe de viento aparta las nubes y asoman a lo lejos La Punta y las islas terrosas de San Lorenzo y el Frontón. Es un paisaje bello, a condición de centrar la mirada en los elementos y en los pájaros. Porque lo que ha hecho el hombre, en cambio, es feo.

Son feas estas casas, imitaciones de imitaciones, a las que el miedo asfixia de rejas, muros, sirenas y reflectores. Las antenas de la televisión forman un bosque espectral. Son feas estas basuras que se acumulan detrás del bordillo del Malecón y se desparraman por el acantilado. ¿Qué ha hecho que en este lugar de la ciudad, el de mejor vista, surjan muladares? La desidia. ¿Por qué no prohiben los dueños que sus sirvientes arrojen las inmundicias prácticamente bajo sus narices? Porque saben que entonces arrojarían los sirvientes de los vecinos, o los jardineros del Parque de Barranco, y hasta los hombres del camión de la basura, a quienes veo, mientras corro, vaciando en las laderas del acantilado los cubos de desperdicios que deberían llevarse al relleno municipal. Por eso se han resignado a los gallinazos, las cucarachas, los ratones y la hediondez de estos basurales que he visto nacer, crecer, mientras corría en las mañanas, visión puntual de perros vagos escarbando los muladares entre nubes de moscas. También me he acostumbrado, estos últimos años, a ver, junto a los canes vagabundos, mujeres vagabundas, todos revolviendo afanosamente los desperdicios en busca de algo que comer, que vender o que ponerse. El espectáculo de la miseria, antaño exclusivo de las barriadas, luego también del centro, es ahora el de toda la ciudad, incluidos estos distritos — Miraflores, Barranco, San Isidro — residenciales y privilegiados. Si uno vive en Lima tiene que habituarse a la miseria y a la mugre o volverse loco o suicidarse.[11]

[A morning jog along the Barranco Sea Wall, when the dew still hangs heavy in the air and makes the sidewalks slippery and shiny, is just the way to start off the day. Even in summer, the sky is gray, because the sun never shines on this neighborhood before ten. The fog blurs the edges of things — the profiles of sea gulls, the pelican that flies over the broken line of cliffs that run along the sea. The seawater looks like lead, dark green, smoky, rough, with patches of foam. The waves form parallel rows as they roll in, and sometimes a fishing boat bounces over them. Sometimes a gust of wind parts the clouds, and out in the distance La Punta and the ocher islands of San Lorenzo and El Frontón materialize. It's beautiful, as long as you concentrate on the landscape and the birds, because everything man-made there is ugly.

The houses are ugly, imitations of imitations, suffocated, in the form of gates, walls, sirens, and spotlights, by fear. Television antennas form a ghostly forest. Ugly, too, is the garbage that piles up on the outer edge of the Sea Wall and spills down its face. Why is it that this part of the city — which has the best view — is a garbage dump? Why don't the property owners tell their servants to stop dumping trash right under their noses? Because they know that if theirs didn't, the neighbors' servants or the workers from the Parque de Barranco would. Even the regular garbage men do: I see them while I'm running, throwing refuse down there that they should be carrying to the dump. That's why people have resigned themselves to the vultures, roaches, mice, and the stinking garbage dump whose birth and growth I've witnessed on my morning runs: a daily vision of stray dogs scratching in the dump under clouds of flies. Over the past few years, I've also gotten used to seeing stray kids, stray men, and stray women along with the stray dogs, all painstakingly digging through the trash looking for something to eat, something to sell, something to wear. The spectacle of misery was once limited exclusively to the slums, then it spread downtown, and now it is the common property of the whole city, even the exclusive residential neighborhoods — Miraflores, Barranco, San Isidro. If you live in Lima, you either get used to misery and grime, you go crazy, or you blow your brains out.][12]

At the outset of this extensive passage we observe a landscape of nearly ideal pastoral beauty, one with the power to transport the witness, taking him to a rhapsodic plane, a privileged, transcendent state. This initial gesture, however, almost immediately reveals itself as a "straw man," put forth only to be refuted by its darker other. The rapture is abruptly transformed into a "spectacle of misery," something closer to the postmodern grotesque or what Lawrence Buell has called "environmental apocalypticism."[13] Where the hand of man enters, the reader is instructed, there appears industrial waste, disorder, corruption, dysfunction, and misery. Present-day urban life equals degradation, pollution and squalor, even for the well heeled. Protracted meditation on the urban wasteland leads to disenchantment, or worse.

In reflecting on the passage, however, it is important to consider not only the object of study but also the voice that projects the image and the eye that sees it. Evidently the narrator is a jogger, a runner who, unlike the *chasquis* who delivered messages and goods up, down, and along the Andes Mountains for the Incas, works out every day before ensconcing himself in his study to write. As such, he does not consider himself to be an integral part of the situation he describes. He runs over the surface of the earth, but he does not make a commitment to the earth. His chosen role is to witness and criticize, not to reform. In brief, the novel begins with poetry in motion, but of a dystopian sort.

In the concluding passage of the same novel, we see the logical outcome of the estrangement built into the narrative posture:

Estoy pensando en las basuras de la barriada de Mayta todavía cuando diviso, a mi izquierda, la mole de Lurigancho y recuerdo al reo loco y desnudo, durmiendo en el inmenso muladar, frente a los pabellones impares. Y poco después, cuando acabo de cruzar Zárate y la Plaza de Acho y estoy en la Avenida Abancay, en la recta que me llevará hacia la Vía Expresa, San Isidro, Miraflores y Barranco, anticipo los malecones del barrio donde tengo la suerte de vivir, y el muladar que uno descubre — lo veré mañana, cuando salga a correr — si estira el pescuezo y atisba por el bordillo del acantilado, los basurales en que se han convertido esas laderas que miran al mar. Y recuerdo, entonces, que hace un año comencé a fabular esta historia mencionando, como la termino, las basuras que van invadiendo los barrios de la capital del Perú [346].

[I'm still thinking about the garbage in Mayta's slum when on the left I see Lurigancho Prison in the distance and I remember the mad, naked inmate sleeping on the immense garbage heap in front of the odd-numbered cell blocks. And shortly afterward, when I am all the way across Zárate and the Plaza de Acho and I'm on Avenida Abancay, on the road that takes me to Vía Expresa, San Isidro, Miraflores, and Barranco, I can already imagine the seawalls in the neighborhood where I have the good fortune to live, and the garbage you see — I'll see it myself tomorrow when I go running — if you crane your neck and peek over the edge. The garbage dump that the cliffs facing the sea have become. And I'll remember that a year ago I began to concoct this story the same way I'm ending it, by speaking about the garbage that's invading every neighborhood in the capital of Peru (309–10).]

The second description of the garbage heap is not only less detailed than the first; it isn't a description at all. It is a prescription. The narrator doesn't even wait long enough to observe the phenomenon. He imagines it, unchangeable, insoluble. This gesture can well be termed *defeatist,* for it declares the war (not the Maoist uprising but the war on garbage) lost before it is even begun. By not recognizing his own complicity with the post-colonial order responsible for the piles of trash that threaten to choke the city, the narrator tacitly collaborates in its perpetuation. While the urban environment declines ever farther into disorder, the narrative arc representing that environment inscribes an inappropriately tidy circle, offering before-and-after snapshots that are indistinguishable one from the other. This may represent a blind spot in the author's worldview, or it may be a question of bad faith; Vargas Llosa has been accused of both. The fact remains that the disconnect between the narrator's eye and the bleak landscape only makes the picture murkier.

As one can see from these two examples, ecocritical analyses are not always available on the surface, nor are they flattering. They deconstruct texts and arrive at conclusions not necessarily intended by a given author (although Quiroga might be pleased to learn he is seen as a proto-environmentalist, Vargas Llosa would surely resist the label of an eco-defeatist). So be it. If necessary, ecological criticism attempts to go beyond an author's conscious intentions, for writers do not necessarily share our values where the priority of the relation between nature and culture is concerned. It is better to beg the pardon of some great writer than to continue to accept the status quo of the natural medium that sustains us and that will, in the end, not pardon any of us.

Humanism has surely been guilty of many errors in its five-hundred-plus-year history. Its roots in anthropocentrism and its widespread acceptance in Western thought are doubtless important sources of the environmental crisis we face today. But make no mistake: humanism and anthropocentrism are not one and the same. We are very likely in an early phase in the development of humanism, whose capacity to mount a holistic vision of the universe positions it optimally to surpass anthropocentrism and take us to the next level: a circumspect and balanced vision of our status within the world.

That vision should be humble and yet proud, one of an integral and collaborative participant, neither an abject subaltern nor an arrogant tyrant. It has been said that the patron saint of the ecological movement is Saint Francis of Assisi, for his simple life style and his peaceful coexistence with the animals of the forest. There should be no illusions as to a possible return to a bucolic, simpler and less technologically sophisticated life. With the exception of oil-rich Venezuela, as the recent (2008) sharp rise in the cost of petroleum and corresponding drop in consumption attest, until our economic interests align themselves with the interests of the natural and physical world, human beings will continue our crazed race toward the sullying of our own nest. What is clear is that, if we don't turn our attention to and don't invest our material resources in that realignment, the system will overheat and melt down. Literature can and should play an important role in the requisite shift in attitudes and priorities. The purpose of ecological criticism — besides producing novel readings of significant texts — is to keep the environment in the discussion, to chip away at the ignorance of and indifference toward the nature that always lies at the base of culture.

The Vortex: Nature's Protagonism

Let us begin this earth-centered exploration of Spanish American fiction by looking at *La vorágine* (*The Vortex*), a 1924 novel by the Colombian José Eustasio Rivera. In order to appreciate fully the significance of *The Vortex* we should introduce an eccentric theory of reading, which for classroom use has been dubbed "reading for the setting." This eccentric strategy of reading displaces anthropomorphic figures to the margins and replaces them with nature, or that part of nature that is not human. In this altered scenario, nature reigns or at least maintains a relationship of equals with mankind and its cultural creations.[14] The shift in focus produces an abundance of unconventional findings.

The narrator of *The Vortex* is Arturo Cova, a promising poet who flees life in the capital city of Bogotá with his underage paramour Alicia because Alicia's family threatens to have him arrested. First the couple takes to the plains, where Cova tries his hand at cattle raising and rustling, but later they feel their future lies in the Amazonian jungle, where they hope to make a fortune — before the advent of petroleum-based tires — by tapping into the burgeoning rubber industry. Cova's basic problem is that he thinks that he is the protagonist or, worse, hero of his own book. In reality — Cova reveals in spite of himself — he is no more than a vociferous and bombastic mouthpiece. From an ecological perspective, he makes a number of decisions that are wrong for his situation, and these errors in the end lead to his — and his entire party's — extinction.

Cova is slow to understand what happens around him and he allows himself to become intoxicated with the illusory notion of making a fortune by exploiting the natives and the jungle. He is disoriented in the plains, where in its immensity every place looks to him like every other place. He is resentful when his friends leave to round up cattle or wild horses, leaving him home with the old men and the women. He does not consider that, beside the wounds that limit him, he lacks the necessary skills to participate effectively in their activities. He complains about women's fickleness, but he does not resist the charms of any of the three he meets, including the wife of his best friend, the aptly named Fidel Franco ("Faithful Candor"). When he is finally reunited with Alicia, he does not treat her as if she were a whole person but rather as a mere incubator for his progeny. On various occasions he reveals himself to be unstable, vengeful, and barbaric. He merits the name Cova (a variant of *cueva*, or cave), for he behaves like a hominid recently emerged from the caverns. In short, Cova is a disaster. Despite his pretensions and antics, he is neither a hero nor even an antihero. He is an *infrahero*, a false protagonist who fails to achieve the sort of centrality necessary to qualify for that category. That title belongs to the stage on which he gesticulates: the land where he treads, and which finally treads on him.

It is generally agreed that the axis of the jungle's protagonism resides in Cova's soliloquy at the beginning of Part Two of the novel. Its first paragraphs read as follows:

¡Oh selva, esposa del silencio, madre de la soledad y de la neblina! ¿Qué hado maligno me dejó prisionero en tu cárcel verde? Los pabellones de tus ramajes, como inmensa bóveda, siempre están sobre mi cabeza, entre mi aspiración y el cielo claro, que sólo entreveo cuando tus copas estremecidas mueven su oleaje, a la hora de tus crepúsculos angustiosos. ¿Dónde estará la estrella querida que de tarde pasea las lomas? ¿Aquellos celajes de oro y múrice con que se viste el ángel de los ponientes, por qué no tiemblan en tu dombo? ¡Cuántas veces suspiró mi alma adivinando al través de tus laberintos el reflejo del astro que empurpura las lejanías, hacia el lado de mi país, donde hay llanuras inolvidables y cumbres de corona blanca, desde cuyos picachos me vi a la altura de las cordilleras! ¿Sobre qué sitio erguirá la luna su apacible faro de plata? ¡Tú me robaste el ensueño del horizonte y sólo tienes para mis ojos la monotonía de tu cénit, por donde pasa el plácido albor, que jamás alumbra las hojarascas de tus senos húmedos!¹⁵

[Oh, jungle, wedded to silence, mother of solitude and mists! What malignant fate imprisoned me within your green walls? Your foliage, like an immense vault, is between my hopes and the clear skies of which I see only glimpses, when the twilight breeze stirs your lofty tops. Where is the loved star that walks the hills at evening? Where are those cloud-sweeps of gold and purple? How often have I sighed as I pictured the sun — far beyond your tangled labyrinths — steeping the distant spaces in purple, there where my native land lies, where the unforgettable plains stretch, where rise mountains on whose foothills I could feel as high above their world as their white-covered peaks.

　　Where is the moon hanging her silver lantern? You stole from me the dreams that spring from the broad horizons. You offer my eyes nothing but the dull monotony of your green roof. Over it flows the peaceful dawn, but never lighting the depths of your humid bosom.¹⁶]

Perhaps what first strikes the reader is the narrator's exalted style, so ill suited to the jungle he inhabits, although probably well received by his urbane, residually *modernista* readers. Despite and beyond that grandiloquence, there are several very important traits on display in this sample. For simplicity's sake I will limit myself to two, however. First, the most obvious, is the feminization of the jungle. Already grammatically feminine in Spanish (*la selva*, *la jungla*), in Cova's vision the jungle is the "mother of solitude and mists." And upon describing the wilderness's green canopy, Cova cannot resist the temptation to cast it in terms of "your humid bosom." The jungle functions as an unhealthy tomb and womb, an oppressive and claustrophobic receptacle, a dystopia that borders on the infernal.¹⁷ It is an earthly and lethal force, a siren that actively tempts man with its beauty and its promise of wealth. But once its prey is seduced, the vertiginous force of the jungle does not permit him to leave. The suction of her uterine vortex retains everything that dares approach its abyss.

　　Cova's attempts to save his life by escaping from the jungle are tantamount to his trying to escape from nature itself.¹⁸ This separation — always illusory since despite culture's achievements it is always subject to the laws of nature — is doomed to failure. Not only is Cova inside the jungle; the jungle is inside Cova. He lacks an identity apart from his surroundings, and ultimately he dissolves within its viscera. When, at the novel's conclusion, the faithful and experienced guide Clemente Silva (or "merciful forest") declares that "The jungle has swallowed them!" (371), what he means is that the jungle and its intruders have fused into one. Cova's defeat, as regards his dreams of enrichment and literary triumph, is total and absolute. His other aspiration, that of taking revenge on his rival Barrera (read, "barrier" or "obstacle"), he does achieve, but that goal is not so much civilizing as recidivist, since it devolves him to a brutal, bestial state. Let us face it, setting aside the cultural achievement of the novel itself, in the nature-versus-culture wars of early twentieth-century Spanish America reflected within its covers, nature wins, hands down.

Doña Barbara: Culture's Reaffirmation

To pronounce the title of the novel *Doña Barbara*, by the Venezuelan Rómulo Gallegos, first published in 1929, barely five years after Rivera's *The Vortex*, is practically synonymous with articulating the polarity of civilization and barbarism that dominated Latin American thinking throughout much of the nineteenth century. This binary was powerfully put forth in the first half of the nineteenth century by the Argentine Domingo Faustino Sarmiento in his celebrated essay *Facundo: Civilization and Barbarism* (orig. *Facundo: Civilización y barbarie*).[19] What we should underscore now, contrary to conventional wisdom, is that Gallegos's text does not dramatize a conflict between civilization and barbarism *per se*, but rather a vexed relationship between Western culture (primarily European, but with a certain American prairie inflection) and irrationally destructive aspects of *human nature*. Non-human nature, in contrast, is relegated to a realm of the theatrical and the symbolic.

In order to support this thesis we must take into account that Sarmiento's dualism basically defines the difference between Latin America and its North American neighbors. In Latin America, where modernization and development have not yet been consolidated, conquering the American continent presents itself as the most crucial of missions to this day. Once Spain's former colonies had gained their independence (largely accomplished by 1836), this "civilizing" quest obsessed thinkers and politicians, and it still tends to frame many a debate today. At a recent professional meeting at the Universidad Nacional de Bogotá, where I gave a paper on ecological aspects of Gabriel García Márquez's novel *El amor en los tiempos del cólera (Love in the Times of Cholera)*, I was asked if it wasn't fair that all this environmental thinking was coming into style just when countries like Colombia were poised to enter into a more robust form of development. Whereas the industrialized nations could now afford the luxury of curtailing their pollution and exploitation of natural resources (many of these coming from the so-called "Third World"), poorer countries were again being penalized and constrained from rising out of their relative poverty. The best answer I could devise was to say that, unfortunately, nature does not make exceptions, that despoiling one's resources is one's own worst punishment, but the questioner's point about environmental (in)justice was not entirely lost on me. From the standpoint of societies that are still developing, industrialization and urbanization still look a lot like civilization, and any defense of nature against development can look like protracted barbarism, which is another term for eco-injustice.

In our treatment of *The Vortex*, we saw how a fierce nature dominates Arturo Cova's pathetic attempts at imposing his urbanizing vision. It is of paramount importance to distinguish that situation from that of *Doña Barbara* and its protagonist Santos Luzardo ("Holy Light"). First, Luzardo is not a bohemian dandy poet but a person who is educated in a deep sense (not just trained in a specialty but broadly cultured, with integrity and respect for others). Born on the prairie and raised there until he went to the capital city in order to pursue his university studies, Luzardo does not have to learn all the practicalities of life on the plains. He just needs to recall them. Furthermore, he is of an even-tempered, rational disposition, not inclined to the narcissistic excesses proper to Cova. And, perhaps most important, the plains are not the jungle. The plains lend themselves to serving as a stage for human dramas, coloring the atmosphere of their episodes and symbolically reinforcing the turns of their plots. In such a setting it would be implausible for the landscape to assume a protagonistic role, for its domestication (first in the form of maps, and then with boundary stakes and fences) is not an insuperable challenge. And these conditions, while repugnant to today's deep ecologists, dovetail perfectly with Gallegos's progressive agenda.

The binary pair "civilization" and "barbarism" warrants careful scrutiny. As Gallegos and Sarmiento understood those terms, they were absolute and universal entities. Either one is civilized or one is not. To our eyes, however, the issue is not so cut and dried. What is commonly called civilization is, rather, modern Western culture, with its Judeo-Christian roots and its faith in reason, science, and technological advancement. Those positivistic values entail a disdain — unannounced, to be sure — toward other modes of thought and other ways of living. They imply a rejection of non–Western cultures, such as that of the Arabs, previously expelled from the Iberian Peninsula by the forces of the Spanish Reconquest, as well as those of sub–Sahara Africans and the native cultures of the Western hemisphere, among many others, long since decimated and enslaved. What is called civilization often implies large doses of impassioned violence, a violence that is often accepted by the masses because of official sanction and because of the densely organized and technologically complex means of its imposition.

Turning to the other term of the pair, we must be sure to understand that "barbarism" is not taken as synonymous with "nature." Descriptions of the Venezuelan plains in the novel, where men work in an orderly and harmonious way with the natural cycles, tend toward the sublime. In many senses the novel is an homage to the beauty and purity of the natural scenery, for it provides all the necessary conditions so that man may, in the words of the narrator, "love, suffer, ... and hope" ("amar, sufrir ... y esperar").[20] This is the Promised Land that God supposedly gave to man in the Creation, or it would be if not for barbarism: the forces of evil. Within the framework of *Doña Barbara*'s positivistic, Christian, Eurocentric narrator, those forces are malevolent because they relentlessly tempt man to contravene the will of the Creator.

From these observations one can conclude that the novel's problematics are not a conflict between man and nature (in the sense of taming horses or clearing land for cultivation) so much as a struggle within human nature itself (or the modern Venezuelan version of masculine human nature). If there is discord, it is within Santos Luzardo, who does not know if he should obey the lessons of urbanity that have polished his peace-loving side or follow the violent and even homicidal impulses that he also embodies. In particular, the disjunction is between seeing (with clarity) and feeling (dark and murky emotions), as represented in the names of the two bordering ranches: Santos's *Altamira* (high view) and Doña Bárbara's *El Miedo* (fear).

All this is rather obvious, since the text indicates so with a symbolism that strikes us today as heavy handed and overdetermined. What is less patent, however, is that in associating Doña Barbara with the baser emotions, the text also removes her from the visual arena, from light and luminousness. She does not just steal, bribe, and kill. She also practices sorcery and considers herself to possess supernatural powers, so as to be able to know what is happening in other places or what will happen in the future. We should underscore that she herself believes in the superstitions she spreads. She deceives herself, believing that, via a medium (called a "socio"), she imparts occult knowledge, controls remote events, and, above all, determines the behavior of certain men. Doña Barbara's evil is based not so much on her link with supposed satanic forces as on her distance from the rationality of Western culture. Her evil resides less in her malevolent intentions (although she manifests these in abundance) than in her misguided and aggressive engagement with a world that she fails to understand.

That misunderstanding is the source of her barbarism, and attentive readers know the reasons for her condition: as a child she was brutally raped by pirates who, in order to achieve their ends, murdered her true love Asdrúbal. And behind that trauma is another: she is the daughter of an indigenous woman who was possessed by a European man. The fruit of the forced coupling of a Spanish conquistador with a native woman, Doña Barbara represents the dominant racial type of Latin America, genetically *mestizo* and open to all possible destinies. Her great defect, according to the narrator (a white, Eurocentric male, after all), is her inability to make rational decisions. Because of the traumas of her youth, she cannot decide between love and hate, or between order and chaos. And the drama of the process of making the decisions necessary to defining herself, to establishing an ecology of the self, an integrated and balanced identity — where the person is cognizant of who she is and how she fits into her environment — is elaborated before the immense and imposing backdrop of the American prairie. Culture is thus reaffirmed, not only by its triumph over mankind's confused, dark side, but also through the use of the Venezuelan plains as a grand symbolic stage upon which a nation's identity is forged. Whether nature and culture can achieve a sustainable relation, however, remains to be seen.

The Storyteller: Postmodern Eco-indigenism

Having observed the reaffirmation of Western culture's supremacy over nature embodied in *Doña Barbara*, and not forgetting the dystopian opening scene from *The Real Life of Alejandro Mayta*, we should now turn our attention to a more contemporary way of looking at the fraught relationship between mankind and our environment. In our trash-strewn world, the last thing we need are more jargon terms for literary sub-genres, such as "postmodern eco-indigenism." Yet it is compelling to employ them at this precise critical juncture, where a paradigm shift is most definitely needed, and that shift requires seeing and saying things differently. But to understand their sense in this context, we need to consider what transpires in world history between the 1920s, when *The Vortex* and *Dona Bárbara* were published, and the late 1980s, when Mario Vargas Llosa wrote *The Storyteller* (the original, titled *El hablador*, first appeared in 1987). To name a few earth-shattering events, commercial aviation, the exploitation of nuclear energy, radio and television (with corresponding changes in the way people listen and look), the exploration of outer space, and the incorporation of cell phones, the computer and wireless internet access in the daily lives of hundreds of millions of people. All that, and more, can be summarized in one word: globalization. That term may echo differently in different ears, but here are a few phenomena that may come to mind: multi-national corporations, outsourcing jobs, the homogenization of tastes, increased dependency on international shipping, unmonitored exploitation of natural resources for industrial development, and increased pressure on the enclaves of small cultures reluctant to abandon their values and traditional practices. Globalization tends to divide the world into two groups, the haves and the have-nots. And these groups correlate strongly with those who are willing and those who are not willing to participate in this monolithic, technologically supported system. One defends one's own regional, national, or ethnic identity at one's own risk.

Again Newton's Second Law of physics comes to mind: for every force in the universe there is another force of equal magnitude whose vector points in the opposite direction. The contrary vector generated in the sixty years between one text and another arises from the notion of limits, where the exploitation of natural resources is concerned. It has not been easy to arrive at this vision, since certain resources have the appearance of being inexhaustible. Think of the image of the jungle in *The Vortex*, for example. That sample of nature is so immense and fierce ("protagonistic" is the term we have used) that it seems impermeable and invulnerable to the vain efforts of the human being. That same vision has been applied (always erroneously) to petroleum, oxygen, water, the ice caps of the two poles, etc. The positivism and progressivism represented by the figure of Santos Luzardo, despite his luminous name, suffer from that same myopia. Nothing, neither the fertile plains of the Venezuelan *pampa* nor the dense vegetation of the Amazon jungle, is limitless; everything is finite. What can always expand is the human desire to dominate, to consume, to seek gratification. And that desire brings us ever closer to the point of exhausting those resources. In short, what has been traditionally called the "novel of the land" (*novela de la tierra*) moves in *The Storyteller* toward the "novel of the Earth" (*novela de la Tierra*, with an upper-case "E" in English and "T" in Spanish). The difference lies in being aware of the finiteness of our planet.

A brief sketch of the plot of Vargas Llosa's novel is in order. The narrator, a cosmopolitan writer — a Peruvian who finds himself in Italy — discovers some photos of Indians from the Machiguenga tribe, of the Peruvian Amazonian jungle. In the snapshots there appears a magnetic figure, a man who is evidently the center of attention, around whom all the other indigenous people sit, as if nailed there in fascination.

What is strange about the particular situation is that the narrator believes he recognizes personally the charismatic man, who looks very much like a former classmate of his from San Marcos University, one Saúl Zaratas, alias Mascarita ("Little Mask"), a Latin American Jew who had a large and ugly birthmark that covered half of his face. But how could a Westerner, a member of a culture that is not only different but even pushing hegemonically against that of the Machiguengas, who are going extinct under the pressure of global development, have managed to secure the privileged position of storyteller among the natives? That is part of the story that the writer wishes to tell.

To tell that story, the writer needs to go to the jungle and know it first hand. There one can see the evolution, or maturation, Western man has undergone, for the distance in his attitude and his strategies from those of Arturo Cova in *The Vortex* could not be greater. In this case the writer becomes aware of the problematic presence of missionary linguists, who translate the Bible to the Machiguenga language in order to spread the word of the Christian God (an echo of the Spanish Conquest cannot but come to mind). Simplifying the issues somewhat, let us pose this question: what happens when a society changes suddenly from fostering oral knowledge to literate record keeping? Many researchers believe that when a small community takes that fateful step, its sense of meaning passes from the nature that supports and surrounds them to the written word. And if that occurs, in that particular environment, its extinction surely follows close behind. If that tribe has not been corrupted yet — if it does not understand the value of money, if it does not understand the concept of "saving time" — is it fair for Western culture to contaminate it with those impulses? In the name of what? What value is being defended in imposing a system of living — we can all confirm — that often confuses quantity (of hours worked, of wealth accumulated, of SUVs upgraded, etc.) with quality of life? Those are the sorts of questions debated between Mascarita and the writer, or within the very mind of the writer.

The novel, nonetheless, is not satisfied with a more-or-less objective exposition of the problems faced by the vulnerable Machiguenga people. It goes a step further and offers a sample of the worldview of one such culture, through the voice of the storyteller Mascarita. For the sake of brevity, we won't get into all the potentially interesting and relevant passages. But a couple of brief examples should suffice to represent the flavor and texture of a vision alternate to the one that impels the West.

First, let us look at a quotation that establishes the desperate situation of the Machiguengas, who suffer from imminent annihilation as a result of the expansive development of the dominant strain of Peruvian culture. Please observe the odd terms and the type of logic that are employed.

> Esta tierra se fue quedando sin hombres. Unos se volvieron pájaros, otros peces, otros tortugas, otros arañas, y se iban a hacer la vida de los diablillos kamagarinis. "Qué nos está pasando, qué desgracias son estas," se preguntaban, aturdidos, los sobrevivientes. Estaban miedosos y ciegos, no se daban cuenta. Una vez más, se había perdido la sabiduría. "Vamos a desaparecer," se lamentaban. Tristes, tal vez. Entonces, en medio de tanta confusión, los mashcos les cayeron encima e hicieron una gran matanza. Les cortaron las cabezas a muchos y se llevaron sus mujeres. Parecía que las catástrofes no terminarían nunca. Entonces, en su desesperación, a uno se le ocurrió: "Vamos a visitar a Tasurinchi."[21]

> [The earth was running short of men. Some had turned into birds, some into fish, others into tortoises or spiders, and went to live the life of little kamagarini

devils. "What is happening to us? What misfortunes are these?" the ones who survived asked themselves, bewildered. They were helpless with fear and blind, but they didn't know it. Once again, wisdom had been lost. "We are about to disappear," they moaned. They were sad, perhaps. And then, amid all the confusion, the Mashcos fell upon them and there was a great massacre. They cut off the heads of many and carried off their women. It seemed that there would be no end to the catastrophes. And then it all of a sudden occurred to one of them, in his despair: "Let's go visit Tasurinchi."][22]

The errancy alluded to at the end of the excerpt, this time in search of Tasurinchi, turns out to be the Machiguengas' true destiny. It implies, among other things, not owning real estate or more than they can carry, curiously anchoring them, as they walk toward the east, to the rising sun and, consequently, to the cosmic order. If things deteriorate, it is because they have not fulfilled their responsibilities, "perhaps." (Notice the humility, the possibility of having misunderstood, the humanity of the speaker, whose fate it is not only to walk but also to tell stories). Mutually dependent interaction with the natural surroundings,[23] continuous movement across its surface, respect for one's cosmic duties, the contingent quality of identity and of pronounced truth: all these elements, alien to globalization's dominant discourse and very akin to planetary environmental thinking, are proffered through the quasi-indigenous storyteller.[24]

The process of negotiating between radically different cultures is very complicated, however. The pressures are not felt in one lone direction, and not even in just two directions. A sort of hybrid mediator, the storyteller himself suffers the impact of all the cultures imposed on him. No matter how much he would wish to participate in the preservation of the Machiguengas in their pure state, he cannot help but incorporate some of the myths and values of his Judeo-Christian upbringing. In one of the versions of the Machiguengas' stories, his wandering fate is conflated with that of the Jews, and the name of the supreme creator is transformed into Jehovah-Tasurinchi. The storyteller speaks as follows:

> Sería que, pese a todo lo que le ocurrió, el pueblo de Tasurinchi-jehová no se desemparejó de su destino. Cumpliría su obligación, siempre. Respetando las prohibiciones, también. ¿Por ser distinto a los demás sería odiado? ¿Por eso no lo aceptarían los pueblos entre los que estuvo? Quién sabe. A la gente no le gusta vivir con gente distinta. Desconfiará, tal vez. Otras costumbres, otra manera de hablar la asustarán, como si el mundo fuera confuso, oscuro, de repente. La gente quisiera que todos fueran iguales, que los demás se olvidaran de sus costumbres, mataran a sus seripigaris, desobedecieran las prohibiciones e imitaran las de ella. Si lo hubiera hecho, el pueblo de Tasurinchi-jehová habría desaparecido. No hubiera quedado de él ni un hablador para contar su historia. Yo no estaría aquí hablando, tal vez [211].

[Could it be that despite everything that happened to it, Jehovah-Tasurinchi's people never was at odds with its destiny? Always fulfilled its obligation; always respected the prohibitions, too. Was it hated because it was different? Was that why, wherever it went, people would not accept it? Who knows? People don't like living with people who are different. They don't trust them, perhaps. Other customs, another way of speaking would frighten them, as though the world had suddenly become confused and dark. People would like everyone to be the same, would like others to forget their own customs, kill their seripigaris, violate their own taboos, and imitate theirs. If it had done that, Jehovah-Tasurinchi's people would have disappeared. Not one storyteller would have survived to tell their story. I wouldn't be here talking, perhaps (219–20).]

Not that postmodern texts tend to be strong on moral lessons, but the surface-level message here could hardly be starker: in a shrinking world, where different cultures enter into contact with each other with growing frequency, the only way to avoid constant conflict is through tolerance (or better, acceptance) of the other. In less preachy terms, there are no cultures that are better or worse, only cultures that are adequate or inadequate to their respective contexts. And all cultures can learn something from the other cultures with which they come into contact: forgotten lessons and roads not taken in the headlong rush to reach the future. The discourses of biodiversity and cultural diversity do not, of course, share all the same goals and values, but *The Storyteller* shows how their interests can indeed overlap.

The foregoing explains the term used at the start of this section: eco-indigenism. This would entail the possibility of entering into a fertile relationship with non–Western cultures — ones that were not technologically advanced, not globalized, not conspicuous consumers of the diminishing natural resources of our biosphere — in order to learn from them what our limited perspective does not allow us to see.[25] But where does "postmodern" enter into the equation? Throughout the entire process, really. The passages narrated by the storyteller are not what they seem to be. They cannot be the very words of the storyteller, for the Machiguengas belong to an oral culture, and these words reach us in written form. Everything that appears to belong to Mascarita is a construct, the *simulacrum* of a quasi-indigenous discourse devised by the intermediary cosmopolitan writer, that Vargas Llosa-like Peruvian who finds himself in Italy.

Postmodernism means many things to many people. But one of the features on which all theorists of Postmodernism agree, in addition to our linguistically and digitally mediated hold on reality, is that Postmodernism breaks with the progressivist vision of the rationalists of the French Enlightenment. Faith in the modernist project of the West has been shaken, and in its place a deep skepticism toward innovation has taken root. Our period in cultural history is marked by an ever-accelerating rhythm of change, but if those changes are moving in a positive direction for culture and nature is open to question. And doubts of this sort lead to a relativization of truth, or of truths.

Amidst the confusion of multiple truths, for the Machiguengas, there are always the storytellers, who remind their listeners of the unbroken thread that ties them to their past and of the community to which they belong. Among contemporary Westerners, the equivalent is our poets or writers, whose role is analogous, although significantly degraded. *Poiesis* means creation, and it is the mission of all writers to create, to create mirrors (however distorted) in which we see our reflections, not necessarily as we would like to see ourselves, but as we may have to admit we are. And our present condition reveals itself to be lamentable. We are alienated from the natural medium that sustains us, we do not respect it, nor do we know how to listen to it or interpret its needs. Of course, as children of the Enlightenment, we cannot return to the animism and magic of our pre-modern ancestors or of our infantile offspring. Having created science, we are now creatures of science, as far as our mode of thinking is concerned.

In his conclusion to *The Future of Environmental Criticism*, Lawrence Buell expresses hope for a general sense of "environmentality" being spread through the humanities, academia in general, the public, and eventually into global policy. "It will have been achievement enough," he writes, "if environmentality becomes seen as indispensable to how one reads literature — whether the specific project at hand be the environmental literacy of a text, its way of situating itself locally and/or globally, its attention or inattention to the non-human sphere, or its ideological valence(s) with regard to receptivity or opacity to social justice issues."[26] Likewise, Arne Naess, the founder of the Deep Ecology movement, is upbeat about eventually achieving broad ecological sustainability, even if things get considerably worse before they get better around the year 2101.[27]

Despite the differences in their areas of interest (Buell's is more literary, Naess's more environmental), it is clear that they both live in and tend to concentrate on what in global ecology has come to be known as the North. Prospects for the South — and not just in Latin America but also, as the work of Ramachandra Guha shows,[28] in India and elsewhere in Asia, Africa, etc.— may not be so bright. Pressures to "develop" (i.e., industrialize and grow the gross domestic product) may be too great in many parts of the institutionally maturing world for ecological purity to hold sway. In these settings — if the biosphere is to be given any consideration at all — Deep Ecology will surely yield to environmental justice (a fair share of the material wellbeing brought about by industrialization) as the prevalent mode of thought and action.

Given the relative material deprivation of the South, one must beware of disproportionate and excessive responses possible on behalf of nature. Green sabotage and eco-terror in the name of the environment are no less ignobly destructive than damage wrought in the name of other fundamentalist movements. One visionary Chilean author, Fernando Raga Castellanos, has — in *Los hijos de Gaia* (Gaia's Children)— already envisaged a circumstance in which, by hijacking the discourse of environmentalism, a Stalin-like leader is able to achieve totalitarian control over much of the industrialized world.[29] Whereas Buell anticipates for the North a trickle-down effect in ecocritical thought from the academy to society at large, in Spanish America — as the case of Raga indicates — we academics may be among the last to know of such developments. Writers, artists, journalists, public intellectuals, labor organizers, and citizens in general may well lead the way in fostering a more horizontal or grassroots environmentality — and especially in demanding environmental justice — in zones where universities or other institutions of the state are relatively weak.[30]

As demonstrated in Vargas Llosa's "Novel of the Earth," *The Storyteller*, a constructive strategy for ecological criticism in what remains of the twenty-first century could be to translate the values of cultures that are politically and economically less powerful and technologically less complex — but which may be psychically and environmentally more balanced than ours — into terms that are intelligible to the North, within a framework of rational and economic viability. This is not "sustainable development," as that term is conventionally understood in its "Shallow Ecology" sense. Let us think of something closer to "sustainable environmentality," whereby generalized ecocentrism is protected from being drowned out by a few very loud voices. Only in that way can we reasonably expect, as a species, to still be around to tell and hear the stories of the *nietas* (granddaughters) of our *nietas*.

NOTES

1. Glotfelty and Fromm, *The Ecocriticism Reader*, xviii–xix. Lawrence Buell, almost ten years later in *The Future of Environmental Criticism* sees ecocriticism as "an umbrella term [...] used to refer to the environmentally oriented study of literature and (less often) the arts more generally, and to the theories that underlie such critical practice." Buell goes on to distinguish between "first-wave" and "second-wave," or revisionist ecocriticism, "in recognition of a growing diversification of critical method and broadening of focus from an original concentration on such genres as nature writing, nature poetry, and wilderness fiction toward engagement with a broader range of landscapes and genres and a greater internal debate over environmental commitment that has taken the movement in a more sociocentric direction" (138). This "sociocentric direction," which implies an insistence on environmental justice rather than on preservation of wild places, is, according to Wolfgang Sachs, what distinguishes predominant environmental discourses of the South (shorthand for less-industrialized societies) from those of the North (highly industrialized societies). See Sachs, "Global Ecology." My own hybridized discourse hopes to avail itself

of both waves of environmental criticism and both regional discourses mentioned by these scholars.

2. *An Inconvenient Truth*, Paramount Pictures, 2006 (Featuring Al Gore; David Guggenheim, Director).

3. Here I am aligned with Lynn White, Jr., who asserts in "The Historic Roots of our Ecologic Crisis" that "We shall continue to have a worsening ecologic crisis until we reject the Christians' axiom that nature has no reason for existence save to serve man." Glotfelty and Fromm, *The Ecocriticism Reader*, 13.

4. Ibid., 5–12.

5. Drengson and Inoue, in the introduction to their collection *The Deep Ecology Movement: An Introductory Anthology*, identify the Norwegian Arne Naess as the originator of the "Deep Ecology Movement" and reproduce his seven-point summary, set in opposition to "Shallow Ecology" (the fight against pollution and resource depletion, whose central objective is the health and affluence of people in the developed countries). Those points entail: (1) Rejection of the human-in-environment image in favor of the *relational, total-field image* (emphasis in original); (2) *Biospherical egalitarianism*— in principle; (3) *Principles of diversity and of symbiosis*; (4) *Anti-class posture*; (5) Fight against *pollution and resource depletion*; (6) *Complexity, not complication*; and (7) *Local autonomy and decentralization* (3–6).

6. See Commoner, *The Closing Circle: Nature, Man, and Technology*, 33.

7. George B. Handley, for example, studies signs of the "Adamic imagination" in the poetry of Pablo Neruda in his *New World Poetics*.

8. Quiroga, "El hombre muerto," *Los desterrados* (1925; Buenos Aires: Losada, 1970), 73–74.

9. Quiroga, "The Dead Man," in *The Decapitated Chicken and Other Stories*, trans. Margaret Sayers Peden (Austin: University of Texas Press, 1984), 105–06.

10. Buell includes the notion of "the environment as a process rather than as a constant or a given" in the text as one of the criteria for helping to identify environmentally oriented works. *The Environmental Imagination*, 7–8.

11. Vargas Llosa, *Historia de Mayta* (Buenos Aires: Seix Barral, 1984), 7–8.

12. Vargas Llosa, *The Real Life of Alejandro Mayta*, trans. Alfred Mac Adam (New York: Vintage, 1986), 3–4.

13. See chapter nine of Buell's *The Environmental Imagination*.

14. This reading strategy is consistent with the notion of Deep Ecology that encourages "an egalitarian attitude on the part of humans not only toward all *members* of the ecosphere, but even toward all identifiable *entities* or *forms* in the ecosphere." See Fox, "The Deep Ecology — Ecofeminism Debate" in *Deep Ecology for the 21st Century*, 269.

15. Rivera, *La vorágine* (1924; Mexico City: Porrúa, 1984), 55.

16. Rivera, *The Vortex*, trans. Earle K. James (Bogotá: Panamericana, 2001), 155.

17. At this point I must recognize my Rutgers colleague Jorge Marcone for his outstanding work in the environmental analysis of the novel of the Peruvian Amazon jungle and beyond. See bibliography for several articles by Marcone on this topic.

18. Jhan Hochman makes a very useful distinction between "Nature" and "nature" (or "*worldnature*") in his introduction to *Green Cultural Studies*. The first term (with an uppercase "N") designates the undomesticated world when "construed as transcendentally metaphysical or immanently essential" (2). The second term (with a lower-case "n" or the Germanically inflected neologism w*orldnature*) is used "in a more worldly fashion in order to collectivize individual plants, nonhuman animals, and elements" (2).

19. Domingo Faustino Sarmiento, *Facundo: Civilización y barbarie* (1845) ed. Roberto Yahni (Madrid: Cátedra, 1990).

20. These concluding words, perhaps too melodramatic for the translator's taste, are absent from the published translation but present in the original Spanish. Gallegos, *Doña*

Bárbara (1929; Mexico City: Orión, 1967), 423. Gallegos, *Doña Barbara* trans. Robert Malloy (New York: Peter Smith, 1948).

21. Vargas Llosa, *El hablador* (Barcelona: Seix Barral, 1987), 63.

22. Vargas Llosa, *The Storyteller*, trans. Helen Lane (New York: Farrar, Straus & Giroux, 1989), 64.

23. Dana Phillips contends that "ecological research has shown that ideas that nature seeks to establish balance and harmony and that everything in nature is interconnected are no better than platitudes. Ideas like these are belied by the natural world's tendency to chaos, competition and evolution." *The Truth of Ecology*, viii. Phillips' strategy appears to entail fighting platitudes with counter-platitudes. Competition in nature is undeniable, and evolution is evolving ever closer to being an incontrovertible fact. To prefer chaos to balance and harmony, however, is to choose the darker half of a story that appears unruly in the short term and on its surface. A more circumspect view would admit a balance of both harmony and cacophony within nature's complex and dynamic order.

24. Similar difficulties are reflected in Luis Sepúlveda's novel *The Old Man Who Read Love Stories* (*Un hombre que leía novelas de amor*), in which the protagonist Antonio José Bolívar, a mestizo who is wise in the ways of the Shuar Indians of the Ecuadorian Amazon, but who has avenged the death of Shuar by killing the murderer with a firearm instead of a traditional blowgun, is told by an elder, "You are not one of us but you are like us." Mascarita would appear, improbably, to have bridged the cultural differences that prohibit Bolívar from integrating completely with the indigenous people.

25. It is tempting to identify these comments with what Shawn Miller has called the "Pristine Myth, which depicts pre-contact America as an unspoiled, lightly peopled wilderness in environmental harmony and ecological balance." See *An Environmental History of Latin America*, 9. It should be clear that we are not idealizing the indigenous as modern-day Noble Savages, for even the passages included herein speak of their near extinction, their disorientation, their wars, and the competition between tribes for women. Rather, they are portrayed as cultural others who have survived and prospered without wreaking the magnitude of gratuitous damage on their natural surroundings that Western societies have done.

26. Buell, *The Future of Environmental Criticism*, 131.

27. See Naess, "Deep Ecology for The Twenty-Second Century."

28. See Guha, "Radical American Environmentalism and Wilderness Preservation: A Third World Critique."

29. Fernando Raga Castellanos, *Los hijos de Gaia* (Gaia's Children) (Buenos Aires: Ediciones Distal, 2005).

30. Contemporary Spanish American creative writers to watch in this regard, in addition to Sepúlveda (see also his *Mundo del fin del mundo* and *Patagonia Express*), include, among others, the Mexican Homero Aridjis (*El hombre que amaba el Sol*), the Honduran-Nicaraguan Giaconda Belli (*Waslala*), the Cuban-Puerto Rican Mayra Montero (*Tú, la oscuridad*), and the Costa Rican Anacristina Rossi (*La loca de Gandoca*).

Works Cited

Aridjis, Homero. *El hombre que amaba el Sol*. Mexico City: Alfaguara, 2005.

Belli, Gioconda. *Waslala: La búsqueda de una civilización perdida*. 1996. Barcelona: Seix Barral, 2006.

Buell, Lawrence. *The Environmental Imagination: Thoreau, Nature Writing, and the Formation of American Culture*. Cambridge: Harvard University Press, 1995.

_____. *The Future of Environmental Criticism: Environmental Crisis and Literary Imagination*. Blackwell Manifestos. Oxford: Blackwell, 2005.

_____. *Writing for an Endangered World: Literature, Culture and Environment in the U.S. and Beyond*. Cambridge: Harvard University Press, 2001.

Commoner, Barry. *The Closing Circle: Nature, Man, and Technology*. New York: Knopf, 1971.

Drengson, Alan and Yuichi Inoue, eds. *The Deep Ecology Movement: An Introductory Anthology*. Berkeley: North Atlantic Books, 1995.

Fox, Warwick. "The Deep Ecology-Ecofeminism Debate and Its Parallels." In Sessions, *Deep Ecology for the 21st Century*, 269–89.

Gallegos, Rómulo. *Doña Bárbara*. 1929. Mexico: Porrúa, 2000. Translated by Robert Malloy. New York: Peter Smith, 1948.

Glotfelty, Cheryll and Harold Fromm, eds., *The Ecocriticism Reader: Landmarks in Literary Ecology*. Athens, GA: University of Georgia Press, 1996.

Guggenheim, David (Director). *An Inconvenient Truth*, Paramount Pictures, 2006 (featuring Al Gore).

Guha, Ramachandra. "Radical American Environmentalism and Wilderness Preservation: A Third World Critique." *Environmental Ethics* 11 (1989): 71–84.

Hochman, Jhan. *Green Cultural Studies: Nature in Film, Novel, and Theory*. Moscow, ID: University of Idaho Press, 1998.

Marcone, Jorge. "De retorno a lo natural: *La serpiente de oro*, la 'novela de la selva' y la crítica ecológica." *Hispania* 81 (1998): 299–308.

_____. "*El hablador* de Mario Vargas Llosa y la imagen de la Amazonía en el Perú contemporáneo." In *La Chispa '93 Selected Proceedings*, edited by Gilberto Paolini, 134–40. New Orleans: Tulane University, 1993.

_____. "Historia secreta de una novela de Vargas Llosa o *La casa verde* y el viaje 'Retorno a lo natural' en la 'Novela de la selva' hispanoamericana." *Monographic Review/Revista Monográfica* XII: 379–92.

_____. "Jungle Fever: Primitivism in Environmentalism: Rómulo Gallegos's *Canaima* and the Romance of the Jungle." In *Primitivism and Identity in Latin America: Essays on Art, Literature, and Culture*, edited by Erik Camayd-Freixas and José Eduardo González, 157–72. Tucson: University of Arizona Press, 2000.

Miller, Shawn William. *An Environmental History of Latin America*. Cambridge: Cambridge University Press, 2007.

Montero, Mayra. *Tú, la oscuridad*. Barcelona: Tusquets, 1995. Translated by Edith Grossman as *In the Palm of Darkness: A Novel*. New York: Harper Collins Publishers, 1997.

Naess, Arne. "The Shallow and Deep, Long-Range Ecology Movement: A Summary." In Drengson and Inoue, *The Deep Ecology Movement*, 3–6.

_____. "Deep Ecology for the Twenty-Second Century." In Sessions, *Deep Ecology for the 21st Century*, 463–67.

Phillips, Dana. *The Truth of Ecology: Nature, Culture, and Literature in America*. New York: Oxford University Press, 2003.

Quiroga, Horacio. "El hombre muerto." In *Los desterrados*. 1925. 4th ed. Buenos Aires: Losada, 1970. 69–74. Translated by Margaret Sayers Peden as "The Dead Man" in *The Decapitated Chicken and Other Stories* (Austin: University of Texas Press, 1984).

Raga Castellanos, Fernando. *Los hijos de Gaia*. Buenos Aires: Ediciones Distal, 2005.

Rivera, José Eustasio. *La vorágine*. 1924. 7th ed. Mexico City: Porrúa, 1984. Translated by Earle K. James as *The Vortex* (Bogotá: Panamericana, 2001).

Rossi, Anacristina. *La loca de Gandoca*. 1992. San José: Centroamericana, 2000.

Sachs, Wolfgang. "Global Ecology and the Shadow of 'Development." In Sessions, *Deep Ecology for the Twenty-First Century*, 428–44.

Sarmiento, Domingo Faustino. *Facundo: Civilización y barbarie*. 1845. Edited by Roberto Yahni. Madrid: Cátedra, 1990.

Sepúlveda, Luis. *Mundo del fin del mundo*. Barcelona: Tusquets, 1994.
_____. *Patagonia Express*. Barcelona: Tusquets, 2002.
_____. *Un viejo que leía novelas de amor*. Barcelona: Tusquets, 1989.
Sessions, George, ed. *Deep Ecology for the 21st Century: Readings on the Philosophy and Practice of the New Environmentalism*. Boston: Shambhala, 1995.
Vargas Llosa, Mario. *El hablador*. Barcelona: Seix Barral, 1987. Translated as *The Storyteller* by Helen Lane. New York: Farrar, Straus & Giroux, 1989.
_____. *Historia de Mayta*. Barcelona: Seix Barral, 1984. Translated by Alfred Mac Adam as *The Real Life of Alejandro Mayta* (New York: Vintage, 1986).
White, Lynn, Jr. "The Historic Roots of Our Ecologic Crisis." In Glotfelty and Fromm, *The Ecocriticism Reader*, 3–14.

Nature and the Discourse of Modernity in Spanish American Avant-Garde Fiction

Adrian Taylor Kane

As Octavio Paz has affirmed, the concept of modernity has been a prominent concern of Latin American intellectuals since the nineteenth century.[1] Indeed, several literary critics have taken Spanish America's position within modernity as the central focus of their histories and broad analyses of Spanish American literature.[2] Among such critics, Raymond L. Williams has observed that during the 1920s and 30s authors interested in modernity generally went in one of two directions.[3] On the one hand, authors such as José Eustasio Rivera, Ricardo Güiraldes and Rómulo Gallegos explored the aesthetic possibilities presented by the unique natural landscapes of Spanish America. Their novels, *La vorágine* (*The Vortex*) *Don Segundo Sombra* and *Doña Bárbara* continued many of the aesthetic principles associated with nineteenth-century European realism and naturalism, and form what could currently be considered the canon of the *novela criollista*, also known as the regional or telluric novel. On the other hand, novelists such as Macedonio Fernández, Arqueles Vela and Martín Adán employed more innovative narrative strategies in their creation of an experimental avant-garde aesthetic that challenged many previous suppositions about the conventions of the novelistic genre.[4]

One important distinction between the telluric novel and the avant-garde novel is their varied representations of nature.[5] The telluric novel is often discussed in the context of the relationship between nature and national identity. Indeed, John Brushwood suggests that the regional novel was born of the persistent necessity to identify and name the objects and circumstances of the "New World" and the experience of living with them.[6] The discourse of modernity influenced Spanish American avant-garde novelists' representations of nature in a different way.[7] For Paz, the Spanish American avant-garde embodies the desire for rupture that is inherent in the concept of modernity.[8] Indeed, in their desire to modernize Latin American culture, many vanguardists rejected what they perceived to be outdated realist and naturalist tendencies. The result was a notable reduction in the images of the natural world, an increased interest in modern urban technologies and spaces, the occasional juxtaposition of urban and natural images and, in general, a new "dehumanized" representation of nature.[9] By presenting re-readings of several avant-garde narratives, the present essay seeks to explore the various ways in which the discourse of modernity affected the representation of nature in fiction from this time period.

To readers familiar with the aesthetic tendencies of Spanish American avant-garde fiction, ecocriticism might initially seem an unlikely approach to this corpus of literature. However, as Scott Slovic has suggested, ecocriticism is not limited to the study of explicitly environmental texts. It also includes, according to Slovic, "the scrutiny of ecological implications and human-nature relations in any literary text, even texts that seem, at first glance, oblivious of the nonhuman world."[10] Similarly, Richard Kerridge asserts that "The ecocritic wants to track environmental ideas and representations wherever they appear, to see more clearly a debate which seems to be taking place, often part-concealed, in a great many cultural spaces."[11]

While many of the works analyzed in this essay are, to varied extents, aware of their physical surroundings, none of them could easily be classified as nature writing.[12] Nevertheless, examining the cultural discourse of modernity and its various manifestations in these texts helps provide a historical context for the environmental challenges that Latin America faces today. For, as Jill Ker Conway, Kenneth Keniston and Leo Marx have argued, "if we are to understand and devise effective solutions for today's environmental threats, we must locate them within their larger historical, societal, and cultural setting."[13] Their perspective is aligned with the concept of deep ecology, which "examines the *roots* of our environmental/social problems [...] to achieve a fundamental ecological transformation of our sociocultural systems, collective actions, and lifestyles."[14] In demonstrating how the roots of the discourse of modernity run through avant-garde fiction, this essay aims, furthermore, to illustrate how this discourse has affected human attitudes toward nature in Spanish America.

Vicente Huidobro is perhaps the most widely recognized figure from the Spanish American avant-garde. His theory of *creacionismo* is an example, *par excellence*, of the vanguardists' desire to break from a literary aesthetic that mimetically represents the physical world. In "Non serviam," a manifesto read by Huidobro in Santiago, Chile in 1914, he expresses his weariness of poetry that extols the beauty of nature's creations. Written in the form of a short narrative, "Non serviam" presents the monologue of a poet who confronts Mother Nature by refusing to serve her, and urges his fellow poets to follow his lead. From the beginning of the manifesto, the poet makes clear to Mother Nature that he no longer intends to serve her. He shouts, "No te serviré," (I will not serve you) and later reiterates, *"Non serviam.* No he de ser tu esclavo, madre Natura; seré tu amo" (*Non serviam.* I must not be your slave, Mother Nature; I will be your master).[15] To the poets he laments:

> hasta ahora no hemos hecho otra cosa que imitar al mundo en sus aspectos, no hemos creado nada. [...] Hemos cantado a la Naturaleza (cosa que a ella bien poco le importa). [...] Nunca hemos creado realidades propias como ella lo hace o lo hizo en tiempos pasados, cuando era joven y llena de impulsos creadores.[16]

> [Until now we have done nothing but imitate nature in her aspects, we have not created anything. (...) We have sung to Nature (which matters very little to her). (...) We have never created realities of our own like she does or did in the past, when she was young and full of creative impulses.]

It is thus clear that for Huidobro the role of literature is no longer to copy what has already been created by nature.

Huidobro's 1916 poem "Arte poética" supports the ideas of *"Non serviam"* by proclaiming that a poet's ability to create should to be used to produce imagery previously unseen in the physical world. He exhorts his fellow poets to invent new worlds and concludes the poem by affirming the poet's power of creation in his well-known verse, "El poeta es un pequeño Dios" (The poet is a little God).[17] His theory of *creacionismo* is also stated concisely in his 1921 essay "Época de creación" in which he declares: "Debemos crear. El hombre ya no imita. Inventa, agrega a los hechos del mundo, nacidos en el seno de la Naturaleza, hechos nuevos nacidos en su cabeza" (We must create. Man no longer imitates. He invents, he adds to the world's creations, born in Nature's womb, new creations born in his head).[18] Although Huidobro is recognized more for his poetry than his fiction, his theory of *creacionismo* embodies the anxiety among avant-garde authors of all genres to break with the tradition of mimesis.

Jaime Torres Bodet, one of many vanguardists who published works in several genres, set forth his ideas about avant-garde fiction in "Reflexiones sobre la novela" (Reflections on the Novel). In this 1928 essay Torres Bodet expresses a desire for literary innovation similar to that of Huidobro. With regard to the literary traditions of the nineteenth century he states:

> El siglo XIX parece haberse complacido en dejarnos el mayor número de tradiciones que contrariar. Sería declararnos vencidos querer persistir en los cauces de las ideas aceptadas por los hombres del ochocientos. Las obras producidas bajo el imperio del positivismo ortodoxo pudieron ser bellas. No les neguemos nuestra admiración; neguémosles nuestra obediencia.[19]

[The nineteenth century seems to have satisfied itself by leaving us a great number of traditions to resist. To continue the course of the ideas accepted by the men from the 1800s would be to declare ourselves defeated. The works produced under the empire of orthodox positivism may have been beautiful. Let us not deny them our admiration; let us deny them our obedience.]

The defiant attitude, characteristic of the literary movements of the avant-garde, is quite obvious here. Torres Bodet takes specific aim at the philosophy of positivism that dominated intellectual thought at the turn of the century in Latin America. Based on the tenet that true knowledge could only be obtained through observable scientific data, positivism had a profound impact on the political and literary spheres in Latin America. As Williams observes, "the novelistic outcome of this more scientific worldview was the realist and naturalist novel."[20] Lengthy and detailed descriptions of the physical environment, both natural and man-made, often filled the pages of these novels to achieve a verisimilar representation of a particular place or situation. As Torres Bodet implies in the above quote, Spanish American avant-garde novelists sought a rupture with the realist-naturalist tradition that flourished under what he refers to as "the empire of positivism." They achieved this goal through a variety of narrative strategies that will be discussed below in the analysis of several texts from this period, but one obvious aesthetic change was a decrease in mimetic representations of the natural world.

For Spanish American avant-garde novelists, to depart with realist-naturalist tendencies was a way of modernizing their countries through culture. As theorists of the avant-garde have observed, technology also played a role in rendering nineteenth-century realism outmoded. Peter Bürger, drawing on the work of Walter Benjamin, asserts that "Because the advent of photography makes possible the precise mechanical reproduction of reality, the mimetic function of fine art withers."[21] Similarly, Renato Poggioli contends that "There is no doubt that pictorial realism, especially in the genres of portrait and landscape, has been destroyed by the invention of the camera. [...] [The artist's] aim now is not what was once called imitation; it is deformative representation or, indeed, just that abstract art which polemically gets labeled nonrepresentational."[22] Poggioli's and Bürger's respective observations with regard to the waning importance of mimetic representation coincide with José Ortega y Gasset's 1925 essay *La deshumanización del arte* (*The Dehumanization of Art*).

The title of Ortega y Gasset's essay alludes to a radical shift in the direction of European arts and literature. For Ortega y Gasset, the human aspect of a work refers to the repertoire of elements that comprise the natural or physical world in which we live. This, he suggests, includes a hierarchy of three levels: humans, living beings and inorganic objects.[23] Thus, despite the negative connotation of the word "dehumanization," Ortega y Gasset's observations refer to a denaturalized or anti-realist aesthetic, not to a creative act that is somehow less human. He asserts:

> Lejos de ir el pintor más o menos torpemente hacia la realidad, se ve que ha ido contra ella. Se ha propuesto denodadamente deformarla, romper su aspecto humano, deshumanizarla. [...]
> No se trata de pintar algo que sea por completo distinto de un hombre, o casa, o montaña, sino de pintar un hombre que se parezca lo menos posible a un hombre, una casa que conserve de tal lo estrictamente necesario para que asistamos a su metamorfosis, un cono que ha salido milagrosamente de lo que era antes una montaña, como la serpiente sale de su camisa. El placer estético para el artista nuevo emana de ese triunfo sobre lo humano; por eso es preciso concretar la victoria y presentar en cada caso la víctima estrangulada.[24]

> [Far from going more or less clumsily toward reality, the artist is seen going against it. He is brazenly set on deforming reality, shattering its human aspect, dehumanizing it. (...)
> The question is not to paint something altogether different from a man, a house, a mountain, but to paint a man who resembles a man as little as possible; a house that preserves of a house exactly what is needed to reveal the metamorphosis; a cone miraculously emerging — as the snake from his slough — from what used to be a mountain. For the modern artist, aesthetic pleasure derives from such a triumph over human matter. That is why he has to drive home the victory by presenting in each case the strangled victim.][25]

Ortega y Gasset perceives in avant-garde art and literature the embodiment of Huidobro's declaration that the role of the poet is no longer to reflect the reality in which he lives, but rather to invent what does not yet exist. Although Ortega y Gasset wrote from Spain about European art and literature, *La deshumanización del arte* was an important essay for many Latin American vanguardists whose work entered into a trans-Atlantic dialogue with many of the authors and movements that were taking place on the continent.

André Breton was another European figure whose ideas undoubtedly contributed to the dialogue on modernity in Latin American art and literature during and beyond the years of the historical avant-garde. Similar to Torres Bodet, Breton viewed positivism as a discourse that stifled the creative potential that art and literature inherently possess. His theories of surrealism can thus be understood, in part, as a way of liberating art and literature from what he views as "the reign of logic" and "absolute rationalism" that dominated intellectual discourse in Europe "under the pretense of civilization and progress" until the First World War.[26] Surrealism's response to positivism was to explore the potential of the human imagination and subconscious to reveal truths that might not be proven by reason alone. In his 1924 "Manifesto of Surrealism," Breton suggests that "The imagination is perhaps on the point of reasserting itself, of reclaiming its rights. If the depths of our mind contain within it strange forces capable of augmenting those on the surface, or of waging a victorious battle against them, there is every reason to seize them — first to seize them, then, if need be, to submit them to the control of our reason."[27] With regard to literature, he ultimately proclaims that "it is time to have done with the provoking insanities of 'realism.'"[28] Breton therefore clearly coincides with his trans-Atlantic contemporaries' call for a new aesthetic that would not be bound by scientific discourse or representation of the physical world. As theorists of the avant-garde Ortega y Gasset, Poggioli and Bürger have all observed, this fundamental shift is one of the defining characteristics of avant-garde literature and art. The following section of this essay examines the ways in which several Spanish American works of fiction embody the theories of avant-garde aesthetics discussed above.

Guatemalan author Luis Cardoza y Aragón was one of many Spanish American intellectuals who traveled to Europe during the 1920s to participate in the literary movements that were sweeping the continent. In his quest for literary modernity, Cardoza y Aragón associated with major literary figures such as César Vallejo, Vicente Huidobro and Ramón Gómez de la Serna, who demonstrated to him the possibilities of the avant-garde aesthetic for the Spanish language.[29] Furthermore, through his friendship with Tristan Tzara, André Breton, Paul Eluard, Robert Desnos and Antonin Artaud, he was introduced to surrealism, and thus to a new vision of literature, life and knowledge. During his time in Europe, Cardoza y Aragón developed an avant-garde impulse that pervades his early work.[30]

Cardoza's 1926 novel *Maelstrom: films telescopiados* (Maelstrom: telescoped films) is the story of a poet named Keemby. The structure consists of five chapters that are mainly episodes in Keemby's life. Four of the five chapters include intercalated poems, and there is no chronological or causal relationship between each episode. Several events in the novel reveal a belligerence towards nature's conventional role in art. In the second episode, for example, Keemby decides to destroy an airplane by jumping on top of it. As the plane turns to smoke, Keemby descends into Pompierlandia, described as "la tierra donde no ha sucedido nada nunca" (the land where nothing has ever happened).[31] The citizens of Pompierlandia have no national flag, but when Keemby shows them a Picasso painting, they quickly adopt it as their national emblem. Their new flag inspires rapid change in Pompierlandia. Significantly, nature's resentment of art visibly diminishes, and women begin giving birth to cubist babies. The transformation of Pompierlandia, inspired by the Picasso painting, can be understood as a call for a new form of art that revolutionizes society. The narrator notes: "Disminuía, visiblemente, el rencor que guarda la Naturaleza por el arte" [Nature's resentment of art was visibly diminishing] (32). He thus implies that nature took offense to the previously dominant mimetic forms of realism and naturalism, and is relieved by the presence of avant-garde art.

The second chapter draws further attention to the contentious relationship between art and nature when Keemby publishes his book *Insultos a nuestra madre naturaleza* (Insults to our Mother Nature). Reminiscent of Huidobro's refusal to continue serving nature in "Non serviam," the title of Keemby's book embodies the vanguardists' desire to transcend the representation of that which already exists. Indeed, as Ramón Gómez de la Serna asserts in his prologue to *Maelstrom*: "Hay que fumigar la naturaleza con imágenes nuevas" [We must fumigate nature with new images].[32] *Insultos a nuestra madre naturaleza* is described as "Obra comprensible únicamente por pasión (¡oh, nunca por inteligencia!): el Sueño es la verdadera vida" [A work only understandable through passion (oh, never through intelligence!): Dreams are the true life] (32). The former half of this sentence can be understood as a rejection of the scientific discourse of positivism. The latter comment, "el Sueño es la verdadera vida," is one of many examples of the influence of surrealism in *Maelstrom*. Pompierlandia's transformation, triggered by avant-garde aesthetics, is consistent with the Surrealists' belief in the revolutionary role of art in society.

Insultos a nuestra Madre Naturaleza is about Keemby's love affair with his partner Paisaje. The symbolism of Paisaje's name (landscape in English) lends itself to playfully ironic and metaphorical interactions between art and nature. At the beginning of the fourth chapter, for example, Paisaje expresses his boredom with nature: "Mi madrastra, Madame la Nature, me trata muy mal... Desde que vivo tengo cuatro trajes que me aburren ya: Otoño, Estío... Tú conoces los otros dos. ¡Cómo desearía vestirme con ropas de Poiret, bufandas de Léger o Delaunay, cuadros de Diego Rivera o Carlos Mérida!" [My stepmother, Madame Nature, treats me very badly... Since I was born I have had four suits that now bore me: Autumn, Summer... You know the other two. How I would love to dress with clothes by Poiret, scarves by Léger o Delaunay, paintings by Diego Rivera or Carlos Mérida!] (76–77). Paisaje's desire to be transformed by avant-garde fashion-designers and painters is a metaphor for the vanguardists' eagerness to go beyond mimetic representation of the physical world.

A similar notion is expressed later in the same chapter when Paisaje reacts to a photographic camera with great trepidation. Keemby recounts: "Entonces, deseando agradar a Paisaje, armé mi Kodak. Al verlo empezó a gritar desesperadamente. Temblaba de pavor. ¡Teníale más miedo que a un revólver!" [Then, desiring to please Paisaje, I armed my Kodak. Upon seeing it he began to scream desperately. He was trembling with fear. He was more afraid of it than a revolver!] (75). Paisaje's reaction to the camera once again implies a rejection of realism. The analogy between the camera and the revolver suggests that realism does violence to nature. This image is repeated later when a would-be-seducer locks Paisaje in his house and begins taking snapshots. The camera is described as "feroz como una ametralladora," (ferocious like a machine-gun) and Paisaje is wounded several times (81). In the same chapter, the police chase Paisaje with their Kodaks after spotting him on Keemby's roof. Paisaje is captured, handcuffed, inserted in a glass frame and sent to the Louvre. For the predominantly future-minded vanguardists, a museum was equivalent to a prison. Thus, Keemby and a cohort of cosmopolitan authors, artists and composers committed to innovation decide to liberate Paisaje from the Louvre. Included among his rescuers are Jean Cocteau, Pablo Picasso, Igor Strawinksy, Andre Bretón and Max Jacob. Upon his escape, Paisaje and Keemby return to Pompierlandia, a land that has been emancipated by avant-garde art.

In the last passage of the novel, Keemby holds a character named Belleza at gunpoint, steals her pearl necklace and decapitates her breasts with kisses. Belleza's mutilation clearly symbolizes the transformation of art and the concept of beauty that the implied author has consistently promoted throughout the novel. As the narrator states: "Lo perfecto, lo bilateral, lo simétrico, lo completo, lo disciplinado, lo par, lo lógico, lo exacto, lo congruente, lo natural, lo razonable, lo plural, lo... no es nunca magnífico" [That which is perfect, bilateral, symmetrical, complete, disciplined, even, logical, exact, congruent, natural, reasonable, plural... is never magnificent] (104). The new concept of beauty posited in this quote and throughout *Maelstrom* is the deformed or dehumanized aesthetic that Ortega y Gasset keenly observed in avant-garde art.

From the beginning of *Maelstrom*, there is a clear departure from the realist-naturalist tradition. Throughout the novel, the empirical world and the notion of objective reality are juxtaposed with dreams and imagination. Indeed, taken as a whole, *Maelstrom* can be interpreted as a manifesto or *ars poetica* of its own. Realism and naturalism give way to an overabundance of free-flowing imagery. Reason is replaced by the absurd, and positivism is challenged by surrealism. By privileging imagination and incorporating surrealist elements in *Maelstrom*, Cardoza implicitly undermines the positivist basis of the realist-naturalist novel. Ultimately, a new relationship between art and nature is presented through a series of playful, symbolic rejections of conventional mimetic representations of the physical world.

Published one year after *Maelstrom*, Jaime Torres Bodet's 1927 novel *Margarita de niebla* (Margarita of Mist) also presents a departure from the realist-naturalist tradition. As a member of the Mexican avant-garde group the *Contemporáneos*, Torres Bodet was committed to modernizing Mexican literature and culture. He viewed the group's flagship publication, *Contemporáneos: revista mexicana de cultura* (1928–1931), as a cultural bridge between Europe and the Americas, as well as a forum for dialogue on the innovative literary and artistic movements that were occurring on both sides of the Atlantic.[33] In their attempt to modernize Mexican literature, the *Contemporáneos* faced two specific challenges. First, by moving towards more universal themes, they sought to distance their work from what they viewed as an overly parochial focus in the novels of the Mexican Revolution. Second, they aimed to undermine the positivist suppositions of realism and naturalism through experimentation with new aesthetic possibilities. These strategies inevitably affected the representation of nature in their novels.

As Vicky Unruh and Gustavo Pérez Firmat have indicated, Spanish American avant-garde literature often served as a forum for writers to discuss art.[34] Consequently, much of the fiction from this era demonstrates an interest in presenting an artistic idea, rather than telling a story, which is precisely the case of *Margarita de niebla*. The premise of the story is that the narrator Carlos Borja, a young professor of Spanish, falls in love with a German-born student, Margarita Millers. The situation becomes complicated when Carlos becomes attracted to Margarita's best friend, Paloma, and is further compounded when Paloma falls in love with Margarita's former boyfriend, Otto Schmiltzer. The story, however, serves as a mere pretext for presenting new novelistic possibilities and promoting a change in aesthetics.

Throughout *Margarita de niebla*, Torres Bodet alludes to a shift in artistic spirit that characterizes the avant-garde era. While discussing music with Margarita's mother, for example, Borja remarks: "no podemos seguir siendo devotos de una música que corresponde a una manera espiritual que ya no es nuestra, a la sensibilidad de un mundo desaparecido" [we cannot continue being devotees to a music that corresponds to a spiritual way that is no longer ours, to the sensibility of a disappeared world].[35] Borja's comment echoes the consistent call of the *Contemporáneos* and other vanguardists for a modernization of Latin American culture. Further along in the novel, Borja gazes into a mirror and perceives an aesthetic transfiguration in his own reflection:

Un cambio de escuelas en el arte decorativo del espejo. La tela impresionista del amanecer ha ido endureciéndose, enfriándose hasta lograr el esqueleto y la temperatura del cubismo. La niebla que es la carne de los personajes fluidos de María Laurencin, cedió el puesto a un sol oblicuo y psicológico. Como en ciertos cuadros de Picasso, los árboles del fondo resuelven el problema de sus volúmenes con una habilidad geométrica y mi semblante, que parecía hasta hace media hora el retrato de Daudet por Carrière, se ha enrojecido en los pómulos y se ha limitado con un grueso óvalo de sombra hasta adquirir semejanza con El Americano de Grigorview [68].

[A change of schools in the mirror's decorative art. Dawn's impressionist cloth has been hardening, cooling off until it achieves the skeleton and temperature of cubism. The fog that is the flesh of the fluid characters of María Laurencin yielded to an oblique and psychological sun. As in certain paintings by Picasso, the trees in the background resolve the problem of their volume with a geometric ability, and my semblance, which until half-an-hour ago looked like the portrait of Daudet by Carrière, has reddened in the cheeks, bordered by a thick oval of shadow until acquiring the likeness of Grigorview's "The American."]

In this passage, Borja is witness to the cultural transformation that the vanguardists so ardently desired to see in their own countries. The image is a transition from nineteenth-century impressionism and symbolism to the more dynamic aesthetic of twentieth-century cubism.[36] The metaphorical implication is a modernization of aesthetic sensibility. In the background, the trees are described in geometrical terms and compared with Picasso's paintings. The vision created by this description is an excellent example of one way that nature is dehumanized in *Margarita de niebla* for creative purposes. This interest in creating a more dynamic aesthetic was common among Spanish American vanguardists. The Argentine *Ultraístas*, for example, in their "Manifiesto de Ultra" establish the theory behind such an aesthetic. They assert, "Existen dos estéticas: la estética pasiva de los espejos y la estética activa de los prismas... Guiado por la segunda, el arte se redime, hace del mundo su instrumento, y forja — más allá de las cárceles espaciales y temporales — su visión personal" [There are two aesthetics that exist: the passive aesthetic of mirrors and the active aesthetic of prisms... Guided by the second, art redeems itself, it makes the world its instrument, and forges — beyond spatial and temporal prisons — its personal vision].[37] Such representation of the physical world poses a stark contrast with the natural imagery in the Spanish American telluric novels of the same period. Whereas the telluric novel attempts to convey the realities of life in the natural settings of Latin America via lengthy descriptions and realist imagery, the avant-garde novel frequently presents nature in abstract terms.

The most striking form of abstraction in *Margarita de niebla* is the use of what Gustavo Pérez Firmat has called the "pneumatic effect." He states:

> In the most general terms the pneumatic effect shows through in images which, in one way or another, convey a sense of dissolution or weightlessness. It represents an ascensional movement and a centrifugal force: up, and away. Pneumatics comprehends that branch of physics that studies the properties of air and other gases. The pneumatic effect, consequently, is the informing principle of imagery that embodies some of these properties.[38]

In *Margarita de niebla*, natural elements such as fog and mist are used to create a pneumatic aesthetic. For example, the clothing of young girls walking through a park is described as water and air: "Algunas se han hecho los tra-jes con dos metros de brisa. La más esbelta va vestida de agua" [Some have made their suits with two meters of breeze. The thinnest goes dressed in water] (48). Such imagery creates the effect of a world that is somewhere between existent and nonexistent. It is visible yet impalpable. The pneumatic aesthetic created in *Margarita de niebla* coincides with the protagonist's sensibility, who declares his disdain for a reality that is immediately accessible to the physical senses. Borja exclaims, "La realidad de lo que puedo inmedi-atamente oler, tocar, sentir, me desagrada como un compromiso" [The reality of what I can immediately smell, touch, feel, displeases me like a commit-ment] (54). This comment by Borja echoes the novelistic preferences expressed by Torres Bodet in "Reflexiones sobre la novela." In this essay he asserts that a perfect novel would be one that kills the reader from "asfixia de la realidad, por sustitución de su atmósfera a la nuestra" (suffocation of reality, by sub-stitution of its atmosphere for ours).[39] Ultimately, this is the effect that is achieved in *Margarita de niebla*. Through a series of innovative narrative tech-niques, Torres Bodet subverts the positivist suppositions of the realist-natu-ralist tradition. The natural world in *Margarita de niebla* is either abstracted through cubist imagery or dissipates into the nebulous reality created through the pneumatic effect.

Max Jiménez's *Unos fantoches* (1928; Some puppets), like *Margarita de niebla*, offers the possibility of a new novelistic aesthetic. The principal dif-ference between the two works is that while Torres Bodet subtly demonstrates his artistic ideas through techniques such as those discussed above, Jiménez directly communicates his strategies via metafictional commentary. As Álvaro Quesada Soto has observed, the plot of *Unos fantoches* develops simultane-ously on two narrative planes.[40] The first level is based on an apparent love triangle between a playwright, his wife and a friend of the couple. This trite, melodramatic storyline, however, is a mere pretext for the creation of the sec-ond narrative plane in which the characters known as *El autor* and *El público* appear.

It is on this plane that the text reveals the possibility of a new anti-real-ist novel. The character named *El autor* lays bare the novel's techniques through continuous interjections about the creative process. He confirms his avant-garde posture at the beginning of the novel, as he declares his prefer-ence for doubt and obscurity over "la desnuda crueldad de la verdad pura" (the naked cruelty of the pure truth).[41] He reaffirms his predilection for ambi-guity at the end of the first half of the novel when he decides to end the story without resolving any conflict. Elsewhere he confesses that his inclination towards brevity stems from his desire to be modern: "Culpa es de la vida moderna que nos exige variedad; la actividad en que vivimos no da lugar a escritos que pasen de cierto límite [...] La tendencia es general: reducir volumen y aumentar calidad" [It is the fault of modern life that demands variety, the activity in which we live leaves no place for writings that exceed a certain limit [...] The tendency is general: reduce volume and increase quality] (25). *El autor* further reveals the novelistic process as he spontaneously creates the characters of the first narrative plane. The scarcely-developed characters resemble cardboard figures more than life-like personages, and are not given names. They are simply known as *Él, Ella* and *El amante*. This technique of decharacterization is a rejection of the nineteenth-century tradition of well defined characters.[42] The ultimate effect of *El autor*'s metafictional commentary is to defamiliarize the text. The reader is constantly reminded that *Unos fantoches* is a literary invention, not a recreation of reality.

The anti-realist aesthetic of *Unos fantoches* inevitably affects the novel's representation of nature. As much of the text's focus is on the metafictional plane, nature is nearly completely eliminated. There are only two passages in the novel that make reference to the physical environment. The first is a description of the sort of night during which the supposed lovers from the first narrative plane would take walks together: "una noche clara en que los árboles juegan de fantasmas, en que la luna es una uña desprendida al Creador, en que a lo lejos las chimeneas son a manera de dedos salidos a la tierra que acarician suavemente el cielo con su color rosa" [a clear night in which the trees play ghosts, in which the moon is a fingernail detached from the Creator, in which the chimneys in the distance are like fingers protruding from the earth that gently caress the sky with their rose color] (19). Here nature is presented through playful personification and audacious metaphorical imagery. Rather than a verisimilar description of the landscape, the effect achieved through such imagery is more akin to a surrealist caricature.

The second significant reference to the natural world appears in the last paragraph of the novel. *El autor*, having traveled from Latin America to Europe, reflects upon the universality of *Unos fantoches*'s theme of a whimsical destiny by comparing the landscapes on both sides of the Atlantic. Here too nature is presented through personification and metaphor: "allá en la América, allá en el trópico, con sus atardeceres que acarician la palmas hijas del Mago Sol, o acá en Europa, entre las tardes de triste plata, en el otoño que desviste a los árboles después de marchitar su túnica" [Over there in America, over in the tropics, with their sunsets that caress the palms, daughters of the magician Sun, or here in Europe, among the sad, silver afternoons, in the autumn that undresses the trees after their tunic has withered] (50). The image of the tropics initially appears to resemble mimetic representation, but becomes fantastic when the sun is presented as a magical character. Moreover, the vision of European foliage as a tunic is precisely the type of unusual, unexpected imagery that the vanguardists sought to create by emphasizing the importance of invention.

While nature is largely elided in *Unos fantoches*, the few references that do appear remain faithful to the anti-realist agenda set forth in this novel. *El autor* alludes to this notion as he contemplates, "la realidad de las cosas [¿]para qué profundizarla?" [the reality of things, why go into to depth about it?] (18). Brevity, spontaneity, ambiguity, decharacterization, metafiction, defamiliarization and metaphorical imagery are the ingredients in Jiménez's recipe for subverting novelistic conventions. Nature in *Unos fantoches* is relegated to a nearly non-existent role, as the text is dominated by the metafictional musings of *El autor*.

Macedonio Fernandez's *Papeles de recienvenido* (1929; Papers of a newcomer) is similar to Jimenez's novel in several ways. It is a compilation of miscellaneous writings of various genres that, as Hugo J. Verani observes, is characterized by humor and an apparent incoherence: "Macedonio vacía la ficción de referencialidad, rehusando contar una historia [...] interpone prólogos, notas del editor, cartas, notas al pie de página, digresiones, paradojas, mensajes contradictorios, paréntesis a los paréntesis" [Macedonio empties fiction of its referentiality, refusing to tell a story (...) he inserts prologues, editor's notes, letters, footnotes, digressions, paradoxes, contradictory messages, parentheses to the parentheses.][43] Like *Unos fantoches*, Fernández's text is replete with self-reflexive passages. The reader, directly addressed as "mi lector," becomes an accomplice in the creative process.[44] However, rather than creating ambiguity to defy positivism, *Papeles de recienvenido* relies upon the illogical and the absurd, which contribute to the work's ludic tone. In its radical experimentation, *Papeles de recienvenido* takes an iconoclastic stance towards any form of literary tradition. Plot, character and setting fall victim to the destruction of novelistic conventions. Nearly devoid of references to the physical world, *Papeles de recienvenido* subverts mimetic representation. As in *Unos fantoches*, the natural world is effectively eliminated.

Felisberto Hernández's short story "Genealogía" (1926; Genealogy) pushes the limit of experimentation even one step further. In this text, characters are replaced with geometrical shapes. Divided into six one-paragraph fragments, the plot consists of the interaction between these shapes, as well as their continual transformations. A circumference, for example, becomes an ellipse, which is subsequently enclosed in a quadrilateral. When the shapes eventually die, they lose their form and become horizontal lines. There is no reference to nature (human or non-human) in this story; the setting is simply space. Hernandez's text participates in the avant-garde quest for modernity by challenging literary conventions. In "Genealogía" ecology is nowhere to be found.

"Genealogía," *Papeles de recienvenido, Unos fantoches, Margarita de niebla* and *Maelstrom* display a common rejection of the positivist suppositions of the realist-naturalist tradition. In the first half of the present essay, therefore, we have seen that through a variety of narrative strategies, the above-mentioned works of fiction avoid mimetic representation of the physical world, and therefore of nature. The remainder of this essay will demonstrate that a second way in which Spanish American avant-garde fiction engaged with the discourse of modernity was to explore the aesthetic possibilities of the rapidly-growing urban spaces and the new technologies that were transforming them. While in many cases this interest resulted in texts in which the natural environment had little or no importance, in other instances it led to intriguing juxtapositions of natural and urban imagery.

One excellent example of the transition in Spanish American avant-garde fiction toward a more urban aesthetic is Salvador Novo's novella *El joven* (1928; The young man). In this brief narrative, the young protagonist experiences the outside world again after an illness, and is thus given the opportunity to see with fresh eyes the city that he knows so well. His musings begin with a reflection on the ways in which Mexico has been transformed in the wake of the Revolution. He ironically observes, for example, that before the Revolution, one could cross the street without concern for the excessive quantity of "hijos de Ford" (sons of Ford) that now dominate it.[45] As he traverses the city, his thoughts continually drift from one topic to another. They range from modern science to groups of university students to American film and Mexican literature. As the storytelling function is lost amidst the narrator's rambling from one topic to the next, the text could accurately be described as a glimpse of a young man's perception of the modern world. In *El joven* nature is largely elided, and replaced with imagery of the modern city. In the opening passage, the narrator observes that "desde el alba, en vez de los gallos higiénicos que hubiera amado oír, había sentido la voz de los autos" (Since dawn, rather than the hygienic roosters that he would have loved to hear, he had sensed the voice of the automobiles.)[46] The cars' replacement of roosters, an image that is also repeated at the end of the text, is a cogent symbol of the cultural transition that Mexico City was experiencing during the 1920s. Novo, as a member of the *Contemporáneos* group, was interested in promoting the modernization of Mexican culture. The exploration of the aesthetic possibilities of urban spaces in *El joven* is evidence of the vanguardists' desire for a more cosmopolitan aesthetic and their interest in a new form of subjectivity.

Also writing in Mexico during the 1920s, the *Estridentistas* drew heavily on the aesthetic ideas of F.T. Marinetti, the Italian leader of the Futurist movement. The Futurists, who employed lavish imagery glorifying the force and velocity of mechanized technology, vehemently rejected anything associated with the past. The *Estridentistas* varied from the Futurists by emphasizing the present (revolutionary Mexico) rather than the future, but exhibited a common interest in the aesthetics of modern machinery. For Marinetti, machinery formed part of a bellicose fascist agenda, whereas for *Estridentista* Manuel Maples Arce, it was associated with the proletarian revolution. Like the *Contemporáneos*, the *Estridentistas* sought a modernization of Mexican society through cultural renovation and revolutionary aesthetics. In the *Estridentistas'* first manifesto, Maples Arce proclaims:

> Es necesario exaltar en todos los tonos estridentes de nuestro diapasón propagandista, la belleza actualista de las máquinas, de los puentes gímnicos reciamente extendidos sobre las vertientes por músculos de acero, el humo de las fábricas, las emociones cubistas de los grandes trasatlánticos con humeantes chimeneas de rojo y negro [...] el régimen industrialista de las grandes ciudades palpitantes [...] toda esta belleza del siglo [...] comprendida por todos los artistas de vanguardia.[47]

> [It is necessary to exalt in every strident tone of our propagandist fingerboard, the presentist beauty of machines, of our athletic bridges sturdily extended over the waters by steel muscles, the smoke from the factories, the cubist emotions of the great transatlantic ships with smoking chimneys of red and black [...] the industrialist regime of the large, palpitating cities [...] all of this century's beauty [...] understood by all of the avant-garde artists.]

According to this view, modernity offers a new form of beauty, and the role of the vanguardist is to create an artistic or literary rendering of it. For the *Estridentistas*, even exhaust fumes are beautiful because they reek of modernity.[48] As declared in "Manifiesto Estridentista Número 2," the exaltation of machinery is part of their march towards the future.[49] Therefore, unusual imagery such as car tires, sparkplugs and gasoline are incorporated into the *Estridentistas'* aesthetic.[50] The ultimate goal of the group is summed up in well in the phrase "Cosmopoliticémonos" (Let us become cosmopolitan) from the group's first manifesto.[51] With respect to the environment, it is noteworthy that in the *Estridentistas'* zeal for representing dynamic urban settings and powerful machinery, their manifestos demonstrate a lack of sensitivity to the noxious environmental effects of the technologies that they praise. A twenty-first century reading of the *Estridentistas'* manifestos clearly reveals a cultural desire for a form of modernity that would eventually have significant implications for the natural environment.

   Estridentista novelist Arqueles Vela published *El café de nadie* in 1926 with the subtitle "Novelas." It includes three separate works: "El café de nadie," *Un crimen provisional* and *La señorita etc.* As discussed below, these short novels continue the *Estridenistas'* engagement with the discourse of modernity.

All three could be grouped with the novels analyzed in the first half of this chapter for their rejection of realist tendencies, but "El café de nadie" and *La señorita etc.* are also of interest for their exploration of the connection between urban spaces, modernity and subjectivity.[52]

"El café de nadie" is a radically fragmented narrative about the surreal ambience of a Mexico City café. The subjectivity of Mabelina, one of its customers, is also a central concern. The text begins and ends with the image of the café's door to the city opening and closing. The image of the threshold is an appropriate metaphor for the intermediate space that is created by the text as a whole. This space is found somewhere between reality and unreality, consciousness and subconsciousness, present and past. Brushwood has observed that in Vela's novel, "Material objects exist in some half recognized state that is removed from reality and is still not quite unreal [...] the characters themselves are somewhere between real and unreal."[53] At the end of the novel, before leaving the café, Mabelina presses an electronic button, "queriendo llamar a la realidad" (trying to call reality), but the question of what is real and what is not in "El café de nadie" is never resolved.[54]

Although the majority of the narrative is set inside of the café, the third and fifth fragments include images of the city beyond the café. As Mabelina and her companion speed through the streets of Mexico City in their car, they quickly change direction when they decide to go to the café. In one of the few references to nature in the text, the narrator observes that "Los árboles, despertados violentamente por la carrera del auto, se iban tropezando a lo largo de la rápida perspectiva" [The trees, violently awoken by the rushing automobile, went stumbling along the rapid perspective] (25). Given the *Estridentistas'* interest in portraying the dynamics of modern technology, it is not surprising that in this image, the trees appear to be dominated by the automobile's velocity. Vela, however, takes a more critical approach to the concept of technology than the view presented in the *Estridentistas'* manifestos. Whereas, according to their manifestos, the *Estridentistas* are enamored of modern technology's force, Vela's novels raise the question of how urban industrial life transforms the human experience. "El café de nadie" hints at this theme by describing the mechanized motions of two of the café's regular customers, but in *La señorita etc.* the theme of the modern human condition is even more prominent.[55]

In *La señorita etc.* an unidentified narrator recounts his experiences with the eponymous character, who is at once an individual and a multitude of subjects. His encounters with her may occur in memories, dreams, imaginations or empirical reality. Similar to "El café de nadie," the structure of *La señorita etc.* is open and fragmented with no causal link between fragments. Throughout the narrative, the city becomes an active agent in the plot, rather than a passive setting.[56] The narrator states, for example, "La vida casi mecánica de las ciudades modernas, me iba transformando. [...] Me acostumbraba a no tener las facultades de caminar conscientemente. Encerrado en un coche, me perdía en el sonambulismo de las calles" [The almost mechanical life of modern cities was transforming me. I was growing accustomed to not having the faculties to walk consciously. Enclosed in a car, I would lose myself in the somnambulism of the streets] (87). He subsequently discovers that la Señorita Etc. has also become mechanized: "Era en realidad, ella, pero era una mujer automática. [...] Sus movimientos eran a líneas rectas, sus palabras las resucitaba una delicada aguja de fonógrafo... Sus senos, temblorosos, de 'amperes'" [It was in reality she, but she was an automatic woman (...) Her movements were in straight lines, her words were resuscitated by a delicate phonograph needle... Her breasts, shaky from amperes] (87–88). While *La señorita etc.*, like other avant-garde texts, manifests its modernity by incorporating new technologies, the above passages suggest that the twentieth-century metropolis was capable of eroding some aspect of its citizens' humanity. However, due to the highly ambiguous nature of the text, the precise causes of such erosion remain unclear. Katharina Niemeyer argues that the city in *La señorita etc.* is the center of a ubiquitous modernity that leaves no space for individual subjectivity.[57] For Elizabeth Coonrod Martínez, La señorita etc. is the artistic muse of modernity and technology.[58] This novel is an example, *par excellence*, of Spanish American avant-garde fiction's focus on urban spaces rather than the varied landscapes of the regional novel.

The city also plays a prominent role in Roberto Arlt's first novel *El juguete rabioso* (1926; *Mad Toy*). It is the story of adolescent protagonist Silvio Astier as he negotiates the merciless streets of 1920s Buenos Aires while simultaneously searching for his own identity. Much of the novel focuses on Silvio's suffering due to difficult socio-economic conditions, but its attention to more universal existential questions prevent its characterization as a purely social novel.[59] The city in *El juguete rabioso* is filled with automobiles, trolleys, electric lights and tall buildings, but the novel is not an ode to modern technology or cosmopolitan society. Rather, the city's description often helps illuminate distinctions in social classes. The following quote, for example, describes an upper-class shopping district:

> Eran las siete de la tarde y la calle Lavalle estaba en su más babilónico esplendor. Los cafés a través de las vidrieras veíanse abarrotados de consumidores; en los atrios de los teatros y cinematógrafos aguardaban desocupados elegantes, y los escaparates de las casas de modas con sus piernas calzadas de finas medias y suspendidas de brazos niquelados, las vidrieras de las ortopedias y joyerías mostraban en su opulencia la astucia de todos esos comerciantes halagando con artículos de malicia la voluptuosidad de las gentes poderosas en dinero.[60]

[It was seven in the evening, and Lavalle Street was at its Babylonian best. The coffeehouses were crammed with customers, the elegant idle stood around in the lobbies of theaters and movie houses, and the display windows of clothing stores, where legs sheathed in fine stockings hung from nickel-plated bars, the show windows of orthopedic shops and jewelry stores exhibited in their opulence the cunning of all those businessmen who pandered to the lust of the wealthy with smart merchandise.][61]

In this passage, Silvio peers into a segment of society from which he has been marginalized. This presents a marked contrast with the outskirts of Buenos Aires where he walks his daily route as a paper salesman. He describes these streets as "las chatas calles del arrabal, miserables y sucias, inundadas de sol, con cajones de basura a las puertas" (wretched and dirty, sun-drenched, with garbage bins at the gates), and contrasts them with the "arco de cielo más limpio y diáfano" (127) [clean, clear sky] (121). As demonstrated in these examples, the city in *El juguete rabioso* presents remarkably varied realities for different social classes. This creates an ideal setting for Silvio to wrestle with his own misery while pondering the possibility of attaining happiness in life.

In this novel Arlt also captures several images of nature embedded in the cityscape. From an ecocritical perspective, two passages are particularly revealing. The first image is a glimpse of the city from the upstairs window of the bookstore where Silvio works: "Allá lejos, una chimenea entre dos tanques arrojaba grandes lienzos de humo al espacio pespunteado por agujas de agua" (72) [In the distance, a chimney flanked by two tanks belched out great gauzy strips of smoke into space stitched by needles of rain] (60). The second passage takes place at the city's port as Silvio seeks to escape to Europe on an ocean liner shortly after being dismissed from the air force: "por los bordes de los diques caminaba, fijos los ojos en las aguas violentas y grasientas que con ruido gutural lamían el granite" (118) [I walked along the edge of the docks, my eyes fixed on the greasy, violet waters that were licking the granite with a guttural noise] (110). Both descriptions are noteworthy for their attention to the city's pollution, but Silvio's observations of the contaminated air and water are seemingly impartial. The portrayal of the city in *El juguete rabioso* is neutral — it is neither a naïve glorification nor a moralistic condemnation. Significantly, however, both of these passages come in moments of despair, and thus add to the melancholy tone.

As the setting for the protagonist's existential struggle, the modern city weighs heavily on his mind. Shortly before his attempted suicide, he suffers a nightmare in which a madman relentlessly pursues him. The dream begins as follows: "En una llanura de asfalto, manchas de aceite violeta brillaban tristemente bajo un cielo de buriel. En el cenit otro pedazo de altura era de un azul purísimo. Dispersos sin orden, se elevaban por todas partes cubos portland" (110) [On an asphalt plain, stains of violet-colored oil gleamed sadly under a burlap sky. At the zenith, another patch of height was pure blue. Scattered everywhere, cubes of Portland cement rose from the landscape] (102). The space of the dream, with its oil-stained asphalt and cement is conspicuously urban. The omnipresent cement blocks emerging from the land symbolize the city's incipient modernity. Silvio attempts to hide behind them as he flees the grasp of the madman's extended arm. The dream's implication is that the twentieth-century city presents new forms of social and psychological oppression, as presented throughout the novel.

In several instances, nature is presented as an escape from Silvio's harsh reality in the city. He recalls, for example, that as he pondered the sky above the filthy outskirts of Buenos Aires, "Mis ojos bebían ávidamente la serenidad infinita, extática en el espacio celeste (127) [My eyes eagerly drank in the peace, the infinite ecstasy of that heavenly blue space] (121). Tired of walking his route as a paper salesman, he daydreams of idyllic Andalusian landscapes, and in the novel's final passage, he expresses his desire to go south, "allá donde hay hielos y nubes ... y grandes montañas" (156) [Where there are glaciers and clouds ... and tall mountains] (151). Despite the contrast they pose with the harsh imagery of the city, these pastoral longings should not be interpreted as condemnations of the modern metropolis, but rather, as symbols of Silvio's desire for liberation from his existential anguish.

El juguete rabioso's rendering of 1920s Buenos Aires is uncommonly verisimilar for a work of avant-garde fiction — that is, despite the influence of Silvio's subjectivity, the city is not veiled in metaphors or surrealist imagery. From an environmental perspective, it reveals an early artistic sensitivity to some of the problems caused by the contact between nature and modern industrial culture that constitute today's ecological crisis.

In Martín Adán's 1928 novel *La casa de cartón* (*The Cardboard House*) the urban setting also plays a central role. This text boldly blurs the line between fiction and poetry by replacing conventional elements such as plot and characterization with a series of fragments inspired by the narrator's memories. Primarily concerned with producing imagery rather than telling a story, *La casa de cartón* is more experimental than *El juguete rabioso* and contains a significantly higher quantity of references to the natural world. In essence, the forty sketches that comprise the text are poetic prose representations of individual sensorial perceptions of life in Lima and Barranco in the 1920s. Barranco, which was an exclusive seaside resort at the beginning of the twentieth-century, has now been subsumed by Lima's urban sprawl. The geographical and chronological setting of Adán's novel affords juxtapositions of urban and natural spaces that reveal the interplay between technology and the physical environment during this time period.

Unlike other avant-garde novels in which the natural environment is nearly nonexistent, *La casa de cartón* is imbued with images of nature. The ocean, the sun, the sky, and a variety of trees that line the city streets consistently penetrate the narrator's sensibility. However, as Mario Vargas Llosa observes, the novel transmits impressions, sensations, and emotions rather than descriptions.[62] This is achieved primarily through clever and playful metaphors and similes. The sunset, for example, becomes a "cine celeste" (celestial movie house) and "un plátano marchito" (overripe banana).[63] The sun itself is "un gran huevo frito" (359) [a huge fried egg] (9) with "la circunferencia mellada" (380) [a dented circumference] (44). In certain instances, Adán uses geometrical terms to evoke metaphorical images. The "cielo convexo" (convex sky) is a "cáscara de limón vuelta del revés" (414) [a lemon peel turned inside out] (94) and the horizon is a "plano que corta el del mar, formando un ángulo X" (356) [the plane that intersects that of the sea to form angle X] (4). The ocean, the most prominent natural image in the novel, is portrayed differently in each fragment. It too is frequently presented through unusual metaphors and similes. For example, "[una] ola forzuda, crinosa y torpe como un búfalo" (381) [a violent wave, maned and clumsy like a buffalo] (46) carries off a bather's hand. Elsewhere the sea is described as "inútil y absurdo como un quiosco en la mañana que sigue a la tarde la gimkana" (373) [useless and absurd like a bandstand the morning after the afternoon of a sports event] (30). For Ortega y Gasset, the metaphor is the foundation of avant-garde poetics.[64] *La casa de cartón*, through its masterful use of unusual similes and metaphors, ultimately achieves the effect of a dehumanized world — both natural and manmade. As Vargas Llosa observes, *La casa de cartón* is "a profoundly realistic book [...] not a reproduction of exterior reality; it is rather the poetic, sensorial, intuitive, nonrational testimony of this reality."[65] The process of modernization that Lima experienced during this time period is at the center of the reality that is evoked through the narrator's whimsical perceptions.

An important element of Lima's transformation is the alteration of the physical landscape. In the following passage, for example, the city begins to dominate the natural environment as development extends into the countryside:

Al acabar la calle, urbanísima, principia bruscamente el campo. De los ranchos con sus patiecitos y sus palmeras y sus matas de campanillas se caen las matas de retamas, en los montículos de tierra fofa, en las tapias de adobe, en los azules monótonos del cielo... Piaras de asnos en una parda nube de polvo, cargan adobes todo el día de Dios. Aquí, en este suelo fofo y duro, a manchas, yacen las casas futuras de la ciudad, con sus azoteas entortadas, con sus ventanas primorosas de yeso, con sus salas con victrola y sus secretos de amor, quizá hasta con sus habitantes — mamás prudentes y niñas modernas, jóvenes calaveras y papás industriales —. [...] Y en el horizonte, un olor ciego de humo barre la perspectiva de álamos y mamblas — de un pálido color de granito, casi azules — [398–99].

[At the end of the very urban street, the countryside begins abruptly. From the huts, with their little patios and palm trees and campanilla bushes, the broom falls on the hillocks of spongy earth, over the adobe walls, on the monotonous blues of the sky... Droves of asses carry adobe bricks all day long in a gray cloud of dust. Here, in patches on this hard and spongy ground, lie the city's future houses with their tarred roofs, delicate plaster window frames, living rooms with Victorola and love secrets, perhaps even with their inhabitants — prudent mothers and modern girls, daredevil young men and industrious fathers. [...] And on the horizon, a blinding smell of smoke erases the view of poplars and hillocks the pale, almost blue, color of granite (72–73).]

With regard to the environment, this passage is noteworthy for two reasons. First, it describes the expansion of the city into the countryside. Similar to Silvio in *El juguete rabioso*, the narrator takes an impartial stance; neither condemning nor lauding the modernization process. Today's reader, however, will undoubtedly recognize this as the beginning of the urban sprawl that has contributed to the contamination of Lima's natural resources. The image of the trash-strewn streets of Lima described in the passage from Vargas Llosa's *Historia de Mayta*, cited in the first essay of this volume, captures the end result of the urban expansion described in *La casa de cartón*. Moreover, although the origin of the smoke that blankets the sky in the above passage is unclear to the reader, it is likely an allusion to the incipient industrialization of the city given that earlier in the novel the narrator makes a direct reference to a source of air pollution: "Los arrabales de Lima. Una fábrica de aceites hincha su barriga pringosa y sopla como una vieja borracha — Lima" (366) [The outskirts of Lima. An oil factory swells its greasy belly and belches like a drunk old lady: Lima] (20). He later refers to the city as "Lima, la sucia Lima" (388) [Lima, dirty Lima] (58).

Throughout the novel, as in the following passage, there is a constant flow between urban and rural images:

Pero, al pasar por la larga calle que es casi toda la ciudad, hueles zumar legumbres remotas en huertas aledañas. Tú piensas en el campo lleno y mojado, casi urbano si se mira atrás, pero que no tiene límites si se mira adelante, por entre los fresnos y los alisos, a la sierra azulita. Apenas el límite de los cerros primeros, ceja de montaña... Y ahora vas tú por el campo en sordo rumor abejero de rieles frotados aprisa y en una gimnasia de aires deportivos aunque urbanos [355–56].

[As you walk down the street that traverses almost the entire city, you smell the perfume of distant vegetables in nearby gardens. You think of the lush, wet fields: almost urban behind you; limitless in front of you, between the ash and elder trees, towards the bluish sierra. Barely the outline of the first foothills, the mountain's brow... And now you pass through the fields surrounded by muffled beehive sounds of fleeting friction over rails and a flourish of athletic yet urban gymnastics (2).]

Here the narrator captures the contact between the two spaces by paradoxically describing the fields as urban and using an image of nature — the beehive — to evoke the sound of the passing rail cars. In doing so, he successfully transmits his impression of a glimpse of Lima's modernization and the encounter between nature and technology. Moreover, he creates a liminal space that problematizes the city/country dichotomy present in much nineteenth-century writing.

Like Buenos Aires in *El juguete rabioso*, the city in *La casa de cartón* is replete with automobiles, trolley cars, telephone polls and electric lights. However, whereas Arlt makes use of the urban setting to pose social and existential questions, Adán approaches the modern metropolis with a healthy dose of irony. Upon witnessing an automobile speed past a donkey at seventy kilometers per hour, the narrator muses about the effect of modernization on the once-rural animals:

> ¡Ay, los asnos, que son lo único aldeano de la ciudad, se han municipalizado, burocratizado, humanizado...! [...] Los gallos también se humanizan, pero no como los asnos — de una manera cuerda, cívica sensata —, sino de una manera extraña, impertinente, exótica. No volverse hombres sino ingleses. Ahora son los gallos, gringos excéntricos que visten de lana escocesa, practican deportes estúpidos como la caza de gusanos, juegan al golf con huesos roídos y mazorcas de maíz, tiemblan constantemente de frío, se levantan de madrugada y no comprenden a las hembras. Pronto fumarán en pipa, leerán magazines, jugarán al polo, caballeros en un gato, y partirán en viaje de placer a Southampton en un barco de la P.S.N.C. [410–411].

> [Oh these donkeys — the only remaining villagers in the city — have become municipalized, bureaucratized, humanized! [...] The roosters also become human, though not in a sane, patriotic, sensible way like the donkeys, but rather in a strange, impertinent, exotic way. [...] Those roosters, eccentric gringos who wear Scottish wool, who engage in a foolish sport like worm-hunting, play soccer with miserly bones and cobs of corn, constantly shiver from the cold, rise at dawn, and do not understand females. Soon they will smoke pipes, read magazines, play polo — instant gentlemen — and take pleasure trips to Southampton on a P.S.N.C. ship (89–90).]

Aside from its obvious comic effect, the image of the donkey as an outmoded means of transportation subtly alludes to the changing role that nature will play in a mechanized society. The rooster's portrayal, a social commentary on the Eurocentrism of modernity's advocates, also raises the question of how modernity will affect the natural world. For Martínez, Adán's "discourse is based on the shifting forces of life that seldom remain the same except in memory, hence, the cardboard house."[66] The primary force of change in this novel is the process of modernization.

La casa de cartón could hardly be described as nature writing. Nevertheless, as Wallace and Armbuster have asserted, "A viable ecocriticism must continue to challenge dualistic thinking by exploring the role of nature in texts more concerned with human cultures."[67] An analysis of the representation of nature in this text reveals a consciousness of processes associated with modernity that, from the vantage point of the twenty-first century, have clearly contributed to the alteration of local ecosystems.

La casa de cartón and the other avant-garde narratives analyzed in this essay leave no doubt that the discourse of modernity had a tremendous impact on the way in which nature was represented in Spanish American fiction during the 1920s. Modernity, Octavio Paz suggests, is a decision. It is a desire to be different from those who came before and a yearning for the beginning of a new time.[68] *Maelstrom, Margarita de niebla, Unos fantoches, Papeles de recienvenido* and "Genealogía" are evidence of the avant-garde rupture with the mimetic portrayal of the environment in the realist-naturalist tradition. *El joven*, "El café de nadie," *La Señorita Etc.*, *El juguete rabioso* and *La casa de cartón* mark the beginning of a period in Spanish American fiction in which urban spaces come to the fore. In some texts the city replaces nature. In others, urban and rural spheres are juxtaposed. In both cases, modernity forces a reevaluation of the space of subjectivity and the interaction between human beings and their physical environment.

While nature is not the primary concern of any of these texts, they nevertheless offer an invaluable perspective of the cultural memory of this period and nature's role within it. Several of the narratives analyzed in the second half of this essay provide glimpses of the initial stages of modernization processes that have ultimately led to the dire environmental circumstances in which many Latin American cities currently find themselves. Without predicting Latin America's current ecological crises, texts such as *El joven, El juguete rabioso* and *La casa de cartón* allude, at the level of symbol, to the early stages of their causes through imagery of streets overcrowded with automobiles, water and air pollution, and urban sprawl. During the 1920s, these phenomena were manifestations of progress — a notion that environmental historian Shawn Miller acknowledges was still prevalent in the latter half of the twentieth century:

> At the United Nations Conference on the Human Environment held in Stockholm in 1972, many Latin American attendees were surprised by the new perspective on nature expressed by the more developed nations regarding pollution, species diversity, and wilderness protection. One Brazilian official argued that if

anything, Brazil wanted more pollution, for this was an excellent indicator of the progress of national development.[69]

The Brazilian official's attitude in this example embodies the fundamentally paradoxical nature of modernity. For, as Marshall Berman asserts, "To be modern is to find ourselves in an environment that promises us adventure, power, joy, growth, transformation of ourselves and the world — and, at the same time, that threatens to destroy everything we have, everything we know, everything we are."[70] Aware of this paradox, Louis Menand keenly observes that rather than overthrowing the discourse of modernity, "the environmental critique of modernity has to come, and can only come, from within modernity itself. It is romanticism that teaches us that science and rationality are impoverishing, and it is science and rationality that are most likely to produce the technology required to overcome the depredations technology has wrought."[71]

The avant-garde era in Latin America was largely characterized by excitement about the artistic, literary, scientific, technological and social possibilities that modernity appeared to offer. In reflecting what Williams identifies throughout twentieth-century Spanish American fiction as a "desire to be modern," the avant-garde narratives analyzed in the present essay offer a glimpse into the collective memory of a culture that, for more than a century, has been driven by the concept of modernity.[72] Such a retrospective view of the literary production of this period ultimately affords a unique insight into the cultural discourses and processes that have led to the ecological crossroads at which Latin America currently finds itself. The task of Latin American intellectuals in the twenty-first century will be to continue to redefine cultural modernity to include a paradigm for environmentally sustainable living.

NOTES

1. Paz, *Poesía en movimiento*, 5.
2. See, for example, the following studies: Carlos Alonso, *The Burden of Modernity: The Rhetoric of Cultural Discourse in Spanish America* (New York: Oxford University Press, 1998). Fernando Burgos, *Vertientes de la modernidad hispanoamericana*, Serie Literatura (Caracas: MonteAvila, 1995). Patrick Dove, *The Catastrophe of Modernity: Tragedy and the Nation in Latin American Literature* (Lewisburg: Bucknell University Press, 2004). Raymond L. Williams, *The Twentieth-Century Spanish American Novel* (Austin: University of Texas Press, 2003).
3. Williams, "Modernist Continuities," 375–76.
4. Williams, *The Twentieth-Century Spanish American Novel*, 37.
5. I use "nature" in the sense established by Kate Soper in *What Is Nature?* She states: "In its commonest and most fundamental sense, the term 'nature' refers to everything which is not human and distinguished from the work of humanity. [...] I speak of this conception of nature as 'otherness' to humanity as fundamental because, although many

would question whether we can in fact draw any such rigid divide, the conceptual distinction remains indispensable. Whether, for example, it is claimed that 'nature' and 'culture' are clearly differentiated realms or that no hard and fast delineation can be made between them, all such thinking is tacitly reliant on the humanity-nature antithesis itself and would have no purchase on our understanding without it" (15).

6. Brushwood, *The Spanish-American Novel*, 82.

7. I use the term "avant-garde" to refer to the international (and intercontinental) experimental literary and artistic movements comprised of the multitude of *-isms* that roughly correspond with the 1910s and 20s. In Latin America, the avant-garde era lasted from approximately 1916–1935. Literary critics often refer to this period as "the historical avant-garde" to distinguish from posterior experimental movements. I use "vanguardist" to refer to the authors and artists that participated in these movements.

8. Paz, *Poesía en movimiento*, 5. He also suggests that modernity is a desire to be different from those who came before and a yearning for the beginning of a new time. For the vanguardists, this consisted of the desire for an innovative form of literary creation that would contribute to a transformation of other aspects of culture such as those outlined by Nestor García Canclini in "¿Modernismo sin modernización?" García Canclini observes four basic projects that constitute the broad concept of modernity: emancipation (understood as cultural secularization), expansion (of knowledge of nature and circulation of consumer goods), renovation (improvement of relations between society and nature as well as reformulation of signs of distinction eroded by mass consumer culture) and democratization (including emphasis on education and diffusion of art) [165]. The avant-garde authors studied in this essay participated in this broader concept of modernity principally through the last project. For García Canclini, Latin American vanguardism was a re-elaboration (not a transplant) of European avant-garde projects in an attempt to contribute to social modernization of Latin America (176).

9. I use the term "dehumanized" here in the sense proposed by José Ortega y Gasset in *La deshumanización del arte*. This concept is discussed in detail below.

10. Arnold et al., "Forum on Literatures of the Environment," 1102.

11. Kerridge, *Writing the Environment*, 5.

12. In the *Encyclopedia of World Environmental History*, Scott Slovic defines nature writing as "literary nonfiction that offers scientific scrutiny of the world (as in the older tradition of literary natural history), explores the private experience of the individual human observer of the world, or reflects upon the political and philosophical implications of the relationships among human beings and the larger planet"(Vol. 2, 888).

13. Conway, Keniston, and Marx, *Earth, Air, Water, Fire*, 3.

14. Drengson and Inoue, *The Deep Ecology Movement*, xix.

15. Huidobro, *Obras completas* Vol. 1., 715. Unless otherwise indicated, all translations in this essay are my own.

16. *Ibid.*

17. *Ibid.*, 219.

18. *Ibid.*, 750.

19. Torres Bodet, "Reflexiones sobre la novela," 8.

20. Williams, *The Twentieth-Century Spanish American Novel*, 4.

21. Bürger, *Theory of the Avant-Garde*, 32.

22. Poggioli, *The Theory of the Avant-Garde*, 179.

23. Ortega y Gasset, *La deshumanización del arte*, 30–31.

24. *Ibid.*, 27–28.

25. Weyl, trans. *The Dehumanization of Art* by José Ortega y Gasset, 21–23.

26. Breton, "Manifesto of Surrealism," 10.

27. *Ibid.*

28. Breton, *What Is Surrealism?*, 82.
29. Pacheco, Prologue, *Poesías completas y algunas prosas*, 9.
30. Monsiváis, "Ni biografía ni campaña justiciera," 10.
31. Cardoza y Aragón, *Maelstrom: films telescopiados* (Paris: Excelsior, 1926), 29. All subsequent in-text page references to this work are from this edition. The name Pompierlandia is presumably derived from the French word *pompier* meaning pompous or pretentious. *L'art pompier*, also known as academic art, refers to a form of nineteenth-century art influenced by neoclassicism and romanticism that was associated with the French Académie des beaux-arts.
32. Gómez de la Serna, Prologue, *Maelstrom*, 9.
33. Torres Bodet, *Tiempo de arena*, 253.
34. In the introduction to *Latin American Vanguards*, Unruh asserts that Latin American vanguardism as a whole is characterized by "its drive toward a 'rehumanization' of art," and thus constitutes a dialogue a with European artistic ideas such as Ortega y Gasset's *La deshumanización del arte* (21). See also Pérez Firmat's chapter "The Vanguard Novel as a Discursive Category" in *Idle Fictions*, 3–39.
35. Torres Bodet, *Margarita de niebla* (Mexico City: Cultura, 1927), 29. All subsequent in-text page references to this work are from this edition.
36. Xavier Villaurrutia, another member of the *Contemporáneos*, includes a strikingly similar image of a dehumanized landscape in his 1928 novel *Dama de corazones*: "De pronto un nuevo paisaje se detiene, se solidifica, se parte en bonitos trozos geométricos superpuestos, aislados, que no recuerdan nada humano y que producen idéntica sensación agradable que la muda inteligencia de dos personas en un solo momento, frente a un suceso imprevisto, conectadas por un solo brillo de la Mirada. En seguida, firman el cuadro siete letras que hacen una palabra: PICASSO" (27). [Suddenly a new landscape stops, solidifies, divides into beautiful geometric pieces superposed, isolated, that do not recall anything human and produce an identical pleasing sensation as the mute intelligence of two people in one single moment, confronted with an unforeseen event, connected by a single sparkle of the Gaze. Immediately following, seven letters that make one word sign the painting: PICASSO].
37. Sureda et al., "Manifiesto del ultra," 86.
38. Pérez Firmat, *Idle Fictions*, 42.
39. Torres Bodet, "Reflexiones sobre la novela," 16.
40. Quesada Soto, "Texto fantoche," 33.
41. Jiménez, *Unos fantoches* (San José: Convivio, 1928), 16. All subsequent in-text page references to this work are from this edition.
42. Pérez Firmat discusses this technique in *Margarita de niebla* at length in chapter 4 of *Idle Fictions*.
43. Verani, "La narrativa hispanoamericana de vanguardia," 42.
44. Fernández, *Papeles de Recienvenido*, 33.
45. Novo, *El joven*, 4.
46. *Ibid.*, 1.
47. Maples Arce, "Actual Número 1," 43.
48. *Ibid.*
49. Maples Arce et al. "Manifiesto estridentista número 2," 49.
50. Maples Arce, "Actual Número 1," 44.
51. *Ibid.*, 45.
52. The second of *El café de nadie*'s three novels, "Un crimen provisional," is a parody of conventional detective fiction that is set entirely in the house where the alleged crime occurred. It is not analyzed in this essay as it makes no reference to the environment outside of the house in which it takes place.

53. Brushwood, *Narrative Innovation*, 17.

54. Vela, *El café de nadie* (Jalapa: Horizonte, 1926), 41. All subsequent in-text references to "El café de nadie" and *La Señorita Etc.* are from this edition.

55. Beatriz González interprets the mechanization of characters in "El café de nadie" as a process of human alienation and disintegration due to a schizophrenic dependency on material objects in modern society. "*El café de nadie* y la narrativa del estridentismo," 57.

56. The precise city is unknown, but in the first chapter the narrator states that it is a city on the Gulf of Mexico.

57. Niemeyer, *Subway de los sueños*, 81.

58. Martínez, *Before the Boom*, 27.

59. Brushwood, *The Spanish-American Novel*, 52.

60. Arlt, *El juguete rabioso* in *Novelas completas y cuentos*, Vol. 1 of 3 (Buenos Aires: Compañía General Fabril Editora, 1963), 86. All subsequent in-text page references to this novel are from this edition.

61. Aynesworth, trans. *Mad Toy*, by Roberto Arlt (Durham: Duke University Press, 2002), 75. All subsequent in-text page references for translations of this novel are to this edition.

62. Cited in Verani, 66.

63. Adán, *La casa de cartón* in *Narrativa vanguardista hispanoamericana*, ed. Verani (Mexico City: Universidad Nacional Autónoma de México, 1996), 380, 364. Silver, trans. *The Cardboard House*, by Adán (St. Paul: Graywolf, 1990), 45, 18. All subsequent in-text page references to the novel and its translation are from these editions.

64. Ortega y Gasset, *La deshumanización del arte*, 36.

65. Quoted in Silver, Introduction, *The Cardboard House*, viii.

66. Martínez, *Before the Boom*, 93.

67. Wallace and Armbuster, *Beyond Nature Writing*, 4.

68. Paz, *Poesía en movimiento*, 5.

69. Miller, *An Environmental History of Latin America*, 206.

70. Berman, *All That Is Solid Melts into Air*, 15.

71. Menand, "Modernity and Literary Theory," 316.

72. Williams, "Modernist Continuities," 369–93.

WORKS CITED

Adán, Martín. *La casa de cartón*. 1928. In Verani, *Narrativa vanguardista hispanoamericana*, 355–421.

Arlt, Roberto. *El juguete rabioso* in *Novelas completas y cuentos*. Vol. 1. Buenos Aires: Compañía General Fabril Editora, 1963. Translated by Michele McKay Aynewsorth as *Mad Toy* (Durham: Duke University Press, 2002).

Arnold, Jean, et al. "Forum on Literatures of the Environment." *PMLA* 114 (1999): 1089-1104.

Berman, Marshall. *All That Is Solid Melts into Air: The Experience of Modernity*. New York: Simon and Schuster, 1982.

Breton, André. "Manifesto of Surrealism" in *Manifestoes of Surrealism*. 1962. Translated by Richard Server and Helen R. Lane. Ann Arbor: University of Michigan Press, 1969.

_____. *What Is Surrealism?* 1936. Translated by David Gascoyne. New York: Haskell, 1974.

Brushwood, John S. *Narrative Innovation and Political Change in Mexico*. New York: Peter Lang, 1989.

_____. *The Spanish-American Novel*. Texas Pan-American Series. Austin: University of Texas Press, 1975.

Bürger, Peter. *Theory of the Avant-Garde*. Theory and History of Lit. 4. Translated by Michael Shaw. Minneapolis: University of Minnesota Press, 1984.

Cardoza y Aragón, Luis. *Maelstrom: films telescopiados*. Paris: Excelsior, 1926.

Conway, Jill Ker, Kenneth Keniston, and Leo Marx, eds. *Earth, Air, Water, Fire: Humanistic Studies of the Environment*. Amherst: University of Massachusetts Press, 1999.

Drengson, Alan, and Yuichi Inoue, eds. *The Deep Ecology Movement: An Introductory Anthology*. Berkeley: North Atlantic Books, 1995.

Fernández, Macedonio. *Papeles de Recienvenido*. 1929. Buenos Aires: Centro Editor de América Latina, 1966.

García Canclini, Néstor. "¿Modernismo sin modernización?" *Revista Mexicana de Sociología* 51.3 (Jul.-Sep. 1989): 163–89.

Gómez de la Serna, Ramón. Prologue. *Maelstrom*. By Luis Cardoza y Aragón.

González, Beatriz. "*El café de nadie* y la narrativa del estridentismo." *Texto crítico* 34–35 (1987): 49–64.

Huidobro, Vicente. *Obras completas*. Vol. 1. Santiago: Andrés Bello, 1976.

Jiménez, Max. *Unos fantoches*. San José: Convivio, 1928.

Kerridge, Richard. Introduction. *Writing the Environment*, edited by Richard Kerridge and Neil Sammells, 1–9. London: Zed Books, 1998.

Maples Arce, Manuel. "Actual Número 1: Hoja de vanguardia: Comprimido estridentista de Manuel Maples Arce," in *El estridentismo: México 1921–1927*, edited by Luis Mario Schneider, 41–48. Monografías de arte 11. Mexico City: Universidad Nacional Autónoma de México, 1985.

_____ et al. "Manifiesto estridentista número 2," in *El estridentismo: México 1921–1927*, edited by Luis Mario Schneider, 49–50. Monografías de arte 11. Mexico City: Universidad Nacional Autónoma de México, 1985.

Martínez, Elizabeth Coonrod. *Before the Boom: Latin American Revolutionary Novels of the 1920s*. Lanham, MD: University Press of America, 2001.

Menand, Louis. "Modernity and Literary Theory." In Conway, Keniston, and Marx, *Earth, Air, Fire, Water*, 305–19.

Miller, Shawn William. *An Environmental History of Latin America*. New Approaches to the Americas. Cambridge: Cambridge University Press, 2007.

Monsiváis, Carlos. "Ni biografía ni campaña justiciera: Asturias según Cardoza." Review of *Miguel Ángel Asturias. Casi novela*, by Luis Cardoza y Aragón. *El Nacional*. 5 September 1992: 9–10.

Niemeyer, Katharina. *Subway de los sueños, alucinamiento, libro abierto: la novela vanguardista hispanoamericana*. Colección Nexos y Diferencias 11. Madrid: Iberoamericana, 2004.

Novo, Salvador. *El joven*. Mexico City: Editorial Popular Mexicana, 1928.

Ortega y Gasset, José. *La deshumanización del arte*. 1925. Madrid: Alianza, 2000. Translated by Helene Weyl as *The Dehumanization of Art and Notes on the Novel* (Princeton University Press, 1948).

Pacheco, José Emilio. Prologue. *Poesías completas y algunas prosas*. By Luis Cardoza y Aragón, 7–26. Mexico City: Fondo de Cultura Económica, 1977.

Paz, Octavio. *Poesía en movimiento: México, 1915–1966*. Mexico City: Siglo XXI, 1966.

Pérez Firmat, Gustavo. *Idle Fictions: The Hispanic Vanguard Novel, 1926–1934*. Durham: Duke University Press, 1982.

Poggioli, Renato. *The Theory of the Avant-Garde*. Translated by Gerald Fitzgerald. Cambridge: Harvard University Press, 1968.

Quesada Soto, Álvaro. "Texto fantoche." In *Max Jiménez: Aproximaciones críticas*, compiled by Quesada Soto, 32–36. San José, C.R.: Editorial de la Universidad de Costa Rica, 1999.

Silver, Katherine, trans. *The Cardboard House: A Novel.* By Martín Adán. Palabra Sur. St. Paul: Graywolf, 1990.

Slovic, Scott. "Nature Writing." In *Encyclopedia of World Environmental History,* edited by Sheperd Krech, John Robert McNeill, and Carolyn Merchant, Vol. 2, 888. New York: Routledge, 2004.

Soper, Kate. *What Is Nature? Culture, Politics and the Non-Human.* Oxford: Blackwell, 1995.

Sureda, Jacobo, et al. "Manifiesto del ultra." 1921. In *Textos recobrados 1919–1929.* By Jorge Luis Borges. Edited by Sara Luisa del Carril, 86–87. Buenos Aires: Emecé, 1997.

Torres Bodet, Jaime. *Margarita de niebla.* Mexico City: Cultura, 1927.

_____. "Reflexiones sobre la novela." In *Contemporáneos: notas de crítica,* 7–21. Mexico City: Herrero, 1928.

_____. *Tiempo de arena.* Letras Mexicanas 18. Mexico City: Fondo de Cultura Económica, 1955.

Unruh, Vicky. *Latin American Vanguards: The Art of Contentious Encounters.* Latin American Literature and Culture 11. Berkeley: University of California Press, 1994.

Vargas Llosa, Mario. "La casa de cartón." *Cultura peruana* 19. November, 1959.

Vela, Arqueles. *El café de nadie.* Jalapa: Horizonte, 1926.

Verani, Hugo J. "La narrativa hispanoamericana de vanguardia." In *Narrativa vanguardista hispanoamericana,* edited by Verani. Mexico City: Universidad Nacional Autónoma de México, 1996, 41–73.

Villaurrutia, Xavier. *Dama de corazones.* Mexico City: Ediciones de Ulises, 1928.

Wallace, Kathleen R., and Karla Armbuster, eds. *Beyond Nature Writing: Expanding the Boundaries of Ecocriticism.* Under the Sign of Nature: Explorations in Ecocriticism. Charlottesville: University Press of Virginia, 2001.

Williams, Raymond L. "Modernist Continuities: The Desire to Be Modern in Twentieth-Century Spanish-American Fiction." *Bulletin of Spanish Studies* 79 (2002): 369–93.

_____. *The Twentieth-Century Spanish American Novel.* Austin: University of Texas Press, 2003.

Nature in the Twentieth-Century Latin American Novel (1900–1967) and in *Cien años de soledad* of García Márquez

Raymond L. Williams

The vast majority of critical readings of *Cien años de soledad* (1967; *One Hundred Years of Solitude*) and the Latin American novel of the 1960s and before appeared in the 1970s and 1980s, well before the recent rise of ecocriticism.[1] A pioneer ecocritical theorist, Lawrence Buell, published his seminal book on this subject, *The Environmental Imagination*, in the early 1990s, and since then a growing number of scholars and readers are increasingly aware of the multiple roles, functions and representations of nature in literature.[2] Inevitably, many discussions of nature in literature lead to parallel considerations of elements that are not considered part of the natural world: culture and technology. In this study, I will begin with a discussion of background canonical literary texts published from 1900 to 1967 (including one nineteenth-century novel) and then move to an ecocritical reading of García Márquez's work, with emphasis on *Cien años de soledad*. What is ecocriticism? I would bring to the discussion a 1999 definition constructed by the editors of a special issue of *New Literary History* on ecocriticism that emphasizes focus on the non-human.[3]

Many studies on nature and Latin America deal with the Colonial period, when the foundational texts for writing about nature were published. Within Latin American literary studies, a recent study by Jennifer French, *Nature, Neocolonialism, and the Spanish American Regional Writers* (2005), is an illuminating analysis of early twentieth-century cultural discourse and nature. She studies the British Colonial Empire in Latin America and how neo-colonialism affected discourse on nature. In her introduction, she proposes that neo-colonialism becomes visible in Spanish American cultural discourse only when Britain's international hegemonic formation begins to break down in the post–World War I era.[4] In this study of nature in the literature of the early twentieth century, she focuses on the stories of Horacio Quiroga, and the novels *La vorágine* by José Eustacio Rivera and *El inglés de los huesos* by Benito Lynch. She concludes that neo-colonialism is not simply a matter of colonized and colonizer, but a much more complex and nuanced triad made up of land, labor and capital. In her study of these regionalists, she also concludes that some of the canonical writers of this period recognized the limits of the neo-colonial order.

The key word for an initial approach to the Latin American novel is the word "land"—*tierra*. Indeed, this is an important word for the classic Latin American *novelas de la tierra* of the 1920 and 1930s, for most *novelas indigenistas* of the 1930s and 1940s and for the novel of the northeast region of Brazil. In the Portuguese language, the term *terra* refers back to the Iberian Peninsula and the Latin *terra*. This word *terra* is the historical backdrop to most discussions of the land in Latin America: the reconquering of the *tierra* of the Iberian Peninsula was the precedent to the conquering of the *tierra* of the Americas. Carlos Fuentes's novel *Terra Nostra* (1975) is the most elaborate novelistic consideration of *terra* on both sides of the Atlantic Ocean from the *reconquista* of the Iberian Peninsula to the *conquista* of the *terra* and, in turn, of the destruction of the land. Fuentes establishes the historical roots for exploiting the land in Spain.

The word *terra* is present in the opening of one of the most elaborate novels about the land of the twentieth century, *Grande Sertão: Veredas* (1956; *Rebellion in the Backlands*) by João Guimarães Rosa. This *terra* in the opening line of the novel evokes the image of land as vast and infinite on the Brazilian *sertão*. In addition to being seemingly infinite, the *sertão* has no figure of authority, making it a utopian land for the gun slinging main character. The *terra* of the *sertão* extends both infinitely and indefinitely—a radically new rethinking of nature with indefinite and ambiguous lines of extension and definition.

The natural world of *Grande Sertão* is divided into two regions, two discrete spaces that have as their common boundary the São Francisco River. The territory of the *jagunços* (hired guns) in this land is an ordered and rationally understandable space in comparison to the lack of geographical boundaries, lack of precise names, and characters who seem to have emerged from an unknowable place and time. This space evokes numerous images of hell; rather than images originating in nature, however, those evocations of hell are from literary sources.

The characters' names might also emerge from this novel's abstract and essentially unknowable *terra* that resonates of the past but is imprecise in the present. All in all, *Grande Sertão: Veredas* is a complex and innovative statement about nature, a construct that offers more ambiguities and imprecision than had been the case for more realist approaches to the subject, and with a multiplicity of sources.

García Márquez also constructs an elaborate and complex web of nature of multiple sources, many of which are human rather than non-human parts of nature.[5] Of the human sources, three of the most noteworthy with respect to the representation of nature are other literary texts, oral tradition and the visual arts. Critical studies on *Cien años de soledad* with ecocritical underpinnings have been limited to relatively brief commentaries on the presence of varying climatic conditions in García Márquez's work, as well as commentary on the role of nature in the Colombian author's masterpiece. In an introductory study of climate in the fiction of major Spanish-American writers, George McMurray notes that the hyperbolic rains in *Cien años de soledad* remind us of the purifying biblical flood and cause Fernanda's day-long tirade directed at her husband.[6] In his study, McMurray also refers to climate in García Márquez's other work, and concludes that weather change is sometimes a source of humor in the fiction of García Márquez. All in all, McMurray offers a close reading of García Márquez, with an awareness of nature as he carries out his close reading.

In an article on nature and natural sexuality in *Cien años de soledad*, Patricia Struebig points to the differences between sexuality as it is manifested in the natural world of nature and natural human instinct in Macondo, as well as how sexuality plays itself out within the confines of conventional social mores. She notes how natural behavior, acts of nature and nature are portrayed as a threat to the Buendía family and the town of Macondo and, consequently, metaphorically, to civilization itself. Struebig emphasizes García Márquez's "approval of the natural or original state of things."[7] Indeed, nature engages in war with man to reclaim the space taken by both traditional "civilization" and modern technological progress. Struebig concludes that, in the end, García Márquez affirms nature and condemns the incursions of civilization. Thus, García Márquez, according to this reading, does privilege the non-human. Indeed, García Márquez is critical of many aspects of the modern progress associated with the rise of the modern capitalistic nation-state. *Cien años de soledad*, however, is not as unambiguously and consistently supportive of the natural world and unequivocally critical of the modern. To the contrary, this novel is also a celebration of the modern on several levels. For example, *Cien años de soledad* is a celebration of literary modernism, and all of García Márquez's work represents a triumph of modern innovation over the forces of traditionalism.[8]

In a study of broader scope and more closely connected to the current ecological concerns of ecocriticism, Ursula Heise has explored how literary texts, including *Cien años de soledad*, negotiate issues of ecological globalism and localism and how they link issues of global ecology with those of cultural globalisms. In this study, she discusses how in *Cien años de soledad*, García Márquez translates scenarios of global connectivity and ecological alienation.[9] Heise is interested in how literary texts can re-imagine earth from a perspective that does not privilege human voices over all others. In the end, however, her conclusions deal less with *Cien años de soledad* than novels that have drawn upon this novel for ecological wisdom. Several book-length studies offer commentary on nature and ecology in *Cien años de soledad* or make allusions to them. Gene H. Bell-Villada's book on García Márquez, *The Man and His Work* is typical of many introductory studies that point to the presence of science and technology as the antithesis to the natural environment in *Cien años de soledad*.[10] Bell-Villada notes that — to some degree — nature is a threat, as manifested in the five-year rainstorm that brings ruin to Macondo, and the constant impulse toward incest that threatens to create a member of the family with a pig's tail.

García Márquez, of course, is not a pioneer in the imaginative fictionalization of nature which, in reality, can be traced back to the original Colonial *crónicas* (chronicles) that he occasionally parodies in *Cien años de soledad*. The most broadly read and influential of the early writings on nature in Colombia were authored by the German scientist and explorer Alexander von Humboldt. Among his voluminous writings were lengthy descriptions and commentaries on the flora and fauna of Latin America, including those made during a trip to Nueva Granada, the Spanish colony that geographically encompassed the present-day territory of Colombia. Von Humboldt prided himself as a man of the Enlightenment who not only wrote with scientific rigor, but was also at the vanguard of his day on certain social issues. Thus, he was a strident critic of slavery and liked to think of himself as a friend and protector of the North American indigenous peoples in the Americas, North and South. Present-day readers will note, however, that Von Humboldt was actually a racist who sometimes contradicted his own campaign to free the indigenous and African peoples from slavery, a practice he abhorred. Despite the numerous contradictions of his writings, he was a foundational figure for much of our understanding and some of our misunderstanding of nature in the Americas. It can be argued that Von Humboldt laid the foundations for environmentalism in the nineteenth century as a thinker who was well-known by American intellectuals such as Thoreau and Emerson.[11]

Cien años de soledad shows several traces of Von Humboldt's texts, as suggested by the narrator who states in the novel's fourth chapter, in reference to the parchments of Melquíades, "En realidad, lo único que pudo en las parrafadas pedregosas, fue el insistente martilleo de la palabra equinoccio

equinoccio equinoccio, y el nombre de Alexander von Humboldt" (In reality, the only thing that could be isolated in the rocky paragraphs was the insistent hammering on the word *equinox, equinox, equinox,* and the name of Alexander von Humboldt).[12] With this sentence, García Márquez not only reveals his awareness of Von Humboldt, but he also alludes to the title of the Spanish translation (widely available in Colombia) of his book *Viaje a las regiones equinocciales del Nuevo Continente.* In his *Personal Narrative,* Von Humboldt vacillates between two general methods of articulating nature. On the one hand, he insists on a highly "scientific" account of his observations, with abundant lists and categories of flora and fauna in the New World, often inserting words in Latin, as evoked in the word "*equinoccio.*" This is the voice of "Von Humboldt the scientist" that is the predominant voice of the text. On the other hand, however, Von Humboldt occasionally betrays the "scientific" voice with comments that are more closely allied with the literature of Romanticism. In both his *Personal Narrative* and his later summa of scientific writings, *Cosmos,* for example, Von Humboldt states that the view of nature ought to be "grand" and "free," and that humans get to know the external world through the organs of the senses. Phenomena of light, according to Von Humboldt, proclaim the existence of matter in remotest space and the eye is the medium through which one may contemplate the universe. In another passage that reveals the Romantic rather than scientific voice, he states that Nature (sic) reveals itself to the single mind and feelings of man as something earthly, and closely allied to himself. In his *Personal Narrative,* then, Von Humboldt assumes the voice of both the scientific rationalist and the Romantic writer in his construction of nature.

After the writings of Von Humboldt, an important text for the construction of nature in Colombia and for *Cien años de soledad* is the canonical Romantic novel *María* (1867) by Jorge Isaacs. This novel continues the Romantic voice articulated in Von Humboldt's writings and portrays nature as part of an idyllic setting for a love affair. Numerous studies have demonstrated the fact that this idyllic nature was filtered through the lens of European Romantic fiction, the most important of which was Chateaubriand's *Atalá,* thus adding another level of literariness of nature. Isaacs wrote *María* from 1864 to 1866 while living in the mountains, often isolated. Despite this proximity to nature, however, *María* is unquestionably the product of the Greater Cauca region's sophisticated and elitist writing culture of the time, which was closely allied to European literary tradition.[13] Nature serves as a backdrop for the protagonist, Efrain, to overcome his childhood and display his masculinity, after numerous descriptions of him as a child and of childhood as an ideal state. Nature is central. His displays of masculinity involve his hunting in the wilderness: his prizes of ferocious beasts are presented as supposedly impressive proof of what social ideals deem genuine manliness. A brief analysis of these masculine deeds, however, reveals a character who is not convincingly effective in this traditional masculine role in nature. Once in the wilderness, for example, Efraín does not measure up to the hearty Emigdio. When the protagonist picks some flowers, Emigdio warns him: "Do you want everything to smell of roses? Men should smell like goats."[14] We note here, in addition, the contrast between a writing-culture value (Efraín's flowers in poetry) and what Walter Ong would identify as an oral-culture value (Emigdio's human life world of goats). Once involved with the actual hunt, his prize is not the awesome bear that Efraín's father had demanded but an effeminate cat. It is described in the diminutive (*gatico*) and is wounded and weakened before Efraín finally delivers the death blow. This act clearly does not measure up to the aggressive dominance that Efraín desires and believes he needs in order to fulfill his traditional role. He has failed to overcome nature and the natural setting in his desire to demonstrate his masculinity. Isaacs uses nature to communicate the novel's outcome: the protagonist Efraín remains the eternal child, even within the rigid and traditional nineteenth-century societal structures. As such, he remains incomplete — the potential writer who never dictates, the lover who never consummates his desires.

Before the appearance of the cornerstone of the Latin American and Colombian literary representations of nature and one of the other texts to inform *Cien años de soledad*, José Eustacio Rivera's *La vorágine* (1924; *The Vortex*), is Spanish American *modernismo*. Well known by García Márquez and parodied in *El otoño del patriarca* (1975; *The Autumn of the Patriarch*), the *modernistas* embraced some aspects of Romanticism, but their renovation of the poetic tradition in the Spanish language was not only a rejection of the major tenets of Romanticism, but also a rejection of the Romantics' appreciation of nature. More specifically, the *modernistas* embraced art rather than nature as the privileged ideal to be expressed and attained, and the very concept of ecocritical understandings of nature is difficult to accommodate with the main currents of *modernista* thought and literary production. In general, then, writers such as Rubén Darío and José Asunción Silva are not of great ecocritical interest.

A novel often described as a classic text of Spanish American *criollismo*, *La vorágine* by Rivera promotes the *criollista* agenda of tying national identity with the land, so nature necessarily has some importance in these novels. This specific *criollista* agenda is not as fully developed as in the two other classic *criollista* works *Don Segundo Sombra* (1926) and *Doña Bárbara* (1929), both of which create a more obvious and direct connection between national identity and the land. In *La vorágine*, the protagonist does escape the city and flee to the inland jungle of Colombia, but the jungle never carries the positive connotations attained in *Don Segundo Sombra* (in which the *pampa* is an aspect of the very essence of authentic Argentine identity) or *Doña Bárbara* (in which the *llano* serves as an essential backdrop to Gallegos's elaborate discussion of Venezuela's need to resolve the dichotomy between *civilización* and *barbarie*). To the contrary, the natural setting of the jungle in *La vorágine* serves as the ultimate threat, devouring the protagonist Arturo Cova in the end.

Given the ambiguities concerning this novel's status as a *criollista* text and other ambiguities, the real subject of *La vorágine* has been a matter of considerable debate. Readings have stressed the portrayal of the New World as one of the three classic *criollista* texts: civilization versus barbarity, the evil forces of the universe, and social injustice. Such forces do indeed operate in the fictional world of *La vorágine*. The *costumbrista* cockfight scene and the revelation of exploitation of rubber workers are two of several examples of subject matter that supports such readings. The question, however, is whether these are the primary subject matter — the thematic core of this supposedly *criollista* text so tightly tied to nature. The predominant subject of *La vorágine*— I would argue — is not really the fictional representation of the natural world and rural Colombia in 1924 (with its exploited workers), but rather the self in the process of writing. Read in this light, the novel fits squarely in the realm of self-conscious writing culture as a precedent to *Cien años de soledad* in its representation of technology and nature.

Several problems arise with reading *La vorágine* as a fictionalized replica of Colombia's rural story of the natural world; one basic difficulty with such a reading of this novel as a fictionalized simulacrum of Colombia's rural story is, simply stated, the absence of a nature story. As narrator, Cova constantly vacillates between his role as creator of story and narrator of himself. Many of the novel's narrative segments begin not with the subject matter of the external story (that is, Colombia's rural story) but with intrusions about the self. The reader observes Cova reacting to a world rather than fabricating a story of nature. The novel's first sentence sets the tone and typifies what will take place in the remainder of the work: "Antes que me hubiera apasionado por mujer alguna, jugué mi corazón al azar y me lo ganó la Violencia" (Before falling in love with any woman, I took my chances with my heart, and Violence won).[15] In this sentence, five basic elements are in operation with respect to the self and story: three references to the self and two references with the potential of developing the external story, these being "*mujer*" (love story) and "*la Violencia*" (a Colombian story).

Given the overwhelming presence of the self in this novel, the story is not essentially of the natural world (a *vorágine*, natural phenomena in a New World), but of a self in the process of writing, of establishing a writerly identity that interrupts the narration of a story. Interruptions can appear at the most inopportune moments of the narrative's potential as a story. When a group of Indians drowns, Cova's reaction is "The spectacle was magnificent" (74). This passage shows a radical shift of focus from an adventure story to a writer's story: The Indian's death is portrayed as a relatively unimportant event at the end of a narrative segment; Cova's emotional reaction to it turns out to be the subject of the entire first part of the following narrative segment, centered upon this vision of mass death as "spectacle." The potential story of an adventure had been subverted by Cova's presence from the beginning of the "Segunda Parte." The narrator does not present the Indians as human beings but as the non-human literary figures about whom Cova-the-writer has read: He characterizes them all as being strong, young, and with Herculean backs (56). Indeed, with respect to the orality-writing culture dichotomy, Cova's attitude epitomizes a writing culture appropriating an oral culture strictly for literary purposes.

The narrator of *La vorágine* exploits his subject matter of writing in three ways: by the use of metaphor, by means of literary allusions, and by dramatizing the very act of writing itself. Cova's language is consistently metaphorical: rather than naming the world, he relates what it is "like" (*"como"*). Cova's inconsistent story also strives to acquire the status of "literature" by means of association with classic literary texts or direct allusions to them. Clemente Silva, for example, refers to their trip as "our Odyssey" (82) and Cova himself characterizes his experiences and the book he is writing similarly, referring to them as "my Odyssey" (128). In addition to a series of parallels between *La vorágine* and Dante's *Divine Comedy*, references relate the text to Dante's *Inferno* and Virgil's *Aeneid*.

Another way in which *La vorágine* self-consciously seeks the status of high culture "literature" is the drama of writing that Cova develops. The figure of "José Eustacio Rivera" initiates this drama in the prologue, which features as its preeminent subject neither Arturo Cova nor the unjust life of Colombian *caucheros* (rubber workers) but a manuscript. In the final sections of the novel the significant drama is not Cova's struggle with nature, for neither he nor nature has a sufficiently important fictional status. Rather, the tension involves Cova's completion of his writing. Since he has acquired his status as writer, thus assuring his text's status as literature, the only question remaining is the novel's denouement: precisely how and under what circumstances will the text be completed? In the end, the drama of the text culminates in its being left for Clemente Silva; the fact that Cova has been devoured by the jungle is of little consequence. This is not really a *criollista* text about nature, but a novel about writing and literature.

Undoubtedly *María* and *La vorágine* are key predecessors to García

Márquez's representation of nature and technology in *Cien años de soledad*. Nevertheless, between the publication of *La vorágine* in 1924 and the appearance of *Cien años de soledad* in 1967, numerous other intervening texts of considerable interest in informing *Cien años de soledad* appeared in print. Among the Modernists, two important predecessors with respect to nature and technology were the Argentines Adolfo Bioy Casares and Jorge Luis Borges. Bioy Casares' *La invención de Morel* (1940: *The Invention of Morel*) was a relatively early exploration in Latin America into the possibilities of integrating new technology (at that time, film) into a Latin American novel. Borges's *Ficciones* (1944; *Fictions*), well known as canonical works for García Márquez himself, were as dramatic a revolution with respect to nature and technology in Latin American literature. In these stories, nature is dramatically diminished in value from its privileged role under the guises of the *criollistas* who had dominated the literary scene in Spanish America for over two decades. Even in stories with some natural setting and presence of nature, such as "El Sur" ("The South"), this natural world is understood as artificial and having literary sources: the South of this story is the southern region of Argentina with a literary legacy related to *literatura gauchesca*.

One of the major fictional representations of nature in the first half of the twentieth century was Mario Vargas Llosa's *La casa verde* (1966; *The Green House*). The construction of nature in this novel follows two broad patterns. On the one hand, nature is a fictionalized version of the geographical region of the Amazon centered in the city of Santa María de Nieva in Peru. Human beings who hold a non-human relationship with nature in this region, the *aguarana* Indians, are treated as commercial objects by the military and the church. The design of the novel's plot can be likened to the unfolding of the fluvial web of nature in the Amazon with its maze of main rivers, tributaries, and small streams, appearing and disappearing in the thick undergrowth. This jungle, however, is not the wild and uncontrolled *vorágine* of the *criollista* texts in which human beings are devoured in an irrational chaos. Rather, it is a nature that Vargas Llosa constructs with scientific vigor: "Santa María de Nieva es como un pirámide irregular y su base son los ríos" (Santa María de Nieva is like an irregular pyramid whose base is formed by the rivers'.[16] The use of scientific discourse represents a radical contrast with the descriptions of nature in *criollista* texts.

On the other hand, the other broad setting of *La casa verde* is the dry, sparse and semi-desertic region of northern coastal Peru and the city of Piura. Vargas Llosa undermines the long-standing dichotomy between *civilización* (among other things, urban space) and *barbarie* (among other things, nature) that were the premises of much fiction and critical discourse for well over a century. He uses several strategies to undermine this dichotomy and the

Manichean simplicity that it implies. The reader eventually discovers that the lives and identities of certain characters (particularly Bonifacia and Lituma) blur the boundaries of the "jungle" and "the city." Around the city nature is not the threatening and hostile nature fictionalized in *criollista* novels, but a friendly companion with the mythic overtones to the creation of Piura. The initial descriptions make nature as mysterious and potentially mythical as the main character of *La casa verde*, Anselmo, and the town of Piura itself. In summary, *La casa verde* along with *Grande Sertão: Veredas* is a radical redefinition of nature as ambiguous.

In *Rayuela* (1963; *Hopscotch*), Julio Cortázar sets forth a critique of the very basic tenets of Western Manichean thought including many Western assumptions about reason. It is a critique of Western assumptions about "progress" as a value in itself. As such, *Rayuela* is a noteworthy predecessor to ecocritical thought that raises similar questions and critiques the proposition that humans are the center in opposition to nature, or that the non-human might have a value similar to the human. Cortázar's critique of Western culture's confidence in post–Enlightenment rational thought is the basis for this fundamental indebtedness of later ecocriticism to the Argentine writer.

As an alternative to post–Enlightenment Western constructs of nature, Cortázar explores Eastern understandings of nature that invite a radical rethinking of this concept. In Chapter 151 of *Rayuela*, Cortázar's theorist Morelli proposes a "new vision" of nature ("vegetable life") that is different than it had traditionally been conceived. Morelli speaks of a vegetative life that responds to the voices of Buddhism, Vedanta, Sufism and Western mysticism.

Cortázar questions other Western constructs of nature in Chapter 134 titled "The Flower Garden." The text describes French and English models of parks. These parks are admittedly "artificial." Thus, Cortázar invites the reader to recognize the artificiality of all human constructs of nature, whether in a "natural" setting or in a park. In the case of the humanly constructed nature of parks, "absolute perfection" is an ideal of one typically European concept of nature.

In Colombia, the noteworthy predecessor of this 1960s period was Álvaro Cepeda Samudio's novel *La casa grande* (1962), the author's only novel and one that was situated in the town of Ciénaga, the site of a strike in 1928 and massacre of banana workers by government soldiers. This was the first literary representation of the strike and massacre that had never been officially recognized by the government and had not appeared in official histories as a part of the nation's history. This event reappeared, of course, in *Cien años de soledad*. *La casa grande* also places into question the legitimacy of modernization when it involves the model of foreign capitalist enterprises in Latin

America; this region of Colombia, where Cepeda Samudio and García Márquez were born and reared, is the only one dominated by foreign capitalists in the history of the nation. Its questioning of modernization, foreign capitalism, and the modern values of patriarchal capitalism make it an important ecocritical predecessor to *Cien años de soledad*.

In the case of *Cien años de soledad*, nature, technology and culture are filtered through the texts outlined above, beginning with a nature that connects with Isaacs' nature in *María*. Not only the exuberant nature of *Cien años de soledad* associates with nature in *María*, but a scene in García Márquez's novel directly evokes the classic Romantic novel from Colombia. At the end of the ninth chapter of the novel, a window in the home of Remedios la bella is portrayed as the classic scene of Romantic love, with the enamored young man awaiting the beloved below her window embellished with nature. In García Márquez's version, a lovestruck soldier dies of love beneath the window of Remedios la bella: "El Dia de año Nuevo, enloquecido por los desaires de Remedios, la bella, el joven comandante de la guardia amaneció muerto de amor junto a su ventana" (158). The original Spanish has him "dead of love" whereas the published translation loses some of the Romantic melodrama: "On New Year's Day, driven mad by rebuffs from Remedios the Beauty, the young commander of the guard was found dead under her window" (173). This passage shows a García Márquez parodying the Romantic tradition, and its nature, in *Cien años de soledad*.

Cien años de soledad evokes *La vorágine* as another self-reflective writerly story. In the end, *Cien años de soledad* is not only the story of the Buendía family, but a self-reflective book about literature. Numerous critics have pointed to this novel's multiple sources: the Bible; classical Greek literature; Ariosto's Orlando; nineteenth-century Russian fiction; the novels of Virginia Woolf, Ernest Hemingway, and William Faulkner.[17] In addition, *Cien años de soledad* refers to the act of writing as incessantly as does *La vorágine*, and the latter part of the novel takes the reader to an intensified focus on the text as literature: the references to characters from other Latin American novels, writers, and the discovery that the entire story of Macondo had already been written on the parchments of Melquíades makes *Cien años de soledad* a patently literary text that focuses, in the end, on its metafictional qualities and the text as literature, not as representation of external reality of Colombia or Latin America. With respect to this first point sustaining an ecocritical reading of *Cien años de soledad*, it should be noted that many of García Márquez's sources of nature do not point the natural world itself, but rather to other literary texts, from those of Alexander von Humboldt to those of Jorge Isaacs, José Eustacio Rivera and a host of others.

A second source of García Márquez's understanding of nature is the oral tradition of the Caribbean coastal region of Colombia where he was reared listening to the stories that comprised this tradition. My understanding of "oral tradition" and my explanation of the "magic realist" elements of the novel are based on the pioneer synthetic work of Walter Ong in his ground-breaking study *Orality and Literacy*, which includes this observation concerning oral cultures: "In the absence of elaborate analytic categories that depend on writing to structure knowledge at a distance from lived experience, oral cultures must conceptualize and verbalize all their knowledge with more or less close reference to the human life world, assimilating the alien, objective world to the more immediate familiar interaction of human beings."[18] In the case of *Cien años de soledad*, this "alien" and "objective" world is the world of nature and technology. In his *Historia doble de la costa*, Orlando Fals Borda points to this phenomenon in the Caribbean coastal region of Colombia, such as the belief in the *hombre-hipoteca* (or "tortoise-man") is a real-world example of the close reference to the human life world, one in which the human life world and the life world of nature are assimilated. This particular characteristic of oral cultures, closeness to the human life world, seen in the context of ecology, the environment, and ecocriticism, should be seen as a positive, ecocritically sound practice. In *Cien años de soledad*, this noetic process — with characters that are minimally abstract and remaining close to the human life world, is often the case of Úrsula and other characters, and as this is noted, it should be kept in mind, once again, that this human life world is of nature. Thus, Úrsula's reaction to José Aracadio's declaration in the first chapter that "el mundo es redondo, como una naranja" (the world is round, like an orange) is telling. First, it should be noted that even José Arcadio's "scientific" view is marked by a closeness to nature, with an orange as his metaphor for the world. It is not really the nature of the native natural world of Macondo, Colombia, or the Americas, however, for the presence of the orange in the Americas has to do with the history of Colonialism and Western technology, having been taken to the Americas by the Colonizers in the ships they constructed using the latest marine technology, the cutting-edge technology of the day: oranges were brought to the Americas by Columbus in his second trip to the New World, and first arrived in Haiti in 1493. Úrsula, however, reacts negatively to José Arcadio's scientific understanding of the world, as the narrator explains, following José Arcadio's explanation "El mundo es redondo, como una naranja" with "Úrsula perdió la paciencia" (Úrsula lost her patience).

In *Cien años de soledad*, García Márquez uses situational frames of reference that are minimally abstract in the sense that they remain close the human life world. The narrator assumes this role as an oral-culture person throughout much of the novel, often using down-to-earth and animal imagery, thus remaining close to the living human life world. In some cases the narrator, when he takes such positions, is assuming a role similar to the characters. For example, he describes Amaranta at birth using the following animal imagery: "She was light and watery, like a newt, but all her parts were human" (37).

The narrator assumes other roles typical of an oral mindset. His treatment of Remedios the Beauty is that of an oral person both in form and content. The narrator regularly employs the epithet *la bella* for her in Spanish, a form common in oral storytelling. The scene in which Remedios rises heavenward is a typical description of how a person in an oral culture would view such an event. Another characteristic of this narrator's storytelling is his copiousness. Oral performance demands flow: hesitancy is always a vice, and the copious flow of oral performance is effected through repetition and redundancy. The repetition in *Cien años de soledad* has been well documented. García Márquez has conceived a novel with the copiousness and flow demanded in oral performance, one of the best examples being Fernanda's two-page, single-sentence diatribe (298–300).

In addition to the narrator and Úrsula, the most prominent examples of oral-culture individuals, other characters in this novel are either oral-culture persons or persons who occasionally react as such. By the twelfth chapter, for example, Macondo's inhabitants seem to be lettered and modern. Nevertheless, the chapter begins with a humorous episode describing an oral-culture person's reaction to modern technology: the people of Macondo become outraged and break the seats of the movie house because an actor who died and was buried in one film reappeared later in another alive as an Arab.

Oral cultures are also verbally agonistic. The Buendía family history begins as a result of Prudencio Aguilar's verbal challenge to José Arcadio Buendía, questioning the future patriarch's masculinity. The female characters are a special case with respect to orality and literacy. As is common in many traditional cultures, the males of Macondo are the lettered characters, beginning with Melquíades and José Arcadio Buendía, whereas, in contrast, Úrsula thinks and expresses herself consistently as an oral-culture person. In the latter parts of the novel Macondo's women do begin to read, usually finding themselves uncomfortable in this masculine writing culture. The loss of the feminine oral culture (more closely aligned with nature than masculine writing culture) affects the novel's denouement: the lettered Amaranta Úrsula and Aureliano conceive a baby with a pig's tail not only because he abandoned his studies of the parchments at the point where he would have uncovered their blood relationship but also because neither of them remembers "Úrsula's frightened admonitions." Their failure also represents the final defeat of a lost oral culture and a parallel loss of nature. In our ecocritical reading of *Cien años de soledad*, then, the presence and then gradual loss of oral culture has as its parallel the presence and gradual loss of nature, for oral culture and nature are closely linked.

What has often been identified by the now overused and frequently vague term "magic realism" in this novel is more precisely described as a written expression of the shift from orality to various stages of literacy. The effects of the interplay between oral and writing culture are multiple. García Márquez has fictionalized numerous aspects of his youth in the tri-ethnic and oral culture of the rural Caribbean coastal region of Colombia, one in which the inhabitants lived close to nature when the oral culture was still predominant. The unique traditionalism and modernity of this novel are based on various roles the narrator assumes as an oral storyteller in the fashion of the tall tale, as narrator with an oral person's mindset, and as the modern narrator of a self-conscious written fiction.

My third and final area of exploration for this consideration of nature in *Cien años de soledad* is an introductory analysis of how García Márquez has used the visual arts as a filter for the representation of nature. With respect to the visual arts, it has already been established that García Márquez's writing in general draws from visual art sources. In an interview with the author, he revealed several of these sources, based on drawings of a nineteenth-century French artist.[19] One of García Márquez's observations from this interview was that he writes his novels based not on a concept, a character or a plot, but on a central image that serves as his point of departure. Another interesting point that came from the interview was that the artist of this drawing did not actually base his work on any scientific observation of nature in nineteenth-century Colombia. The French explorers Charles Saffray and Eduard André were in Colombia in the latter half of the nineteenth century, and sent their travel diaries back to Paris, where a French artist who had never actually set foot in Colombia drew the images of nature, such as a scene with the steam ship "Simón Bolívar" floating down the Magdalena River, the river that passes by the real town of Macondo, which is called Aracataca, and flows into the Caribbean sea at the port city of Barranquilla. (This is also the central image García Márquez employed for his novel on Bolívar, *El general en su laberinto* [1989; *The General in His Labyrinth*]).

If one is to imagine Macondo as the town at the edge of the river, on the lower left of this drawing, one observes that Macondo is not surrounded by an exuberant nature, but a sparse mountain in the background. The sparseness of this particular drawing is more indicative of what the Magdalena River region generally looks like rather than as one imagines it reading *Cien años de soledad*, so this particular drawing is more important for the steamboat and the Magdalena River in the novel *El general en su laberinto* than for the

The *Simón Bolívar* steamship on the Magdalena River

representation of nature in *Cien años de soledad*. These drawings were originally published in 1872–73 in the French magazine *Le Tour du Monde*; they
appeared in a book in Spanish published in 1948, when García Márquez was
living in Barranquilla, at the base of the Magdalena Rivera, and beginning to
write his first Faulknerian short texts.

   A drawing in this volume of French artworks titled "Rocks with Hieroglyphs in Pandi" evokes several of the issues at hand in this consideration of
nature and technology in the writing of García Márquez. This drawing shows
an early intrusion of the technology of writing on nature, with an early form
of human script on one of several stones in these drawings that evoke the image
of the novel's second sentence: "Macondo era entonces una aldea de veinte
casas de barro y cañabrava construidas a la orilla de un río de aguas diáfanas
que se precipitaban por un lecho de piedras pulidas, blancas y enormes como
huevos prehistóricos" (1) [At that time Macondo was a village of twenty adobe
houses, built on the bank of a river of clear water that ran along a bed of polished stones, which were white and enormous, like prehistoric eggs] (1). The
prehistoric rocks are like eggs in the early history of Macondo. On the lower
left is a small image of a human being, but whose dress is not one of the indigenous peoples who carved the hieroglyph, but rather is a colonizer clearly overshadowed by the huge dimensions of the rock "like a prehistoric egg," by

Rocks bearing hieroglyphs in Pandi

nature, and by the indigenous past about which he seems oblivious as he walks in the opposite direction. Like García Márquez, then, the artist has momentarily privileged the non-human over the human.

The images of a drawing from this volume titled "Peasants from Guaduas" evoke several scenes from García Márquez's cycle of fiction of Macondo published from 1955 with the appearance of the novel *La hojarasca* (*Leaf Storm*) to the 1967 appearance of *Cien años*. Slaughtered fowl fill the drawing in three areas, underlining the human conquest of nature. The most prominent image of this drawing, however, is of human technology: the cages on the lower left of the drawing are the masterpieces of human technology and art that are the centerpiece of the Macondo story of Baltazar in "La prodigiosa tarde de Baltazar" ("Balthazar's Prodigious Afternoon"), the artist and technician whose day of victory over nature turns into a an evening of ruin. Thus, from an ecocritical point of view, this story questions the very assumption of the human being as the center and non-human nature as periphery.

The spectacular image of the drawing titled "Condor Shooting at the Andes," brings forth several important issues with respect to the representation of nature and human presence in nature. First and foremost, the mod-

Peasants from Guaduas

ern-day observer of this drawing questions if condors are really this large and this menacing. This drawing features the hyperbole of *Cien años de soledad*, using the methods of the oral tradition that emphasizes "heavy" and memorable characters. Thus, this drawing and the next one evoke questions of realism in contrast to magic realism and the like. They also evoke the following question: Is García Márquez's representation of nature hyperbolic, or merely a realist representation of hyperbolic images, such as these drawings, that have surrounded him for much of his writing career?

The image, "Wax Palm Trees in Quindío," invites discussion of García Márquez's oft quoted assertion that he is a "mere realist" who copies reality versus the "magic realist" that many critics use to describe him. The filter of the drawings only complicates this discussion further because of how unreal these trees seem as "nature." The observer is invited to ask, are they nature or art?

The drawing titled "The Old Convent of Santo Domingo in Bogotá," provides an image of the multiple themes in *Cien años de soledad* related to the political, social and ecclesiastical hierarchy in Latin America. This image of the convent presents a powerful portrayal of the centralized political and ecclesiastical power structure (the patriarchal order) that García Márquez sat-

Opposite: Condor Shooting at the Andes

The Old Convent of Santo Domingo in Bogotá

irizes in *Cien años de soledad* as powers that are distant from Macondo and ineffective locally.

This political/ecclesiastic structure in Colombia is the opposite of the environmental adage to think globally and act locally. In *Cien años de soledad*, García Márquez mocks the political and religious order in Colombia, with a narrator who claims that the only difference between the followers of the Liberal Party and the partisans of the Conservative Party is the time they attend mass on Sunday morning. Beyond the institution of the church portrayed here, the presence of nature is radically different from what has been observed thus far. Now, nature is mostly controlled by humans, with nature as a park in the center of a building structure built with the latest in architecture and technology of the Spanish Colonial period, including an Arabic motif that was imported from Spain and implanted in their Spanish colonies.

In conclusion, García Márquez portrays an ambiguous relationship between the non-human and the human world, and actually privileges both. Unlike some books identified as "eco-literature," *Cien años de soledad* portrays a complex web in which the implied author is attracted to and critical of both orality and writing, both technology and nature, both modernity and

Opposite: Wax Palm Trees in Quindío

tradition. More specifically, I offer three areas of concluding remarks. First, *Cien años de soledad* draws from at least three main sources for images of nature: (a) literary texts, (b) oral tradition, (c) visual arts (in the form of nineteenth- century French drawings). Second, *Cien años de soledad* is perhaps less about nature and technology than about oral and writing culture's images of nature and technology. Clearly, the novel has a multiplicity of filters for the representation of nature. Third, *Cien años de soledad* is far more complex than more typical books of "eco-literature" that necessarily privilege nature as center, as already suggested. On the one hand, characters such as Úrsula live in an oral-culture mindset, close to the human life world and close to nature (using homeopathic herbs such as arnica). Finally, *Cien años de soledad* does invite the reader to rethink nature as it was and as it is, as well as our relationship with it as it was and as it is. In this sense, *Cien años de soledad* is a novel that ecocritics can identify as a work of ecological wisdom. Returning to our original definition of ecocriticism, *Cien años de soledad*, like ecocriticism, claims as its hermeneutic horizon the finite environment the reader occupies thanks not just to culturally coded determinants but also to natural determinants that antedate these, and will outlast them.

Cien años de soledad, like *Grande Sertao: Veredas*, *La casa verde* and *Terra Nostra*, far surpasses the simplistic dichotomies and Manichean vision of nature as the Iberian *terra* to be conquered. The nature that we understand in the real world to be finite is not as consistently finite or concise in these three novels (or in many other novels published since 1945) as it is in the empirical world in which we live and in the nature we still inhabit.

NOTES

1. Important studies of *Cien años de soledad* include Gene Bell-Villada, *Gabriel García Márquez: The Man and His* Work; Josefina Ludmer, *Cien años de soledad: una interpretación*; George McMurray, *Gabriel García Márquez*; George McMurray, ed. *Critical Essays on Gabriel García Márquez*; Ricardo Gullón, "Gabriel García Márquez and the Lost Art of Storytelling"; Mario Vargas Llosa, *García Márquez: Historia de un deicidio*; Raymond L. Williams, *Gabriel García Márquez*.

2. The rise of ecocriticism is fundamentally a phenomenon of the 1990s, but can be traced back to the 1960s and works such as Rachel Carson's classic *Silent Spring*, originally published in 1962. Important critical bibliography of key works for ecocritical readings of literature include Leo Marx's early study, *The Machine in the Garden* (1964); Joseph Meeker, *The Comedy of Survival: Studies in Literary Ecology* (1974); Annette Kolodny, *The Lay of the Land: Metaphor as Experience in American Life and Letters* (1975); Leonard Lutwack, *The Role of Place in Literature* (1984); Steven Rosendale, *The Greening of Literary Scholarship* (2002). The third and most recent book by Buell on this subject, *The Future of Environmental Criticism* (2005) and other recent books, such as *Practical Ecocriticism* (2003), by Glen A. Love, are indicators that ecocriticism is a growing field. The aim of Love's book is to initiate a more biologically informed ecocritical dialogue about literature and its relationship to nature and environmental concerns.

3. Early ecocriticism of the 1980s and early 1990s (now referred to as the "first wave") placed emphasis on the non-human over the human. The definition of ecocriticism offered by the editors of the special issue of *New Literary History* is as follows: "challenges interpretation of its own grounding in the bedrock of natural fact, in the biosphere and indeed planetary conditions without which human life, much less humane letters, could not exist. Ecocriticism thus claims as it hermeneutic horizon nothing short of the literal horizon itself, the finite environment that a reader or writer occupies thanks not just to culturally coded determinants but also to natural determinants that antedate these, and will outlast them." See Tucker, "From the Editors," 505.

4. French, *Nature, Neo-Colonialism, and the Spanish American Regional Writers*, 7.

5. As Buell points out in his recent *The Future of Environmental Criticism*, a second wave of ecocritical thought has allowed for the recovery of the human.

6. See McMurray, "The Role of Climate in Twentieth-Century Spanish American Fiction."

7. See Struebig, "Nature and Sexuality in Gabriel García Márquez's *One Hundred Years of Solitude.*"

8. I have discussed the role of García Márquez and the writers of the Boom as Modernists and innovators in *The Twentieth Century Spanish American Novel*, chapter 8, and in "Modernist Continuities: The Desire to Be Modern in Twentieth-Century Spanish American Fiction."

9. See Heise, "Local Rock and Global Plastic: World Ecology and the Experience of Place."

10. See Bell-Villada, *Gabriel Garcia Marquez: The Man and His Work.*

11. See Jenkins, "Alexander von Humboldt's *Kosmos* and the Beginnings of Ecocriticism."

12. García Márquez, *Cien años de soledad* (Buenos Aires: Sudamericana, 1970), 70. All subsequent in-text page references to quotes are from this edition. English translations are from *One Hundred Years of Solitude* translated by Gregory Rabassa (New York: Perennial Classics, 1998), 78.

13. For a more developed analysis of writing culture in *María*, see Williams, *The Colombian Novel: 1844–1987*, pages 151–160.

14. Isaacs, *María*, 1867 (Buenos Aires: Losada, 1972), 62. My translation. All quotations are from this edition. Subsequent page references are included in the text.

15. Eustacio Rivera, *La vorágine*, 1924 (Mexico City: Porrúa, 1972), 5. My translation. All quotations are from this edition. Subsequent page references are included in the text.

16. Vargas Llosa, *La casa verde*, 1966 (Mexico City: Alfaguara, 2000), 33. All in-text page references are to this edition. References to English translations are from *The Green House*, translated by Gregory Rabassa (New York: Avon Books, 1973), 19.

17. For lengthy discussions of the literary sources of *Cien años de soledad*, see Levine, *El espejo hablado: Un estudio de "Cien años de soledad*; and Hood, *La ficción de Gabriel García Márquez: repetición e intertextualidad.*

18. Ong, *Orality and Literacy*, 42–43.

19. See Williams, "The Visual Arts, the Poetization of Space and Writing: An Interview with Gabriel García Márquez."

Works Cited

Bell-Villada, Gene. *García Márquez: The Man and His Work*. Chapel Hill: University of North Carolina Press, 1993.

Buell, Lawrence. *The Future of Environmental Criticism: Environmental Crisis and Literary Imagination*. Blackwell Manifestos. Oxford: Blackwell, 2005.

French, Jennifer L. *Nature, Neo-Colonialism, and the Spanish American Regional Writers.* Hanover, NH: Dartmouth College Press, 2005.

García Márquez, Gabriel. *Cien años de soledad.* Buenos Aires: Editorial Sudamericana, 1970. Translated by Gregory Rabassa as *One Hundred Years of Solitude.* (New York: Harper and Row, 1970).

Gullón, Ricardo. "Gabriel García Márquez and the Lost Art of Storytelling," *Diacritics* 1.1 (1971): 27–32. Translated by José G. Sánchez.

Heise, Ursula K. "Local Rock and Global Plastic: World Ecology and the Experience of Place," *Comparative Literature Studies* 41.1 (2004): 126–52.

Hood, Edward Waters. *La ficción de Gabriel García Márquez: Repetición e intertextualidad.* New York: Peter Lang, 1993.

Isaacs, Jorge. *María.* 1867. Buenos Aires: Editorial Losada, 1972.

Jenkins, Alice. "Alexander von Humboldt's *Kosmos* and the Beginnings of Ecocriticism," *Interdisiciplinary Studies in Literature and Environment* 14.2 (2007): 89–105.

Kolodny, Anette, *The Lay of the Land: Metaphor as Experience in American Life and Letters.* Chapel Hill: University of North Carolina Press, 1975.

Levine, Suzanne Jill. *El espejo hablado: un estudio de* Cien años de soledad. Caracas: Monte Avila, 1975.

Ludmer, Josefina. *Cien años de soledad: una interpretación.* Buenos Aires: Editorial Tiempo Contemporáneo, 1972.

Lutwack, Leonard. *The Role of Place in Literature.* New York: Syracuse University Press, 1984.

Marx, Leo. *The Machine in the Garden.* 1964. 2nd ed. Oxford: Oxford University Press, 1999.

McMurray, George. *Gabriel García Márquez.* New York: Frederick Ungar, 1977.

_____. "The Role of Climate in Twentieth-Century Spanish American Fiction" in Perez and Aycock, *Climate and Literature,* 55–64.

_____, editor. *Critical Essays on Gabriel García Márquez.* Boston: G.K. Hall, 1987.

Meeker, Joseph. *The Comedy of Survival: Studies in Literary Ecology.* New York: Charles Scribner's Sons, 1974.

Ong, Walter. *Orality and Literacy: Technologizing of the Word.* New York: Meuthen, 1982.

Perez, Janet and Wendell Aycock, eds. *Climate and Literature: Reflections of Environment.* Lubbock, Texas: Texas Tech Press, 1995.

Rivera, José Eustacio. *La vorágine.* 1924. Mexico City: Porrúa, 1976.

Rosendale, Steven. *The Greening of Literary Scholarship.* Iowa City: University of Iowa Press, 2002.

Struebig, Patricia. "Nature and Sexuality in Gabriel García Márquez's *One Hundred Years of Solitude,*" *Selecta: Journal of the Pacific Northwest Council on Foreign Languages,* 15 (1984): 58–62.

Tucker, Herbert F. "From the Editors," *New Literary History* 3 (1999): 505.

Vargas Llosa, Mario. *La casa verde.* 1966. Mexico City: Alfaguara, 2000. Translated by Gregory Rabassa as *The Green House* (New York: Avon Books, 1973).

_____. *García Márquez: historia de un deicidio.* Barcelona-Caracas: Seix Barral-Monte Avila, 1971.

Williams, Raymond L. *Gabriel García Márquez.* Boston: G.K. Hall, 1984.

_____. "Modernist Continuities: The Desire to Be Modern in Twentieth-Century Spanish American Fiction," *Bulletin of Spanish Studies,* LXXIX (2002): 369–393.

_____. *The Twentieth Century Spanish American Novel.* Austin: University of Texas Press, 2003.

_____. "The Visual Arts, the Poetization of Space and Writing: An Interview with Gabriel García Márquez," *Publications of the Modern Language Association,* 104.2 (1989): 131–40.

The Long and Winding Road of Technology from *María* to *Cien años de soledad* to *Mantra*: An Ecocritical Reading

Gustavo Llarull

This essay advances two theses that put three seemingly disparate novels — *María* (1867), by Colombian Jorge Isaacs, *Cien años de soledad* (1967; *One Hundred Years of Solitude*), by Colombian Gabriel García Márquez, and *Mantra* (2001), by Argentine Rodrigo Fresán — in fruitful dialogue.[1]

First, a thesis about nature, technology, and the language of self-description: *María* and *Mantra* mirror each other, in the sense that nature and technology are used in opposite ways to describe human life. While in *María* virtually every aspect of human life — conspicuously, human feelings, bodies, and even technological devices — is described in terms of *natural* images and processes, in *Mantra* virtually every aspect of human life is described in terms of *technological* images and processes. In other words, in *María* there is a reduction of the language of technology to the language of nature, while in *Mantra* the language of nature is reduced to the language of technology.[2] Between these two poles, *Cien años de soledad* presents a transitional stance: it contains ironically disguised references to the language of *María*, and at the same time foreshadows the use of language presented in *Mantra*.

The second thesis is more directly related to the views of nature put forth in these three novels. I argue that the implied author in *Cien años de soledad* presents an outlook that rejects simplified, Manichean views on nature and technology. Instead, the implicit ethical-ecological criterion found in *Cien años* is two-fold: first, the quest for increasing intelligibility; second, the quest for the development of human capacities — regardless of whether these aims are achieved through natural or technological means.[3]

This reading of *Cien años* sheds light on the implicit ecological concerns presented in the other two novels. Guided by the aforementioned reading of *Cien años*, one finds in *María* elements that might help us conceive of a role for technology that is not divorced from contemporary ecological concerns — a role that escapes at the same time the stereotypical Romantic conception of the nature/technology system in which this novel is embedded. This role can be summarized in the following judgments (which, as will be shown below, are found in the interstices of *María* and further developed in both *Cien años* and *Mantra*):

(1) Nature is *prima facie* good, but it can surprise us with expressions of fierce, blind, destructive force.

(2) Technology *can* be deemed "good" if used to counter the natural excesses mentioned in (1). In these cases, technology *can* and *does* come to our aid. Also, technology is deemed "good" when it helps satisfy basic human necessities (e.g., shelter, food, transportation), but not when it is used in an unnecessary, superfluous way.

(3) An ethical approach to technology can not only minimize its pernicious effects, but also aid human development. Furthermore, an ethical approach is necessary to avoid relegating human life to the "needs" of technological development *per se*. If left to its own devices (i.e., without ethical guidance), technology might be mistakenly regarded as something intrinsically valuable. When this occurs, social life is subsumed under, and absorbed into, a self-sustaining technological system that the implied author (in the three novels) deems pernicious.

These three pronouncements map onto an ecological view according to which neither nature nor technology is intrinsically good or bad, but, rather, each can be used in good or bad ways. The goodness or badness of these ways is, to reiterate, a function of a search for intelligibility and development of human capacities. This view extends from *María* to *Mantra*. While *Mantra* seems at first sight an unqualified paean to technology, a closer, more careful reading reveals a framework that presents unexpected continuities with the vision of nature found in both *María* and *Cien años de soledad*. Put differently, while the presentation and use of imagery related to nature and technology in *María* and *Mantra* are the mirror-image of each other — the opposite, but incarnating, as said above, two poles in a continuum — the ecological concerns presented in both novels may be seen as presenting a certain continuity. The outlook presented in *Cien años*, then, offers a unitary thread to interpret such seemingly dissimilar novels as *María* and *Mantra*.

I. Natural and Technological Imagery in *María*

Upon a first reading, the narration in general and the descriptive devices in particular that *María* presents seem to pertain exclusively to the well-known (and, many may argue, worn out) features of the nineteenth-century Romantic novel. Thus, the environment is described either as something in accord with the emotions and sentiments of the characters — the famous Romantic projection of feeling onto the external world — or as an always-positive, comforting force. As an example of the first mode, when Efraín — the doomed protagonist who will fall in love with the woman whose name gives the novel its title — feels exultant about his return to the Cauca region of Colombia, nature appears as his ally: "Aquella naturaleza parecía ostentar toda la hermosura de sus noches, como para recibir a un huésped amigo" (Nature seemed to be displaying all her beauty that night, as if to welcome a guest).[4] Conversely, when he feels sad, the valley is gloomy, and "el diostedé saludaba al día con su canto triste y monótono desde el corazón de la sierra" (34) [the *diostedé* hailed the day with his sad and monotonous song] (21). However, it is the second mode that is more widespread: nature is for the most part seen in a positive light. It is a source of consolation in moments of pain, and a fellow companion in moments of happiness: "La naturaleza es la más amorosa de las madres cuando el dolor se ha adueñado de nuestra alma, y si la felicidad nos acaricia, ella nos sonríe" (97) [Nature is the most loving of mothers when grief has taken possession of our souls; and if happiness is our lot, she smiles upon us] (84). There are also references to nature that relate it to a state of Edenic innocence that seems to have been lost.[5]

The addition of María as an almost angelic, untouched and untouchable character that Death takes away from Efraín rounds up the picture — as good a picture of the Romantic novel as one can get. But, fortunately, *María* is more than that. *Everything*, not just the characters' inner lives, is presented in terms of natural imagery — even technological devices. But before moving on to this issue, it is worth addressing an intermediate step, still typical of Romanticism (of a widespread version of Romanticism, at any rate), but which presents interesting features. Nature not only "expresses" the inner lives of the characters, but seems to be fused, blended, and made one with them. At first, María's voice is compared with the singing of birds (117 [105]); her crying face, with dew-covered roses (124 [113]). Likewise, the face of a man is compared with fruits; his nose, with the beak of a bird (77 [61]). The city is said to fall asleep like birds (330 [288]). But, later, the whole area of Cauca is, or becomes, María. That is, María and Cauca — the loved woman and one's land — become one and the same thing (311 [283]).

This is an intermediate step, still in the grip of typical Romantic imagery, because it incarnates the nationalistic strand — the "patrioterismo," as Cortázar refers to it in his 1979 *Un tal Lucas*— of Romanticism. Nonetheless, it is important to observe this fusion of person and nature because it is a further step in the direction of reducing all imagery — even that representing technological devices — to natural imagery. Moreover, this fusion of person and nature is of interest because it is the opposite of what occurs in *Mantra*: the fusion of person and technology.

There is, then, a crescendo that culminates when person and land (i.e., María and the Cauca region) are identified, and when virtually everything else is described in terms of natural phenomena. Consider technological devices. The ship on which Efraín's father brings María to his home — a schooner — is described thus: "La ligera nave ensayaba sus blancas alas, como una garza de nuestros bosques las suyas, antes de emprender un largo vuelo" (30) [The light bark spread her sails, like a heron of our forests beginning a long flight] (17). The image of the ship as a bird, and of its movement as this bird's flight, is an excellent example of the use of the language of nature to describe technology. Also, houses and shelters — expressions of a "primitive" technology of sorts — are not only compared to nature, but actually made of elements whose natural materials are still apparent. Thus, Braulio's house is made entirely of natural elements. Its main room is "cubierta de esteras, de junco y pieles de oso" (36) [had bamboo rush-bottomed seats scattered about, covered with bear-skins] (23); its kitchen, in turn, is "formada de caña menuda y con el techo de hojas de la misma planta" (36) [built of strips of cane and with a roof of the leaves of the same plant] (23).

However, in *María*, the more technology evolves, the more negative the judgment on it seems to become. Thus, there is a gradation (and degradation) of sorts in the movement from natural, rural spaces, to urban ones: Bogotá and London represent the urban pole; Cauca, the natural, rural pole; Efraín's property and the *hacienda* (the estate where Braulio's house is located), an intermediate space between the two poles. In the rural environment, people are viewed as naturally good-hearted. In urban settings, everything and everyone is characterized by superficial sophistication and deceit. It is in the city where Efraín's father is the victim of a scam (163 [154]). It is also in the city where Micaela cheats on Emigdio (72 [62]).

II. Implicit Moral Judgments on Nature and Technology in *María*

There is a single but important exception to the Romantic conception of nature that permeates *María*: the jungle. This exception is central to the role that the implied author assigns to nature and technology when he manages to escape Romantic commonplaces. The jungle is presented as a blind force of nature that can either benefit or harm us. On the one hand, at times the richness and exuberance of the jungle are seen as beneficial. On the other, mosquitoes, bats, and snakes (whose venom dooms the victim to suffer an atrocious death) are also the elements the jungle is made of.[6]

Nature, then, in the form of the jungle, can take away its riches — and even human life — without rhyme or reason. The jungle enables us to sketch a picture of the normative view on nature and technology posed by the implied author in *María*. Despite the abundant examples of a more stereotypically Romantic view presented so far — a Manichean view according to which everything related to nature and the rural environment is "good" and everything related to technology and the urban environment is "bad" — the conceptual space opened up by the jungle does alter this oversimplified view. This more neutral view of the jungle suggests that nature is not the all-good "mother" that protects us, but rather, something that, although *prima facie* is good, can also afford us horrible experiences such as dangerous animals and illnesses. Correlatively, technology is sometimes presented as not being intrinsically bad. The jungle scene, again, provides an excellent example of this: when Efraín has to go through the jungle, on his trip back to the Cauca region, Gregorio and Laureano, the *balseros* (raft guides), master the technology necessary to overcome the threats of the jungle. They are nimble, knowledgeable, and they dominate a rather primitive but effective technological system to guide the *canoas* (barges) and avoid shipwrecks (320–325 [282–287]). But then again, it should be borne in mind that technology and nature are not always, and not necessarily, irreconcilable opposites; for, in order to be able to master the technological system required to guide the barges, the *balseros* must also know how to "listen" to the signs of nature. It is in this sense that Greg Garrand, commenting on another Romantic text — Wordsworth's "Michael: A Pastoral Poem" — writes, "the shepherd's ability to take warning from the 'meaning' he derives from the 'music' of the weather suggests a responsiveness as sophisticated as it is crucial to the survival of his flock."[7] In *María*, the *balseros* master both the technological system required to bypass the perils of the jungle, *and* the "language" of the marshes, without which technology would be barren.

This jungle scene is essential to reconfigure other scenes in the novel and articulate three judgments about the relationship between nature and technology which were first enumerated on page 90 and are elaborated upon here in the context of *María*.

(1) Nature is *prima facie* good, but it can surprise us with expressions of fierce, blind, destructive force (e.g., the river flood during the storm; the jungle).

(2) Technology *can* be deemed "good" if used to counter the natural excesses mentioned in 1). In these cases, technology *can* and *does* come to our aid (e.g., the "technique" of the *balseros* who know how to navigate safely the dangerous river that goes through the jungle). Also, technology is deemed "good" when it helps satisfy basic human necessities (e.g., shelter, food, transportation), but not when it is used in an unnecessary, superfluous way (e.g., the hunt of the tiger; the even more unnecessary hunt of the *venadito* [little deer]; the excesses of life in the city).

(3) An ethical approach to technology can not only minimize its pernicious effects, but also aid human development. Consider, again, the case of the *balseros*. Consider too the agriculturally oriented technology used in Efraín's *hacienda*, which is deemed "good" by the implied author, provided the relationship between the different users of technology abides by certain minimal ethical standards (e.g., servants and slaves in Efraín's *hacienda*—the main workers and users of agriculturally oriented technology—are treated as members of the family).[8] Lastly, an ethical approach is necessary to avoid relegating human life to the "needs" of technological development *per se*. If left to its own devices (i.e., without ethical guidance), technology might be mistakenly regarded as something intrinsically valuable. When this occurs, social life is subsumed under, and absorbed into, a self-sustaining technological system that the implied author deems pernicious. Consider the parallelism of the stories of Nay and Simar, on the one hand, and María and Efraín, on the other. Both couples were separated and doomed because they were instrumentally used as chains in the link of technological and consumerist urban environments: the cotton industry and the related slave-industry in the case of Nay and Simar; the demands of a "successful" urban life in the case of María and Efraín. (Recall that Efraín is sent to Europe in order to pursue a successful urban career; his father tells him that only after he has acquired the requisite knowledge — technical knowledge, since his career will be medicine — can he return to Colombia and marry María. Failing to do this would have, in his father's view, compromised the financial strength of the family).

These three pronouncements[9] map onto an ecological view according to which neither nature nor technology is intrinsically good or bad, but, rather, each can be used in good or bad ways. The goodness or badness of these ways is, as anticipated earlier, a function of a search for intelligibility and development of human capacities.

In these pronouncements there is an implicit rejection of a certain conception of nature. This conception involves conceiving of nature as an entity that is completely independent of human beings and human action, and which is directly accessible to the human gaze and human scrutiny. In other words, this conception involves an ontological claim, and an epistemological claim. The ontological claim states the self-sufficiency of both nature and human beings. That is, nature is one kind of entity (or group of entities), whereas human beings are a different kind. At most, these two kinds of entities interact with each other, but they are in principle distinguishable. The epistemological claim states the possibility of cognitively accessing nature in a "pure" way. Allegedly, human beings can take an objective stance and "see" nature transparently. This knowledge, in turn, results in the possibility of acting on, and thus altering, nature.

The rejection of these two claims is widely accepted nowadays.[10] It is, however, noteworthy that *María* could foreshadow it. Let me briefly discuss why this naïve view of nature has been rejected. The ontological claim is false: there is no such thing as a "purely" natural state that is independent of the realm of the human. Whether or not one endorses one form or the other of the evolutionist theory (or any form of physicalist or emergentist theories), it is uncontroversial that from a biological standpoint the human is embedded in, and springs from, the natural. Thus, the dichotomy between the natural and the human is a conceptual tool, not a statement that correlates to a real state of affairs.

The epistemological claim is also false: human beings do not have a pure, complete cognitive access to natural phenomena. Note that the rejection of this claim does not commit one to any particular view on science in general or perception in particular. One can be an advocate of scientific knowledge, and — let us suppose — wary of sociological explanations and relativistic stances, and still be committed to acknowledging that our grasp of natural phenomena is incomplete at best. Alternatively, if one is more inclined to sociological explanations, there is ample evidence that human beings, socialized in a given culture, perceive natural entities and phenomena from the standpoint of their necessities, which operate as a "filter" of sorts, which, in turn, guides their perception and articulation of perceptual data.[11]

If what has been suggested so far is accepted, it follows that all attempts to "return" to a state of alleged purity — "natural" purity — which in many Romantic versions involves a sort of Eden-like happiness — cannot be more than a wish. However, the impossibility of a Romantic return to nature does not imply that *any* kind of relationship that humans establish with "nature" should be accepted. On the contrary, this preliminary attempt to clear the ground of untenable notions of nature is meant to be the starting point of a more realistic assessment of ecological concerns, for, it will be granted, starting from an erroneous definition of the terms won't help find solutions.[12]

These considerations do not invalidate the three *avant la lettre* pronouncements presented in the above discussion of *María*. While the general view of nature presented in *María* falls prey to the misguided dichotomy between nature and technology, the three implicit, interstitial pronouncements presented toward the end of the last section hold true, among other reasons because they don't depend on this dichotomy.

The main thread of these three pronouncements is the rejection of the view that natural phenomena are necessarily "good," and technological phenomena necessarily "bad." Rather, the evaluative criterion seems to be the pursuit of intelligibility and development of human capacities (positive evaluation) and the entropic tendency (negative evaluation), whether or not these come from "nature" or "technology." The following section demonstrates how García Márquez's *Cien años de soledad* pursues this line of inquiry.

III. *Cien años de soledad*: Overcoming Romantic Stereotypes

In *Cien años de soledad*, the Eden-like appearance of the town of Macondo as it is presented prior to the arrival of the gypsies — a Macondo created by people who want to "flee" from urban culture and "return" to a simpler, more "natural" way of life — cannot be but an ironic use of the old Romantic theme of "the return to Nature." It is in this context of irony that the plethora of judgments such as the following should be read: "Era en verdad una aldea felíz, donde nadie era mayor de 30 años y donde nadie había muerto" [It was a truly happy village where no one was over thirty years of age and where no one had died.][13] Note that even the very foundation of Macondo doesn't fit the Romantic dichotomy between nature and culture in general and nature and technology in particular: the first Buendía — José Arcadio Buendía — designed Macondo in such a way that every house would be equidistant to the river. Every house, too, would receive a decent amount of sunlight. Is this something "purely" natural, or does it involve some sort of "technological" or "technical" use of architectural design? Rather than an opposition between nature and culture (or, again, nature and technology), it is more fruitful to speak of an opposition between the search (and yearning for) intelligibility and development of human capacities on the one hand, and the search (and yearning for) unintelligibility and destruction on the other. The implied author does not "condemn" the initial design of Macondo — again, it is a "happy," quasi-Edenic state (despite the irony with which this state is depicted). And yet, there *is* a technical use of architectural design applied to natural resources in Macondo's construction — guided by an

ethical, social intention, revealed by the just, equitable distribution of sunlight and access to fresh water. Then the gypsies arrive, and Buendía — the
founder — gets lost in his world of magnets, scientific discoveries, and
alchemy — *isolated*, this time, from social interaction and ethical guidance.

From the beginning of the novel, then, it is apparent that, first, there
isn't a "pure" natural state, nor is there a "pure" technological state; and, second — within a continuum of sorts — moving toward the technological end
of the spectrum *does not* entail, for the implied author, a negative evaluative
judgment. Again, technique and technology applied to the design of Macondo
are guided by an ethical parameter and are thus regarded positively, while technique and technology devoid of social and ethical parameters are judged negatively. Later in the novel, the same will happen with other occurrences of
technology. On the one hand, technology frees human beings of the yoke
and whim of weather and climate — people do not depend entirely on the
weather to provide themselves with food — but on the other hand, technology *can* be destructive if it isn't guided by ethical parameters, as the denouement of the banana industry episode shows.

This lack of intrinsic value of technology (i.e., technology isn't intrinsically "good" or intrinsically "bad") runs parallel to a lack of intrinsic value
of nature.[14] Consider sex, that strong natural force that reproduces the lineage of the Buendías. On the one hand, this seemingly beneficial natural force
not only propels the Buendía family forward, but it is a space of playful enjoy-
ment, a natural refuge that helps them overcome the challenges of life. On
the other hand, the blind force of sexual impulse threatens the family with
the ominous but tempting ghost of incest.

The same occurs with other natural phenomena. In the novel, rains can
be beneficial — they help agricultural activities — but they can also be atro-
ciously cruel: the deluge. And, again, it is technology — a certain use of technology — that allows Macondians to control the damage caused by natural
causes. Recall, for example, that when a generalized "illness" (insomnia) hits
Macondo, a rudimentary form of technology ameliorates the situation: a
machine of sorts, designed to retain memories and knowledge and based on
a system of files and cards that resembles the *ars combinatoria* (method or "art"
of combination) of Raimund Lull and G.W. Leibniz (47–48 [47–48]). The
reference to the *ars combinatoria* is very likely a wink to Borges, who wrote
quite often about it, and even incorporated it into the mechanics of some of
his stories.[15] Whether this is a direct allusion to Borges or not, the presence
of the *ars combinatoria* should be a reminder that, despite its "natural" and
allegedly "primitive" setting, there is in García Márquez's novel a most subtle but certainly laudatory "commentary" on Borgesian or Borges-related —
that is, very sophisticated — literary culture. (Consider another potential wink

to Borgesian literature: the ending of the novel, with the revelation of the fantastic function of the manuscripts of Melquíades).

The irony referenced in the above examples does not have as its sole target the allegedly Edenic, natural state of Macondians, but also the blind reliance on technology and culture. The episode of the "magical" artifact that can produce music — and, in particular, its sad destiny of abandonment — is an excellent example of this ironic meta-commentary on technological progress.

To sum up: the novel presents neither an unqualified endorsement of the natural nor an unqualified rejection of the technological. The key is the way in which the implied author treats nature and technology, be it to endorse them or to criticize them. The criterion for this endorsement or criticism is, as I suggested above, the search for intelligibility and development of human capacities. Is the phenomenon in question — be it "natural" or "technological" — tending toward greater intelligibility and/or greater development of human capacities, or is it, on the contrary, tending toward unintelligibility and/or entropy? Think again of sex in the context of the novel: it is (implicitly) commended and celebrated when it operates as a force of creation and recreation, but (implicitly) criticized when it is "tainted" by the entropic tendency that incest would lead to.

This same operation can be tracked throughout the novel. The above criterion that guides this operation could be generalized and — if applied to the whole novel — yield an interesting "map" of the ecological aspects of *Cien años de soledad*.[16] The implied author is very careful when making this two-fold move: he makes ironic use of the more widespread, simplified versions of Romanticism (which, as pointed out earlier, glorify an alleged return to nature), while he follows up and further develops a subtler, more interesting criterion of assessment of the nature/technology system or constellation.

In the previous section of this essay it was shown that this criterion — or at the very least the antecedents of this criterion — can be traced back to the interstices of *María*. In the next two sections, an altogether different kind of novel — Rodrigo Fresán's *Mantra*—will prove to display surprising similarities with regard to the relation between nature and technology.

IV. *Mantra*, or Our Technological Selves

Mantra is divided into three parts. In the first one, the narrator — an unnamed Argentine in his late thirties or early forties — tries to make sense of his life using an old school photograph as a starting point. In the photograph, his childhood friend Martín Mantra is missing. The narrator is fascinated with Mr. Mantra, and he thinks that understanding him will be the key to understanding himself. Ironically, his attempts at self-understanding are threatened by an illness that affects his memory. A tumor gradually destroys all his memories but the memory of the letter "X" — a reduction, concentration, and amplification of Macondo's special illness of insomnia.

From the very beginning, then, hyperbole, irony and parody set the tone of the novel. Besides the reference — the *references*, rather, for there are plenty — to the world of Macondo, note the alliterative names of the character that gives the novel its title. Note, too, the parody of a typical "page-turner" beginning: when the narrator recalls first meeting Martín Mantra, he says, "yo conocí a Martín Mantra o, mejor dicho, Martín Mantra me conoció a mí, me tendió su mano, y en su mano había un revólver" (I met Martín Mantra, or, rather, Martín Mantra met me: he extended his hand to shake mine, and in his hand there was a revolver).[17] Thus ends Chapter One. How can one *not* turn the page and see what will happen?

However, the next page frustrates the reader's expectations. Instead of the continuation of the story, one finds a meta-fictional reflection on the art of storytelling (loosely triggered by the narrator's upcoming impossibility of telling any more stories, given his illness). And then again, once the reader is already immersed in the narrator's train of thought, the reflection is interrupted and rejected: "No tengo tanto tiempo ni conocimientos" [I don't have that much time or that much knowledge (to go on with this reflection or to tell the story in that way)] (18).

One may think that behind these "tricks," that is, once one adjusts to the alternation between fictional and meta-fictional passages, the plot is, after all, fairly straightforward: a particular childhood memory — the memory of Martín Mantra — that triggers the narrative of a life. But this seeming simplicity and straightforwardness soon turn into a very complex textual challenge to the reader, who at times finds it difficult to make sense of who is saying what, who the narrators are, and so on. This confusion, however, has its reasons, as will become apparent shortly. For now, let us continue with an outline of the structure of the novel.

The second part of *Mantra* is narrated by a dead Frenchman as he watches his whole life on television — he is actually chained to the television set — in a limbo, or Hell, or Purgatory of sorts. When he was alive, this narrator was romantically involved with a cousin of Martín Mantra, María Marie. Thus, he offers a new perspective on the life of Mantra and his family. Formally, the second part has the structure of a dictionary or an encyclopedia, with entries disposed in alphabetical order.

The third part is narrated by an android (or a conscious computer of sorts) in the ruins of Mexico City. The android is searching for its creator,

"Mantrax," in turn created by Martín Mantra. Formally, this section is a parody of Juan Rulfo's groundbreaking, and now classic, short novel *Pedro Páramo* (1955).

Lastly, after the third part, there is a list of acknowledgements in a section called "Bajo la máscara (Agradecimientos)" [Under the Mask (Acknowledgements)]. While the author seems to be presenting a non-fictional, neutral, conventional list of acknowledgments, the list ends with Ana, the author's "real" "Mexican friend," which may be construed as an invitation to reread the novel, whose first part is precisely called "The Mexican Friend." Thus, the novel has something of a circular ending not unlike that of *Cien años de soledad*.[18]

The protagonists of the novel want to reach an understanding of themselves: the narrator of the first part wants to re-tell his life-story and assess it, prompted by his incoming loss of memory. The narrator of the second part watches his life on television, re-tells it and reinterprets it with the aid of those images. Finally, Martín Mantra is obsessed with the idea of reaching an understanding of himself, of his family, and of history, by appealing to a filmic narrative or "extraño artefacto narrativo" (strange narrative artifact), as the narrator of the first part calls it (75). In the more essayistic passages of the novel, Martín Mantra explains his "theory." In the more conventionally narrative ones, the reader sees him trying to put that theory into practice, by — among other things — attaching a camera to his head and filming every moment of his life. The result, "Mundo Mantra" (Mantra World), is meant to be a "Film Total" [Total Film] (67).

Things gradually get complicated because of the constant barrage of tidbits of information that may or may not be relevant, which are the result of the hyperbolic exposure of the narrator(s) to mass-media. This exposure threatens the characters' search for intelligibility. Note in this regard that *Mantra* doesn't merely represent or comment on the confusion produced by the barrage of information; it is also a presentation of such barrage: the texture of the novel is saturated with images pertaining to technology and mass-media — from pop songs to *telenovelas* (Latin American soap-operas) to television shows and films. Other factors that contribute to the increasing difficulty in following the plot and the characters are the aforementioned illness of the narrator of the first part (i.e., his gradually deteriorating memory, which leads him to confuse his own words and his own past life with those of Martín Mantra), and the conflation of past, present and future that — in the hyperbolic world of the novel — everybody experiences due to the velocity and sophistication of technological progress.[19]

Recall that in *María*, part of the reverence shown toward nature — besides the already discussed use of natural images to describe human bodies, feelings, and even technological devices — is expressed through the treatment of space. Consider the imposing long distances, and the natural impediments to move from one space to the other (e.g., the long trip to attend Braulio's wedding; Efraín's spending four years in Bogotá without ever being able to visit the Cauca; the Bogotá/Cauca separation; the Colombia/England separation).

In *Mantra*, in contrast, spatial distance has been abolished. As part of the initial exaltation of technology that *Mantra* presents, the narrator seems to take for granted that in a matter of hours any person can be anywhere. It is not by chance that many of the events presented in the novel occur on an airplane. Likewise, in *Mantra*'s postmodern society, since space has lost its interest and challenge (e.g., the space race is reduced to a fancier form of tourism), we are thrown into the inner space of human genome, where all possible spaces are mediated by electronic microscopes and other technological devices (192–93).

Also, recall that human life, in *María*, reaches its peak in the context of the *hacienda*— Rousseau's return to Nature. After Romanticism, Symbolism will claim that human life reaches its peak in a *literary* life — recall Mallarmé's words to the effect that life should be consummated in a book. In *Mantra*, it is neither the bucolic utopia of Romanticism nor the literary destiny of Symbolism. Rather, it is the technologically-charged life of a movie or a television show. Martín Mantra's film, started when he was nine years old, "duraba por entonces unas veinticuatro horas, la duración real de la fiesta en cuestión. Nada podrá convencerme de que no ha seguido creciendo a lo largo de todos estos años y cumpleaños" [lasted around twenty-four hours, the real duration of the party. Nothing will convince me that it hasn't continued growing along all these years and birthdays] (75). As a matter of fact, Martín Mantra lives his life through the camera attached to his head, thus actualizing the ideal of one's life as a movie.

In this sense, television shows, movies, and technological devices function as communicational codes between family members, friends, and lovers. In *María*, these codes were given by natural elements and natural phenomena: think of flowers as a quasi-linguistic code between Efraín and María.[20] In *Mantra*, these codes are always related to technology and mass-media: Martín Mantra pleads for "alguien hábilmente rodserlingforme que nos narre y ordene nuestras existencias" [someone nimbly rodserlingoid who could narrate and put order into our existence] (58), in reference to Rod Serling, presenter of the television show *The Twilight Zone*. Along these lines, consider the following words uttered by Mantra: "En el futuro todos seremos directores de cine; todos filmaremos la película de nuestras vidas. Pienso en un mañana cinematográficamente autobiograforme [In the future we'll all be movie directors; we'll all shoot the movie of our lives. I'm thinking of a cinematographically autobiographoid tomorrow] (67). Just like at past historical junctures people used literary and/or dramatic devices to understand and even constitute their identities (from the times of the Greek tragedy to Elizabethan drama to the real suicidal Werthers in Goethe's time to the Beat Generation in the United States), the implied author in *Mantra* shows that nowadays it is technology and mass-media that help us perform these identity-related tasks.

A brief clarification is in order. The claim is *not* that films, exclusively, have this constitutive role. That films have had this role in the past is no news. Certain types of film-making have long ago gained legitimacy alongside the literary arts. But — a science-fiction television show like *The Twilight Zone*? A *telenovela*? True, many writers and literati have explored the connections between the *telenovela*, mainstream films (as opposed to "art" films), and more prestigious literary forms (think of the paradigmatic case of Manuel Puig), but in *Mantra* this operation takes up a more integral and substantial form. It is not merely another case of what Ellen McCracken has aptly dubbed "bridge texts" between modernism and postmodernism.[21]

This integral form becomes clearer when one bears in mind that the constitution of identities governed by technology and mass-media operates not only on an individual, personal level, but also on a collective, historical one. In *Mantra*, under the heading "Historia (Mexicana)" [(Mexican) History], Fresán writes:

> Imposible de comprender a no ser que se la vea y se la lea con los mismos ojos de un adicto a una de esas alucinógenas telenovelas mexicanas. Una historia que tiembla, que se cae y se hace pedazos y vuelve a construirse con los mismos pedazos pero puestos en distintas partes de la estructura original a la que intentan, con cierta entusiasta dificultad, volver a parecerse [304].

> [Impossible to understand unless it is seen and read with the eyes of an addict to one of those hallucinogenic Mexican soap-operas. A History which trembles, which falls apart in pieces, and is reconstructed with the same pieces, though placed in different parts of the original structure which they try to resemble with a certain enthusiastic difficulty.]

Earlier in the novel, Mantra says with ironic grandiloquence: "la Historia habrá adquirido la textura de un Film Total" [History will have acquired the texture of a Total Film] (67). Despite the humor, the irony, of this last remark, the attempt to write, against all odds, a *novela totalizante* (total novel) is noticeable — though the totality is, this time, made of fragments: fragments of high and "low" (i.e., pop) culture, fragments of stories, histories and History.[22] In sum, fragments of memory — a memory which is, again, mediated by technology: the narrator suffers from amnesia, and has to rebuild his identity through the tapes that he had saved from his conversations with his therapist. A tape-recorder in lieu of the more rudimentary memory aids used by the villagers in Macondo, but a wink to Macondo nevertheless.

Unlike more traditional uses of tapes or recordings in high modernism (e.g., Beckett's 1958 play *Krapp's Last Tape*), in which the recordings question and challenge the character's identity, in *Mantra* the tapes *redefine or constitute* the character's identity. The amnesia of the narrator is also an ironic take on Martín Mantra's quasi-futuristic pronouncements:

> Se nos implantará una minúscula filmadora en nuestras pupilas en el momento mismo de nuestro nacimiento y a partir de entonces registraremos hasta el mínimo detalle de nuestras existencias. Todo podrá ser proyectado más tarde, y, por lo tanto, recordado a la perfección [67].

> [A miniscule camera shall be implanted in our pupils at the very moment of our births, and from then on we shall register even the most minute details of our existence. Everything shall be played later, and, therefore, everything shall be remembered perfectly.]

In sum, if in *María* memory and identity are mediated and constructed through natural elements — recall that María promises Efraín that she will send him flowers while he is in London, in celebration and memory of the understanding that they reached through the "language" of the flowers (which she had arranged for months in Efraín's room)[23] — and in *Cien años* memory is safeguarded by writing (think of Melquíades) and other incipient forms of technology (e.g., the card system — that rudimentary "machine to remember" — during the plague of insomnia), in *Mantra*, instead, memory and identity are constituted by technological devices: a tape that reproduces one's voice; a camera that reproduces one's memory. If Borges's short story "Funes el memorioso" ("Funes, The Memorious") presents the nightmare of a powerful, perfect, and yet formidable personal memory, *Mantra* presents the technologically mediated, perfect memory as an ideal: "ya no sabremos lo que es la memoria ni sus deformaciones que todo lo complican" (we won't know what memory is nor will we know its deformations that complicate everything), because we will be "más sabios" (wiser), given that we will remember, as said above, everything (67).[24] Memory will be like those musical shows in which the singers pretend to sing while a recording is broadcasted:

> La memoria es el *playback* de nuestra vida y, en ocasiones, nosotros no hacemos otra cosa que mover los labios sin emitir sonido alguno, porque es nuestra memoria la que canta a través de nosotros ... la memoria nos ayuda poniendo a girar la música de nuestro pasado, nuestros *Greatest Hits* cada tanto remasterizados, cada tanto incorporando un *bonus track*, versiones alternativas de la misma canción de siempre. Hay un momento imperceptible pero terrible y trascendente en que, pienso, finalmente estamos llenos de pasado, de memoria, por lo

que nuestro presente y lo que nos queda del futuro no es más que un constante actuar — cantar — de acuerdo con lo que nos ordena y nos sugiere todo aquello que tuvo lugar hace tiempo [169–70].

[Memory is the *playback* (Argentinean vernacular for "lip-synching") of our lives, and, on occasion, we don't do anything but lip-synch without emitting any sounds, because it is our memory that sings through us ... Memory helps us by playing the music of our past, our *Greatest Hits*— remastered every now and then, every now and then incorporating a *bonus track*, alternative versions of the same old song. There is an imperceptible but terrible and transcendental moment in which, I think, we are finally filled with past, with memory, and our present and what remains of our future are nothing but a constant acting out — a constant singing — dictated by what took place long ago.]

Now, if all these human features are constituted by and presented through technological imagery, it shouldn't be surprising that in a chapter significantly entitled "D.F. (Historia)" [Mexico City (History)] (236–242), the narrator claims that it is sufficient to click "rewind" to have the memory — the history — "played" backwards, an image that brilliantly blends the idea of the perfect technological memory discussed above (which can "track" every memory-item at will, just like one can track every song at will on an i-Pod, a CD, tape, or record) with the treatment of memory found in fictions like Alejo Carpentier's short story, "Viaje a la semilla" ["Journey Back to the Source"] (1944), and — more literally — with John Lennon's Beatle song "Rain" (1966), whose coda is an indecipherable gibberish that makes sense only if one actually plays the song backwards.

Not only do characters model their lives, or seek understanding of their lives, through the lens of technology and mass-media — put differently, not only are technology and mass-media artifacts and products that operate as heuristic devices — but they also shape the very language and metaphors we use to define and describe ourselves. Not only do we want a Rod Serling to tell the story of (and put order into) our lives, but we want to describe ourselves in the language of technology and mass-media in general, and in the language of Rod Serling in particular. A modern writer would say something like "We want Rod Serling to give a meaningful narrative of our lives." Instead, Fresán uses an image from technology and mass-media to express this aim. Thus, he writes, "Rod Serling como apóstol escritor y productor de nuestras vidas en el horario central de los televisores" [Rod Serling as writer, apostle, and producer of our lives in primetime television] (58). Life is not a literary narrative anymore, but a television show, a *telenovela*, or a film at best — all this, paradoxically, articulated in a text that remains, against all odds, a novel.

Memory and identity, but also communication, among other key features of human life, are transfigured by and described in terms of technology and mass-media. An uncomfortable exchange with his therapist moves the narrator to say "parecemos malos actors" [we're like bad actors] (97). The effect of information on people is like "una ráfaga de palabras como salidas de una feliz ametralladora caliente" [a round of words as if blurted out from a happy warm machine-gun] (235), an image that clearly references John Lennon's Beatle song "Happiness Is a Warm Gun" (from 1968's *White Album*).[25]

Even the most intimate images and metaphors, those of traditional themes such as romantic love and its ineffability, are permeated by technology:

> Entonces, estoy seguro, fue cuando comenzaste a amarme. Lo supe del modo en que sólo pueden saberse esas cosas y se las acepta. Lo supe del mismo modo en que no nos resistimos a, por ejemplo, lo que nos dicen y nos aseguran que es la imagen del eco del big bang tomada por el satélite Cobe [174].

> [Then, I'm sure, you started to love me. I knew it in the way in which only these things can be known and accepted. I knew it in the same way in which we do not object to what we are told and assured is the image of the echo of the Big Bang taken by the Cobe satellite.]

Since, as mentioned above, in Mr. Mantra's utopia every person will have cameras implanted in their eyes, every person's "total film" will include the very intimate expressions of love and friendship: "Intercambiaremos nuestros ojos desmontables y yo veré tu vida y tú verás la mía y, quién sabe, tal vez intentemos una coproducción. El amor y la camaradería serán algo que surgirá a partir de un impulso tan creativo como sentimental, algo estéticamente fotogramiforme [We'll exchange our detachable eyes and I'll see your life and you'll see mine, and, who knows, perhaps we'll attempt a coproduction. Love and comradery will arise from an impulse as creative as it is sentimental — something aesthetically photogramoid] (68). Consider, also, the following passage in which the narrator is talking about his love for María-Marie:

> Así hablabas, María-Marie, como la locutora de un último noticiero transmitiendo desde debajo de las frazadas, donde la tormenta y los meteoros no podrían alcanzarnos porque nuestro amor era algo fuera de este mundo, nuestro amor estaba hecho de iridio, y brillaba en la oscuridad... Iridio y radiactividad. De eso estaba hecho nuestro amor y — cada vez más convencidos de su relación con un orden absoluto de las cosas — nos llevábamos a la cama libros científicos, mirábamos las fotos capturadas por el Hubble del mismo modo en que otros exploran el espacio profundo y lleno de agujeros negros de los álbumes familiares [192].

> [Thus you spoke, María-Marie; like the anchorwoman of the last news program transmitting from under the blankets, where the storm and the meteors couldn't reach us because our love was something out of this world; our love was made

of iridium and shone in the darkness... Iridium and radioactivity. That's what our love was made of. And — more and more convinced of its relation to an absolute order of things — we'd take to bed with us scientific books, we'd watch the pictures captured by the Hubble in the same way in which others explore the space — deep and filled with black holes — of family albums.]

Conventional memory — *our* memory, not Martín Mantra's ideal film-like memory — is described as a deep space filled with black holes; love, as made of radioactivity... the contrast with *María* couldn't be any starker. But the common thread, again, is that in these two novels an opposite reduction is operating: technology is reduced to natural imagery in *María*, and natural phenomena (*all* phenomena) are reduced to technological imagery in *Mantra*. The same goes for the description of the (both psychologically and literarily) prestigious and elusive phenomenon of *déjà vu*, which is depicted in *Mantra* as "la voz desconocida que a veces interfiere en la música de nuestros audífonos, la súbita visión de nosotros mismos como si nos viéramos por televisión en un programa de cuyo nombre no estamos del todo seguros. O tal vez los *déjà vu* sean, simplemente, los comerciales de productos que de alguna misteriosa manera nos incluyen" [the unknown voice that sometimes interferes with the music coming from our headphones, the sudden vision of ourselves as if we looked at ourselves on television, in a show whose name we can't quite remember. Or maybe *déjà vu* phenomena are simply commercials of products that in some mysterious way include us] (233). Like the very phenomenon it captures, this description is surprisingly precise, familiar, and yet novel. This use of technology and mass-media is, at its best, one of the main achievements of Fresán's work.

In sum, technological images absorb and transfigure spatiotemporal points of reference, the identities of characters, and the very language the characters use to describe themselves, along with typically human features such as memory, time, friendship, and love. To reiterate, *María* and *Mantra* are related in the sense of being opposite poles of a spectrum. In *María*, a ship is a bird or a peasant; a crying face, a dew-covered flower. In *Mantra*, memory is a movie that we'll start shooting from our very birth and whose details we can access at will (a movie we can even rewind at will!); love, a coproduction made of iridium and radioactivity. In a sense, *María* can be seen as the dawn of the modern nature/technology system; *Mantra*, as the consummation (and perhaps consumption) of such system.

V. Ecology in *Mantra*: Rupture or Continuity?

Now, is there *anything* in *Mantra* remotely resembling the ecological view put forth in the above analysis of *María* and *Cien años*? Do Martín

Mantra and the narrator(s) not incarnate something like a twenty-first century version of the old Futurist dreams? Isn't technology something to embrace without reservations, or, at most, an inescapable *datum* of life, which we can neither object to nor combat? The reference to the Futurist movement is not a mere analogy. True, *Mantra* seems, on the face of it, to embrace the technological dreams of Futurism — but it also presents its nightmares: war and fascism, in the case of Futurism (for Fascism is, among other things, the technological manipulation of society); the possibility of some kind of apocalypse, in the case of *Mantra*.

Whatever the status of the rather puzzling section entitled "Después: el temblor" (Later: The Tremor; 513) — what *is* this section? A movie by Martín Mantra? A narration or a film by an android? A post-earthquake Mexico City? Causality, identity, and even the status of this narrative within the narrative are left deliberately ambiguous — it seems clear that the desolate view of New Tenochtitlan, or the D. F., or whatever that "city" really is, doesn't fare well. This final section makes it clear that not everything is perfect in *Mantra's* technological utopia: Martín Mantra's dream can turn into a nightmare. Reflection on this section allows the reader to reframe certain implicit claims made throughout the novel. When one rereads *Mantra*, it is not too difficult to find that, alongside the most enthusiastic passages in which technology and mass-media seem to be univocally and unequivocally exalted, there is irony and suspicion and subtle references to potential drawbacks (216ff).

Mantra, then, is not an unqualified paean to technology and mass-media. The already mentioned gap between Martín Mantra's dreams and their flawed realization in the life of his friend, the narrator (one of the narrators, in any case) suggests a view that is quite close to the ecological stance that can be found in the two other novels discussed earlier. Certainly, the implied author of *Mantra* is fascinated by, and welcomes, technological progress. But there is also something akin to resignation and a warning when one sees the failed attempts of the narrator of the first part to retrieve his memory, his identity, only to decide to destroy the tapes and forget it all.

The overwhelming flood of information, of technical devices — conveyed in almost Borgesian enumerations — gives one the sense that, in absence of criteria to determine the relevance of both information and technology, these are pointless. (Hence the narrator's renouncing his own memory). The nightmare of Borges's Funes, after all, may be hidden among the infinite movies of Martín Mantra. This excess is not only pointless, but dangerous: consider the many passages in which, along with the strident hails to technology, there are humbler, unobtrusive but ultimately important comments on pollution, consumerism, excess, lack of meaning — all of which pervade the very texture of the novel, and thus turn it into a very example of what the text is implicitly denouncing.[26] *Mantra* can be overwhelming — even sickening. This is not only due to a new kind of author/reader agreement, as David Daiches[27] would have it (though this is certainly one element of rupture that *Mantra* presents), but it's also due to the very incarnation of what the implied author is trying to convey. In the absence of the aforementioned criterion (i.e., intelligibility and development of human capacities) technology brings chaos and an excess that is linked to entropy. At the end of the day, holding that *Mantra* merely exalts technology is misguided. Again, just as a close reading of *María* reveals, and just as an ecocritical reading of *Cien años de soledad* suggests, in *Mantra* the implied author is postulating that technology *can* be enormously beneficial; that it *does* open entirely new possibilities; but that if what guides our use of technology isn't an ethical concern for intelligibility and development of human capacities (as opposed to unbridled productivity), we will lose touch with what appears to be a very strong need to search for meaning (a need that is deeply ingrained at the very least in our Western world). Moreover, the implied author seems to suggest that, in the absence of the aforementioned criterion and ethical guidelines, this very world may in fact — in a most literal, physical sense — disappear.

NOTES

1. I would like to thank Raymond L. Williams and the editor of this volume, Adrian T. Kane, for very insightful comments on earlier drafts of this essay. The value and helpfulness of their suggestions cannot be emphasized enough, although I fear I may not have done justice to all of them.

2. A caveat about this first thesis: the kind of technology that is presented in these novels represent two opposite poles of an arc that goes from the rudimentary techniques presented in *María*, which are still very much linked to natural elements and natural phenomena, to a more autonomous and artificial sphere of technology — the one of the twentieth and twenty-first centuries — presented in *Mantra*. Nevertheless, this fact does not undermine the thesis for reasons that will become apparent below.

3. There are, then, two separate issues that may overlap but that are conceptually distinct and independent: i. the implicit conception of nature and technology; ii. the imagery, which may lean toward absorbing technology into "natural imagery" (*María*) or which may lean toward absorbing (roughly) natural phenomena into "technological" imagery (*Mantra*).

4. Jorge Isaacs, *María* (Mexico D.F.: Grupo Editorial Tomo, 2002), 18. Jorge Isaacs, *María: A South American Romance* (New York: Harper and Brothers, 1890), 5. All subsequent in-text page references to this novel at its translation are from these editions.

5. Efraín's childhood memories are saturated with images of natural phenomena and child-play in the countryside: Efraín and his sisters picking up fruit that nature generously offers them; Efraín the child enjoying the sight of birds and their nests, and so on (24 and ff. [10 and ff.]).

6. See Chapter 58.

7. Garrard, *Ecocriticism*, 41.

8. A caveat: the very existence of slaves and servants shows that the whole social structure in which this technology is embedded falls short of an ethically acceptable stance.

But, while this is true, it is also the case that these slaves and servants are treated humanely — unlike, for instance, the "free" workers exploited in urban areas.

9. It is worth reiterating, however, that these three pronouncements become apparent in the interstices of the novel. That is to say, in the few moments in which the implied author rids himself of his commonplace version of Romanticism. Still, it is worthwhile to emphasize these moments, for they present a stance that can be connected with both the ecological view of *Cien años de soledad* which is discussed in the next section, and with the ecological view that is presented in *Mantra*, which is discussed in the fourth and last section of this essay.

10. See, for example, Nagel, *The View from Nowhere*, and Dennett, *Freedom Evolves* for a rejection of these claims from the perspective of contemporary analytic philosophy (reliant, for the most part, on contemporary science). For an analogous view from the Continental philosophy camp, see Jay, *Adorno*. From a more recent ecocritical perspective, see Howarth, "Some Principles of Ecocriticism."

11. See, again, the bibliography suggested in the previous note.

12. In this connection, it should be clear now that *María*'s naïve and simplistic dichotomy between nature and technology (a species of the more general — and equally misguided — dichotomy between nature and culture) cannot be a sound starting point to channel ecological concerns. Hence my emphasis on a different, interstitial view on nature that the implied author of *María* presents.

13. García Márquez, *Cien años de soledad* (Buenos Aires: Sudamericana, 2000), 16. García Márquez, *One Hundred Years of Solitude*, trans. Gregory Rabassa (New York: Harper & Row, 1970), 9. All subsequent in-text page references to this novel and its translation are from these editions.

14. It should be emphasized that these terms — technology, nature, culture — do not refer to discrete entities but to a continuum or spectrum of sorts.

15. The story "The Garden of Forking Paths" (1944), for instance, can be read as the application of the *ars combinatoria* to different time-lines or possible worlds.

16. An example: the "first" Buendía — the founder of Macondo — looks for intelligibility in the natural world; Melquíades and the "last" Buendía, for intelligibility in the world of culture — which ends up in the famous *mise-en-abyme* or circular ending, in which the exuberance of the natural and the historical and the technological and, in sum, the cultural, is "swallowed" by the writings of Melquíades.

17. Rodrigo Fresán, *Mantra* (Barcelona: Mondadori, 2001), 17. All subsequent in-text page references to *Mantra* are from this edition. The translation of this and all other quotations from Fresán's novel are mine.

18. *Mantra* plays with the idea of trapping the reader in the text — thus inviting the comparison of the reader with the narrator of the second part, chained to a television set. The narrator is doomed to watch his own life on that television set, *ad infinitum*; the reader, in turn, if she is to follow the circular indications of the text, is doomed to read and reread the novel *ad infinitum*. Analogous moves are made in Julio Cortázar's 1963 *Rayuela* (*Hopscotch*), and in *Cien años de soledad*.

19. In this regard, novelist-critic Edmundo Paz Soldán, who has written one of the most comprehensive and influential pieces on Fresán's novel ("*Mantra* (2001) de Rodrigo Fresán, y la novela de la multiplicidad de la información"), has called *Mantra* a novel of "information multiplicity." This kind of novel, first described by John Johnston in *Information Multiplicity* (1998), appeals to new formal structures in which the most heterogeneous sources of information meet in order to "take stock of new forms of subjectivity that emerge in this media-technological ecology," as Paz Soldán puts it (100).

20. When Efraín returns to the *hacienda* after four days, he sees a withering flower in María's hair — the same flower he had given her right before leaving. Thus, María shows

her sadness before the fact of Efraín's absence. And yet, when he goes to his bedroom, he finds a set of beautiful flowers, which María had refreshed and renewed every day. Likewise, when Efraín is about to leave for London, María tells him that by the freshness or precariousness of the roses she'll know whether he's thinking of her (*María*, 241 [230]).

21. See McCracken, "Hybridity and Postmodernity in the Argentine Meta-Comic."

22. In *Mantra* there are fragments of life-stories of the different characters, fragments of the history of different countries (Argentina and Mexico, most prominently), and fragments of world history and the history of Western culture — hence History is capitalized. In this sense, *Mantra* is a (perhaps skeptical, certainly ironic) heir of Cortázar's *Rayuela* and Fuentes's *La muerte de Artemio Cruz*.

23. Recall too that when Efraín returns to Cauca to learn of María's death, he sees the flowers "withered and half-eaten by insects" (*María*, 343 [298])

24. However, the ironical actualization of Martín Mantra's project in the life of the narrator — already mentioned above when I pointed out that he suffers from amnesia — is accentuated over and over again: the narrator decides to erase the tapes — and, with them, his memory and identity (95).

25. For a more detailed account of Fresán's fascination with pop music in general and with The Beatles in particular, the reader should track his weekly columns in the Buenos Aires newspaper *Página 12*.

26. See, for instance, *Mantra*, 511 and ff.

27. See Daiches, "What Was the Modern Novel?"

Works Cited

Daiches, David. "What Was the Modern Novel?" *Critical Inquiry* 1.4 (June 1975): 813–19.

Dennet, Daniel. *Freedom Evolves*. New York: Viking, 2003.

Fresán, Rodrigo. *Mantra*. Barcelona: Mondadori, 2001.

García Márquez, Gabriel. *Cien años de soledad*. 1967. Buenos Aires: Sudamericana, 2000. Translated by Gregory Rabassa as *One Hundred Years of Solitude* (New York: Harper & Row, 1970).

Garrard, Greg. *Ecocriticism*. London: Routledge, 2004.

Howarth, William. "Some Principles of Ecocriticism." In *The Ecocriticism Reader: Landmarks in Literary Ecology*, edited by Cheryll Glotfelty, Cheryll and Harold Fromm, 69–91. Athens, GA: University of Georgia Press, 1996.

Isaacs, Jorge. *María*. 1867. Mexico City: Grupo Editorial Tomo, 2002. Translated by Rollo Ogden as *María: A South American Romance*. New York: Harper and Brothers, 1890.

Jay, Martin. *Adorno*. Cambridge: Harvard University Press, 1984.

Johnston, John. *Information Multiplicity: American Fiction in the Age of Media Saturation*. Baltimore: Johns Hopkins University Press, 1998.

McCracken, Ellen. "Hybridity and Postmodernity in the Argentine Meta-Comic: The Bridge Texts of Julio Cortázar and Ricardo Piglia." In *Latin American Literature and Mass Media*, edited by Edmundo Paz Soldán and Debra Castillo, 139–51. New York: Garland, 2001.

Nagel, Thomas. *The View from Nowhere*. Oxford: Oxford University Press, 1987.

Paz Soldán, Edmundo. "*Mantra* (2001) de Rodrigo Fresán, y la novela de la multiplicidad de la información." *Chasqui* 31:1 (May 2003): 98–109.

II. Environmental Utopias and Dystopias

Caribbean Utopias and Dystopias: The Emergence of the Environmental Writer and Artist

Lizabeth Paravisini-Gebert

In his often prickly homage to the city of his birth, *San Juan, ciudad soñada* (2005; *San Juan: Memoir of a City*), Puerto Rican novelist Edgardo Rodríguez Juliá writes about the rapid and often devastating changes in the island's rural and urban landscape brought about by the shift from an agrarian to a manufacturing and tourism economy ushered by the Estado Libre Asociado (the Commonwealth) in the 1950s. "Todo el paisaje de mi infancia ha desaparecido" (All the landscapes of my childhood have disappeared), he writes, lamenting the loss of once-familiar landscapes to make way for high-rise office buildings, condominiums for the middle classes, tourist hotels and casinos.[1] He mourns the disappearance of the old road from Aguas Buenas to Caguas, "una de las más hermosas del país, con sombra de pueblo a pueblo a causa de su tupido dosel de flamboyanes y jacarandas" (one of the most beautiful on the island, shadowed from one town to the other by a dense canopy of flame trees and jacarandas) before concluding that "la herida en mi paisaje infantil estremece" (the wound on my childhood's landscape sends shivers down my spine).[2]

Rodríguez Juliá's elegy to this old vanished road, which I remember for the lace-like patterns created on the hot tarmac by the sunlight filtering through leafy trees and the bright-red flowers of the flamboyant tree, reminds us of how, in the Caribbean region, profound and often vertiginous changes ushered by a variety of post 1950s historical events — the collapse of the sugar industry, the shift from agrarian to tourism economies, urbanization and industrialization, deforestation and desertification — have turned Antillean geographies into unrecognizable landscapes, bringing some of the islands dangerously close to their carrying capacity. The rapid deterioration of the environment in the Caribbean region, which has taken place within the lifetime

113

of many of its residents, has led to a "sense of an ending," to the apocalyptic dread of a potential ecological disaster that can erase the islands, their peoples, and cultures from the geographies of the *mare nostrum*. This fear underpins the development of a Caribbean environmentalist philosophy that is inextricably tied to a critique of globalization as the latest manifestation of the forces of rampant capitalism in whose grip the islands have remained since the Columbian encounter. In the Caribbean region, where post-colonial politics, foreign controlled development, and the struggle for economic survival has for many decades forced environmental concerns out of the mainstream of national discourse, writers and artists have responded to increasing fears of global warming, food insecurity, habitat losses, mangrove destruction, and uncontrolled tourism-related development with eloquent defenses of the fragile ecologies of the islands in the name of the nation. As Graham Huggan writes in his essay on "Greening Postcolonialism,"

> From recent reports on the devastating impact of transnational corporate commerce on local/indigenous ecosystems (Young) to more theoretically oriented reflections on the efficacy of postcolonial literatures and/or literary criticism as vehicles for Green ideas (Head), postcolonial [literatures] and criticism [have] effectively renewed, rather than belatedly discovered, [their] commitment to the environment, reiterating its insistence on the inseparability of current crises of ecological mismanagement from historical legacies of imperialistic exploitation and authoritarian abuse.[3]

One of the most urgent questions to emerge from ecocritical discussions in the Caribbean is that of whether fiction and the arts, despite their compelling exploration of the environmental dilemmas facing the islands, can indeed play a role in fostering the necessary changes in people's practices needed to save increasingly vulnerable environments prey to global forces often outside local control. Can literature and the arts play a meaningful role in local and regional environmental struggles or must writers and artists move beyond their creative roles into ecological activism for their unique perspectives on the problems facing the region to be effective in propelling change?

The questionable success of literature in stemming ecological deterioration and effecting positive environmental change can be seen most poignantly in Haiti, where, despite its writers having made the nation's environmental crossroads a central leitmotif— a cornerstone, in fact, of the development of the national novel — the country is believed to have long ago breached its carrying capacity. (The concern with carrying capacity — a concept questioned in other contexts — remains relevant in Haiti given the collapse of the nation's production for export and its inability to import sufficient food for its population). The devastation brought upon the Haitian landscape by continued deforestation, desertification, failed tourism development, and the collapse of agro-business amidst governmental corruption, has become the country's most glaring socio-economic and political problem. Haiti's forests, already depleted for lumber to be sold in the international market in the early twentieth century, have in recent decades been cut down in catastrophic numbers for the charcoal used everywhere for cooking. With forest coverage below 1.5 percent of the national territory, topsoil has been washed to sea, where it threatens marine habitats. The loss of topsoil — "as much a nonrenewable resource as oil" as Wes Jackson reminds us — has rendered large portions of the Haitian land permanently unproductive, exacerbating already serious levels of food insecurity.[4] Its significantly reduced rates of rainfall have left the country prone to severe drought and a high rate of desertification; its vulnerable position in the path of hurricanes, on the other hand, has intensified the impact of severe rainfall, which in the last decade has caused thousands of deaths from flash floods and disastrous mud slides. Haiti is at the very edge of an environmental collapse that threatens its viability as a nation. The most frequent question prompted by its environmental crisis is whether something can still be done to help the land of Haiti regain its ability to sustain its people. The answer is increasingly a resounding "no."[5]

The literature of Haiti has bemoaned the environmental calamity that has befallen its people, denounced the practices that led to this catastrophe, and offered inspiration and ideas for solving the nation's most central problem. It has counseled, above all, political action against exploitative governments as a path towards environmental safety, focusing on the state's inaction as evidence of the slow violence of environmental neglect. From Jacques Roumain's *Gouverneurs de la rosée* (1944; *Masters of the Dew*), a seminal text in the development of the Haitian novel, to Pierre Clitandre's *Cathédrale du mois d'août* (1979; *The Cathedral of the August Heat*), the Haitian novel has been, above all, a chronicle of the nation's unimaginable ecological catastrophe. Roumain brings his hero, Manuel, back to a land parched and dying from a persistent drought caused by acute and unrelenting deforestation and to a village mired in a violent dispute over inheritance of the land and access to water in an increasingly desertified environment.[6] Jacques-Stephen Alexis in *Les Arbres musiciens* (1957; The Musician Trees), speaks of the trees of Haiti's embattled forests "as a great pipe organ that modulates with a multiple voice ... each with its own timbre, each pine a pipe of this extraordinary instrument," hoping to endow them with a mythical protection against escalating destruction.[7] Marie Chauvet, in *Amour* (from *Amour, Colère et Folie*, 1968; *Love, Anger, Madness: A Hatian Trilogy*), dissects the forces that led to the ecological revolution produced by deforestation as a factor in Haiti's internal politics and international economic relationships, especially during the nineteen years of American Occupation, which lasted from 1915 to 1934.

Clitandre chronicles the misery and hope of an exploited peasantry seen as one more cheap commodity to exploit locally or export as labor, as peons in the protracted game of ecological and political mismanagement that has resulted in Haiti's despoiled landscape.

All to little avail. Despite decades of literary denunciation, despite countless foreign interventions and reforestation plans, the Haitian landscape has continued its rapid decline, proving, in the process, that in Haiti, as "throughout the world, environmental hazards have been unequally distributed, with poor people and people of color [the formerly colonized] bearing a greater share of the burden than richer people and white people."[8] Because the Caribbean shares Haiti's history of colonial exploitation and subordinate economic development, the ghost of Haiti haunts the Caribbean imaginary. Its ecological disintegration has become the focal point for meditations on the region's environmental options. It is not surprising, then, that as events have proven convincingly to the world that Haiti's ills could not be cured through foreign aid, investment, or technology — that it would take more than a democracy and a change in leadership to save the nation — we have witnessed growing levels of popular engagement in local environmental movements elsewhere in the Caribbean islands, many of them led by writers, artists, and musicians ready to use their local fame and reputation in the service of stemming the tide of environmental degradation in their home nations. The post–Duvalier period has been marked in the region by the emergence of the Caribbean artist and writer as a committed environmentalist.

The debate over solutions to the region's environmental dilemma is a complex one, however, given that many of the causes of local environmental degradation — global warming, cruise ship pollution, marine-life depletion, to name a few — fall so far outside local control. Local actors in the environmental dilemma have taken note of their inability to control some crucial aspects of their country's environmental situation, seeking instead to focus on the more limited set of problems that are open to local solutions. These have ranged from joining forces with NGOs supported by international environmental groups (although this has often led to clashes between goals formulated in response to outside concerns as opposed to local needs) to forming political organizations to combat measures proposed by local governments (that of fostering tourist development at the expense of local environmental concerns, more often than not). What these local solutions have had in common across the region has been an emphasis on four issues related to the recovery of the islands' agrarian past: restoring pre-development landscapes and habitats associated with a real or imagined past of post-plantation agricultural sustainability (the type of nostalgia Rodríguez Juliá writes about in *San Juan, ciudad soñada*); fostering the return of arable land to small farms that used to produce local foods as the means to alleviate the present state of food insecurity; the return to the remnants of the agrarian past (from former plantations to small cocoa and coffee farms) as sites for eco-tourism; and the creation of social movements to defend landscape resources that served as national symbols. The salient theme in these efforts is that of a return to an often-imagined prior sense of national identity rooted in an agrarian economy that is the pre-requisite for an environmentally sustainable national wholeness.

The nostalgia for lost landscapes of which Rodríguez Juliá writes in *San Juan, ciudad soñada* has led to a number of landscape restoration projects throughout the Caribbean, most of them linked to literary or cultural projects. The restoration of landscapes and habitats of the pre-industrial/tourist development period in the Caribbean has been of particular importance in the islands that remain in close political relations with former colonizing powers, such as Puerto Rico and the French departments of Martinique and Guadeloupe. These are islands where the United States and France, through direct state investments in industrial, tourism, and infrastructure development, have supported relatively high standards of living and high levels of consumerism. They are also islands with relatively active anti-colonial/pro-independence movements that often rely on nostalgia for the post-plantation agrarian past as the foundation of alternative notions of the nation. The Creolité movement, for example, has made the *bétonisation* (cementification) of Martinique a rallying cry in their appeals for political support for the pro-independence cause. The movement, initially focused on fostering the use of the Creole language in the islands' literature, has expanded its areas of interest to environmental protection and landscape restoration. They have supported projects like Les Ombrages, a landscape restoration project in the northern Martinique community of Ajoupa-Bouillon. It is typical of restoration projects aimed at recreating aspects of local colonial history and includes a Creole garden — a laboratory for the reintroduction, preservation, and display of a wide range of herbs and spices, many of them with curative properties, brought from all parts of the world and cultivated locally by slaves. It is also the site for the reintroduction of indigenous parrots that were eradicated from the zone through intense poaching and land development.

A similar habitat restoration project in Ciales, Puerto Rico — associated with the "agrarian" poetry of noted *independentista* writer Juan Antonio Corretjer (1908–1985) — is built on the same set of environmental values and stems from a similar political foundation. The project, located in Puerto Rico's central mountain range, was inspired by Corretjer's environmental activism and poetry. The poet, long known for his *nacionalista* political beliefs and for his celebration of the richness and diversity of Puerto Rico's mountain ecology and history of subsistence agriculture, wrote of his delight at entering "los campos húmedos de crespos pastizales / por donde el río traza su torva geometría" (the moist fields with their crisp grassy greenness / through which the river traces its sinuous geometry) and of penetrating forest groves where he could rub against the bark of the trees and "aspir[ar] el el humo sagrado / que hace la boca profeta" (inhale the sacred smoke / that makes the mouth capable of prophecy).[9] His environmental activism, rooted in counterbalancing the slow violence that had been perpetrated on the environment by American agricultural corporations, had focused on the impact of agro-business on the island's interior. In essays and interviews he decried "the overwhelming encroachment of concrete and the use of poisonous chemicals [insecticides and synthetic fertilizers] in Puerto Rican farming" that had led not only to massive deforestation in the interior, but also to the disappearance of bird, lizard, and butterfly species that had been plentiful in the landscape of his youth and young adulthood.[10] Habitat loss was the most radical impact of rapid urbanization in San Juan's metropolitan area, and concern for vanishing species was shared by Corretjer and fellow writer Enrique Laguerre, both of whose work is associated with rural culture in Puerto Rico.

By the end of his life, Corretjer's beloved "greenblack highlands," especially the lands through which flows the Encantado River with its grand cascades and crystalline pools — the inspiration for many of his poems — had been severely deforested to allow for the intensive cultivation of coffee. Land and water had been contaminated by insecticides and fertilizers. In an ambitious project of habitat restoration, the former plantation is now being returned to its former "complex, healthy and productive ecosystem" by friends and neighbors of the late poet, "using Corretjer's poetry in combination with the most advanced concepts of ecological farming and environmental protection."[11] Now known as Corretjer's Forest, the lands have been planted "with the trees mentioned in Corretjer's poetry, and with numerous native species" — citrus trees, teak, cedar, royal palms, star apples, guava and guamo trees. The aim of the restoration is that of returning the landscape to one the poet would have recognized, and its success has been measured in part by the return of the birds and insects whose absence Corretjer himself had noted with dismay. "The singing bees are already back, we had not seen them for a long time," explains the former coffee planter whose friendship with the poet spearheaded the project, "the *sanpedritos*, which are like miniature parrots and only live in caves, had gone, but since we stopped using chemicals they are back. Once again we can hear the *múcaros* [screech owls] at night."[12] The project reflects a shift (also observed elsewhere) towards "focusing conservation strategies on the restoration of habitat, and not simply on its protection."[13] It also intends to serve as a center for the education of young students in the values and rewards of returning to pre-industrial agrarian spaces as places of practical instruction in the need for achieving food security and reconfiguring the idea of the nation as rooted in the principles Corretjer's poetry addressed.

The restoration of the rural setting loved by Corretjer is designed upon environmental principles that acknowledge the power of certain spaces in the national imaginary — many of them made hallowed by their connection to literary works. The defense of these spaces as "sacred" to the wholeness of the nation endows them with special significance when they are threatened by development, as was the case in St. Lucia when the Hilton chain was given permission by the state to build the Hilton Jalousie Plantation Resort in the valley sloping down to the sea between the Pitons, the two great volcanic cones on the west coast of St. Lucia — "one of the great landscapes of the Caribbean" and now a UNESCO World Heritage Site.[14] Echoing Enrique Laguerre's notion of the environment as "the nation's most valuable patrimony," St. Lucian poet and Nobel Prize winner Derek Walcott joined in vocal opposition to the project on the grounds that The Pitons was undeniably a natural space of great national significance where a hotel would be "aesthetically like a wound."[15] In an interview with George B. Handley, he explained his opposition to the Jalousie scheme as having derived from his perception of the Pitons as a "sacred space," a "primal site" that emanates power and which, having become the object of the people's devotion, should have remained inviolable.[16] The building of a resort in such a space was tantamount to "blasphemy." Writing in a local paper, Walcott argued that "to sell any part of the Pitons is to sell the whole idea and body of the Pitons, to sell a metaphor, to make a fast buck off a shrine."[17] He equated the economic arguments in favor of the resort — that it would provide extra income and jobs — to proposing building "a casino in the Vatican" or a "take-away concession inside Stonehenge."[18] The loss of such a pristine space was the loss of a place that could help people regain a feeling of "a beginning, a restituting of Adamic principles."[19]

The development of the Jalousie resort — which opened in 1994 — is emblematic of the tensions that arise when different notions of what constitutes the nation and of how to exploit its resources are pitted against each other. As a site of national significance that was also a prime locale for potential tourist development, the Pitons became the focus of struggle between foreign developers, a local government seeking to increase foreign investment and foster employment, and a large number of conservation-minded citizens who understood the significance of the space in myriad ways. The debate involved the Hilton Corporation, the Organization of American States (which supported an alternative proposal for a Jalousie National Park at the site), the St. Lucia development control authority, and numerous members of the community — Walcott included — with differing views of the role of the "nation's most valuable patrimony" in the nation's development. The arguments marshaled against the selling of this symbolic space had as a backdrop the growing value of land in St. Lucia fostered by the increasing encroachment of tourism construction and agro-businesses, which threatens the access of St. Lucian farmers and would-be farmers to prime cultivable land. (Local groups, as a result, were unable to buy the Pitons property away from the Hilton Corporation.) The Jalousie resort was duly built, nestled in a "sacred" space from which St. Lucians are now banned, thereby separating the local population from its natural patrimony. Ironically, despite great initial interest, the Jalousie resort has met with questionable success. Although still managed by the Hilton Corporation, the resort is now primarily financed by the St. Lucian government, despite a dwindling tourist base and indifferent returns.

For Walcott, the relinquishing of "sacred spaces" like that of the Pitons to the pressures of development for tourism — and the risk it poses to St. Lucian local food production — threatens the very survival of Caribbean peoples. In "Antilles," he likens the Caribbean native to the sea almond or the spice laurel — "trees who sweat, and whose bark is filmed with salt" — threatened by "rootless trees in suits ... signing favorable tax breaks with entrepreneurs, poisoning the sea almond and the spice laurel of the mountains to their roots."[20] "A morning could come," Walcott warns, "in which governments might ask what happened not merely to the forests and the bays but to a whole people."[21] It is a sentiment echoed by Enrique Laguerre, one of Puerto Rico's most respected twentieth-century novelists, a self-described "ecological humanist" who dedicated the last decade of his long life (he died just short of his 100th birthday in 2005) to the struggle against the destruction of forests and mangroves to make way for broader highways, luxury hotels, and middle-class housing developments. He used his prominence as a writer as a platform from which to argue that Puerto Rico had followed a very shortsighted vision of socioeconomic development that had sacrificed the environment to the pressures of urban sprawl and consumerism. In one of his last interviews he spoke of dreaming "of a Puerto Rico that knows how to contain a rampant urban growth [...] that preludes a sad fate for future generations."[22] True nationalism, he argued, had to be linked to a respect for the geographical spaces that were the nation's most valuable patrimony.

A similar critique of uncontrolled development brings writers like Jamaica Kincaid into the discourse of environmentalism. In *A Small Place* (1988) she bemoans the disappearance of a species of snails — "the best wilks in the world," as she describes them — during the constructions of hotels on the islands' best beaches, beaches from which the locals are now banned. Her concern for threatened species is echoed in the region's first avowedly-environmentalist novel, Mayra Montero's *Tú, la oscuridad* (1995; *In the Palm of Darkness*). This tale of an American herpetologist and his Haitian guide on a quest for an elusive and threatened blood frog, extinct everywhere but on a dangerous, eerie mountain near Port-au-Prince, allows Montero to unveil how the troubled landscape of Haiti has decayed precipitously due to political corruption, violence, institutional terror, murders, brutality, and religious turmoil. The vignettes about the troubling disappearance of frog species throughout the world that we find interspersed throughout the narrative remind us that the price of the continued abuse of the local environment is ultimately extinction.

A salient feature of the emerging literary environmentalism — as Laguerre and Walcott's involvement and Corretjer's influence indicates — an understanding that struggles in the Caribbean, as they are in poor and dependent societies around the world, are ultimately about environmental justice for the peoples of the region. First world environmental solutions that speak of reduced consumption and wilderness preservation, for example, assume options that are not open to Caribbean peoples in small post-colonial economies with few resources other than fertile soil and a highly coveted natural beauty whose exploitation they cannot always control. Their struggles are often as much against outside forces as they are about the tensions between environmentally-sound options and a livelihood. These tensions often translate into local political struggles as governments seek income-bearing investments from abroad to produce employment and profit. Huggan identifies the "ambivalent role of the post-independence state in brokering national economic development" as a crucial factor in the struggle for environmental justice while pointing to "the value of imaginative writing" — to which I would add artistic creativity in general — "as a site of discursive resistance to authoritarian attitudes and practices that not only disrupt specific human individuals and societies, but might also be seen as posing a threat to the entire 'ecosphere' and its network of interdependent 'biotic communities.'"[23]

I would like to look here more closely at two examples of literary and artistic environmental activism as indicative of the multi-faceted nature of local environmental struggles in the Caribbean — that of the Creolité movement's struggle against the *betonization* (cementification) of Martinique and Guadeloupe and the 2001–2003 campaign against the continued bombardment of the small island of Vieques (a part of the territory of Puerto Rico). In both cases, a very vocal and committed participation by writers and artists — who both engaged in community-led protest activities and turned the subject of their writing and art to the support of the cause — has been a crucial factor in engaging a larger community in the process and bringing international attention to the resolution of their environmental dilemma.

In *Landscape and Memory: Martinican Land-People-History*, a documentary by Renée Gosson and Eric Faden, three of Martinique's most salient contemporary authors — Jean Bernabé, Raphaël Confiant, and Patrick Chamoiseau — argue for an understanding of the island's marked environmental degradation as the most disturbing result of France's continued political control — as the disturbing by-product of enduring colonialism. The anxiety over the sustainability of Martinique's physical territory allows these three proponents of the Creolité movement to bridge the gap between the local specificity of their movement's concerns and the increasing interconnectedness brought about by intensifying globalization about which their colleague Edouard Glissant writes in his *Poétique de la relation* (Poetics of Relation). In *Landscape and Memory*, Chamoiseau, Confiant, and Bernabé identify the environmental problems facing Martinique as those same issues confronting the rest of the archipelago to which they belong: food insecurity, since Martinique produces only 2 percent of the food its population consumes; the increasing *bétonization* (cementification) of the land as more land is taken away from agriculture for the building of hotels, supermarkets, shopping centers, and other infrastructure typical of tourism development; the pollution of land and rivers with fertilizers and insecticides used for agro-businesses on the island; the production of larger quantities of garbage than the island landfills can reasonably absorb; the destruction of mangroves and of the wildlife they support from a failure to understand their uniqueness as a "cradle of life"; and the disconnection of the Martinican population from its land and culture, as French television and French-owned media control access to information and entertainment and promote a desire for consumer items that the islands' economy cannot sustain.

Both Chamoiseau and Glissant share Walcott's sense of a potential apocalypse if the region cannot resolve its environmental dilemmas and move to a sustainability only possible with a greater degree of local political and economic control. Despite the clear differences in their approach to Martinique's relationship to the global, both writers agree on the importance of environmental activism as a path to environmental security. In his *Poetics of Relation*, Glissant, although proclaiming his belief in "the future of little countries," finds in "the politics of ecology" the best protection "for populations that are decimated or threatened with disappearance as a people."[24] He sees the politics of ecology as "the driving force for the rational interdependence of all lands, of the whole Earth."[25] Chamoiseau, in his turn, writes in *Ecrire en pays dominé* (Writing in an Oppressed Country) of "the difficulty of writing in and about Martinique when what constitutes the island physically and, more importantly, in the realm of the imagination is threatened with extinction."[26] A cultural ecologist separated from Glissant by "a desire for some measure of control over the cultural and economic commerce between Martinique and the rest of the world," Chamoiseau does not only live a life of multifarious activism in Martinique, which has the environment as a principal focus, but has dedicated his third and most recent novel, *Biblique des derniers gestes* (2002; Scripture of the Last Gestures) to the recreation of a life of environmental activism focused on access to water in Martinique.[27] In the novel, Chamoiseau seeks to give life to ideas he had expressed often in connection to his participation in groups like ASSAUPAMAR, the Association for the Protection of the Martinican Patrimony, an environmental group particularly concerned with agricultural issues, most notably with the increasing declassification of agricultural lands to give way for the construction of shopping malls and gas stations. This declassification, according to Raphaël Confiant, threatens "our economic survival" and leaves "our very food autonomy endangered."[28] The concern about food supplies is a particularly serious one in Martinique, which has only a week's worth of food reserves and where the panic occasioned by the gap in the flow of food supplies caused by the revolts in France in 1968 is still vividly remembered.

Both Chamoiseau and Confiant trust in greater local political autonomy in the restoration and reorganization of land and water supplies as a necessary step towards an environmental balance that ultimately rests on creating a strong agrarian sector devoted to the cultivation of local foods for the local market. Chamoiseau uses his novel *Biblique des derniers gestes*, which has been described by Richard Watts as "an impassioned rant against ecological degradation," to ponder how the island's status between colonization and independence complicates environmental issues, particularly those related to control over resources such as land and water. Like land, on an island that is not politically autonomous and has become a "privileged site for the fulfillment of metropolitan fantasies of vacations in paradise," "water is a local commodity," access to which has become "a global issue."[29] Ultimately, for Chamoiseau as for Confiant, the development of a sustainable agrarian nation appears as the only solution to an economic impasse in which Martinique has only an "Économie-Prétexte" that subsists only on French state subsidies — a pretense, as Confiant has argued, "to give the appearance of an economy, that there are people who go to work, etc., but in reality, our country has been, and is, economically ruined."[30]

The idea of an agrarian nation, which from an environmentalist perspective looms as the only possible space from which Martinique can sustain itself as an autonomous island, emerged in the prolonged struggle of the Puerto

Rican municipality of Vieques against the Navy as the quasi-utopian goal of a political movement that found in environmental arguments a more effective weapon than that of sovereignty over local spaces in the international arena. One of the salient features of the prolonged struggle against the U.S. Navy's presence in Vieques was the ultimate success of the environmentally-focused political campaign after years of a campaign focused on political sovereignty failed to yield the expected results.

In the struggle against the Navy in Vieques, the intense engagement of writers and artists shows the possibilities open when literature and the arts join an environmental justice movement. The use of Vieques as an area for target practice for the U.S. Navy, which had been going on continuously since the 1940s despite continued local protests, was challenged by the larger Puerto Rican community through a campaign of civil disobedience following the death in 1999 of a local man, David Sanes Rodríguez, killed by an errant bomb. At the heart of the protest were the expropriation of land from local residents, the environmental impact of weapons testing, which had been linked by epidemiologists to cancer and other ailments linked to exposure to ordnance and contaminants, and the closing of large portions of the islands to farming and other activities that could contribute to sustainable development. Over the years, the EPA had cited the Navy for 102 violations of water quality standards on Vieques, identifying excessive concentrations of such chemicals as cyanide and cadmium in the coastal waters near the bombing range. The people of Vieques are plagued by unusually high levels of lung, heart, and liver disease, asthma, diabetes, lupus, anxiety, and depression. These are believed to stem from possibly irreparable damages to the environment, which include contamination of the surrounding waters and the poisoning of numerous species that have formed the basis for the local diet for decades. By 1999 it had been amply demonstrated that the Navy's presence threatened the continued existence of the flora, fauna, and people of the island. The intensification of protests that followed the death of Sanes in 1999 included an unprecedented literary and artistic presence. The resumption of bombing after the accident was greeted with proclamations of solidarity from artists, musicians, and writers that would signal the beginning of a sea change in the way local writers and artists have incorporated a concern for the environment in their work. The resulting burst of creativity in the service of an environmental cause marked the Vieques struggle as a unique moment in the history of the fight for environmental justice.

Among the first organized responses to the intensification of the Vieques struggle was that of the AU+MA (Acción Urgente Mail Art) Collective. Their mail-art project, called "Postcards for Vieques," was initiated in June 2000 and consisted of an international call disseminated through the internet and echoed by a variety of mass media to "bomb" the White House with creative postcards asking for "Peace for Vieques." The international collective, linked to Boek 861, an established member of the mail-art network, appealed to the public to send artisanal postcards through the post or creative e-cards through e-mail in a show of solidarity with the environmentally-focused political action organized by the residents of Vieques. As is characteristic of such calls for solidarity, the collective encouraged participants to use art as a weapon against "the very circles of power where important decisions are made."[31] The response was thousands of electronic and artisanal postcards sent to the White House, many of which were broadcast through the media and displayed on a virtual exhibit site on the web.

Of interest to our discussion is the collective's perception of their action as limited in the face of the magnitude of the obstacles facing the people of Vieques. Recognizing the difficulties in trying to oust the U.S. Navy, a powerful institution in one of the most powerful nations in the world, it conceived its efforts as merely "another link in the chain of solidarity."[32] The success of their campaign, then, rested on its promotion of an international creative response in the humanistic tradition to a political situation that may have seemed beyond the scope of individual action. The sponsoring of this creative response, even among people without artistic training or aspirations, was seen by the collective as an indication of how the democratization of art, its "decontextualization from the traditional elitist space" art normally occupies, could become a powerful weapon in support of political and environmental action.[33] To mail-art collectives around the world, the postcard, whether produced through artisanal elaboration or the use of the latest technological resources, remains an accessible creative form, inexpensive to produce and exchange, and "open" in its message. Formally, it saw the use of the postcard, with its local links to a foreign-controlled tourist industry that had replaced the plantation as an economic source of labor exploitation in the region and had contributed to the region's environmental deterioration, as a subversion of the impact of globalization on the people of the Caribbean.

On August 28, 2000 a group of artists, with the support of the Committee for the Rescue and Development of Vieques and the Peace and Justice Camp of Vieques, entered lands restricted by the Navy for an art installation and performance entitled "I Believe in Vieques" whose thematic focus was the fundamental importance of returning the land to the local population for the establishment of an agrarian community, of reaching an agreement with the Navy for thorough decontamination, and of establishing a plan for sustainable economic development. The call for solidarity rested on a depiction of the people of Vieques as displaced farmers eager for the return on their cultivable lands and the resumption of their "natural" agrarian lives.

The event, sponsored by Artists for Peace, was divided in two parts. Those who entered the Navy's restricted zone in an act of civil disobedience produced a "human mural" recreating the landscape of the "Isla Nena" and proclaiming how "from the esthetic point of view the landscape has been, and will be a vital source of inspiration of artistic creation."[34] A second group displayed its support from outside the restricted zone through a second "human mural," this one a recreation of Picasso's famous anti-war painting *Guernica*. A third group boasting some of the most salient Puerto Rican painters and sculptor of recent decades — among them Rafael Tufiño, Antonio Martorell, Lorenzo Homar, Myrna Báez, and Luis Hernández Cruz — issued a simultaneous proclamation of support from the main island. In a press release, the artists explained that their goal was that of "questioning the limits between a traditional work of art and a political act of clear humanist intentions" and of "creating" the "necessary conditions in which the people of Vieques can enjoy their land in peace."[35]

These artistic efforts coincided with a number of literary projects focused on the intensification of protests that followed upon the death of Sanes Rodríguez. Among these was the production in Vieques of *Romeo y Julieta: un amor de protesta* (Romeo and Juliet: A Love of Protest), a version of Shakespeare's play adapted and directed by Juan Carlos Morales in which Romeo, the son of a family of fishermen, falls for Julieta, the daughter of a Navy Commander. The use of the popular and well-known play in its new ideological framework allowed for the dramatic articulation of the island's political dilemma for a broad audience. Romeo's occupation, in its turn, underscored the identity of the people of Vieques as fishermen and farmers, an identity that had become central to the campaign for restoration of the land and the beaches to the local population. Likewise, Jorge González's drama *Vieques*, produced in New York City just a few months later by Repertorio Español and set in the early years of the U.S. occupation, used the ideological framework to highlight the impact of the Navy's presence. This story of a young local woman in love with a Navy sergeant allows González to probe the various responses to the loss of the island's territory to the Navy, while underscoring, among other themes, that of the environmental impact of the occupation, seen here through the health repercussions of the Navy's relentless spread of insecticides to kill the mosquitoes that constitute a health hazard for the Navy personnel. The same ideological framework offers a point of departure for a short story included in the journal *Cultura*'s testimonial issue celebrating the cessation of the bombing in 2003. "Hubiera sido más fácil" (It Would Have Been Easier), a story by Leonor E. Quirorges, pits two childhood friends against each other — one a protester against the continued military occupation of the island, the other a Navy seaman who must watch his friend being beaten by his colleagues as he murmurs repeatedly that he had entered the restricted grounds as a protest to safeguard the health of the children of the island.

As an additional gesture of artistic solidarity, Augusto Marín's "Vieques amado," a serigraph based on an earlier painting commemorating the struggle, was sold as part of a fundraising program to cover the local population's mounting legal costs. In this homage to a "beloved Vieques" strong geometrical forms and earth and sea colors convey both the vortex of the long-running struggle and the hope for a peaceful resolution to the conflict that will restore the small island's ecological balance. Its flowing furrows remind us of the movement's insistence on describing the people of Vieques as a "farming community," despite the fact that the Navy occupied most of the lands that had previously been farmed and the farming population left was minuscule (in 1942 the Navy had expropriated 26,000 of Vieques's 33,000 acres). The insistence on a the return of the Vieques land to a community of farmers that would restore it to sustainable agrarian production was an important claim against the argument proposed by the Navy and its supporters that behind the struggle to end the target practice was a desire on the parts of the local population to capitalize on the high value of coastal lands to the construction and tourist markets in the region.

Similar arguments in favor of the people of Vieques were expressed through the caricatures by the Puerto Rican artists that contributed to *Bieké desde otra perspectiva: Caricaturas por la paz* (Vieques from Another Perspective: Caricatures for Peace) and through the multiplicity of t-shirt designs analyzed by Ramón López.[36] In both cases one finds allusions to the environmental dimensions of the Vieques struggle. The use of caricatures in Vieques included the creation of comic books as vehicles for the dissemination of notions of a post-occupation sustainability.[37] The t-shirts, as López argues, included a variety of motifs, among which we find images alluding directly to the environmental problems facing the island even after the cessation of the bombings. One of the t-shirts analyzed by López, shows in its message "Paramos el bombardeo" (We stopped the bombardments) and its slogan "La lucha continua" (The struggle continues) an awareness that the cessation of the bombing has left the island environmentally devastated. Its simple depiction of the submerged or buried ordnance, the damaged tree, and torn fencing summarizes the environmental catastrophe that has been the legacy of the bombings.

One of the most effective contributions to the struggle against the Navy's continued bombing — measured in terms of its broad international reach and enthusiastic reception — was "Canción para Vieques" (Song for Vieques), an ambitious project initiated in mid–2001 by Tito Auger, lead singer for the

Puerto Rican group Fiel a la Vega. Auger found his inspiration in projects like Band Aid ("Do They Know It's Christmas?/Feed the World"), where artists gathered to combat hunger in Ethiopia, USA for Africa ("We Are the World"), Live Aid, and Artists United Against Apartheid ("Sun City"). Solidarity with the Vieques movement revived the Nueva Trova or song of protest tradition in the region, leading to musical expressions of solidarity from a significant number of world-class musicians. Just within weeks of Sanes Rodríguez's death, in April 1999, King Changó, a musical group from Venezuela, incorporated a "Peace for Vieques" message in their concerts and in June of that year joined one of the first of many protests to come before the White House in Washington. They would later perform a "King Changó for Vieques Concert" and would record "Al rescate de Vieques" (To the Rescue of Vieques) with Ismael Guadalupe, leader of the Committee for the Rescue and Development of Vieques.[38] Puerto Rican Nu metal rock group Puya's song "Pa tí, pa mí," a track in their characteristic mix of salsa and rap metal, protested the U.S. occupation of Vieques and called for environmental justice, linking the Vieques situation to global decolonization movements. Latin jazz flutist Nestor Torres "Paz Pa' Vieques," which drew its inspiration from Afro-Puerto Rican bomba/plena tradition, is among numerous tracks dedicated to bringing the plight of the island to an international audience.

"Canción para Vieques" ("Song for Vieques," written by Tito Auger and Ricky Laureano) is a six-minute music video of political and environmental support featuring a stellar cast of international music stars that included Ruben Blades, Olga Tañón, Gilberto Santa Rosa, Lucecita Benítez, Alberto Cortez, Danny Rivera, the late Tony Croatto, and many of the stars of the Nueva Trova, like Roy Brown, Antonio Cabán Vale ("El Topo"), Silvio Rodríguez, Pablo Milanés, Mercedes Sosa, and Joan Manuel Serrat. It responded, as salsa superstar Santa Rosa described it at the time, to the need to respond as a musical community to an issue that had "brought consensus to all sectors in Puerto Rico."[39] Victor M. Rodriguez sees the return to politically conscious music as a welcome move away from the "homogenized identities" of a global music market. "The artists of my generation," he argues, "are reconnecting with the activism which, because of their commercial success, they had left behind."[40] Unlike projects such as Band Aid and USA for Africa, however, "Canción para Vieques" was not produced for sale, but was distributed free as a declaration of solidarity. "Copyrights were not an issue," Auger explains, "because nobody [was] making money."[41]

Like "We Are the World," the most successful of its predecessors, the musical video shows the solo portions of the performances by the lead singers as recorded in the studio. Unlike in "We Are the World," the entire group does not sing together, as the musicians that appear in "Canción para Vieques" recorded their contributions individually. Like "We are the World," however, "Canción para Vieques" uses the same lyrical format, building in intensity and dramatic effect as the song moves to its climax. The crescendo provided in "We Are the World" by the gradual appearance of all the artists in the same studio is provided in "Canción para Vieques" by the images that appear interspersed with those of the singers. These include a variety of seascapes displaying the small island's natural beauty, images of fishermen that remind us of the villagers' traditional occupation, crowd scenes from some of the many demonstrations in solidarity with the people of Vieques, white crosses standing on a hilltop cemetery as a reminder of the many deaths linked to the island's polluted environment, the word "peace" (paz) written across a sandy beach, and repeated images of children and the elderly looking hopefully towards the camera as the chorus sings of the ultimate triumph of their hopes for a future without the Navy's presence. The song's emotional impact is further reinforced by privileging the presence of Danny Rivera and Lucecita Benítez in the final moments of the video. Rivera and Benítez, Puerto Rican singers long associated with a political commitment to the pro-independence movement on the island, have been at the forefront of solidarity movements of this type throughout their long careers. They are backed by digital voice multiplication and a studio chorus, both of which stress the moral authority their presence brings to the project. The environmental foundation of the renewed campaign to stop the bombardments is addressed directly by the singers in the third of nine stanzas: "Sesenta años con lluvia / De uranio y de municiones / Limpiando ventanas con pólvora sucia / Esperando que el cáncer reaccione" [Sixty years of raining / Uranium and ammunition / Of cleaning windows with dirty gunpowder / Waiting for cancer to kick in.] The environmental topic is underscored through multiple reiterations of the verb "proteger" (to protect), particularly in the final verses, which express, through an increasingly dramatic arrangement, the notion of sustainability — the obligation of those living in the present to safeguard the environment for generations to follow.

Ironically, the correspondences between "We Are the World" and "Canción para Vieques" highlight the differences in the ideological foundations of the two projects. "We are the World" has been criticized as a "colonial" project through which pop music royalty celebrated itself while showing their inability to reflect upon how the people they are seeking to help may "hear" them. Their project could be read simultaneously as an inspired act of splendidly successful philanthropy or as "a stunning act of narcissism for an industry so invested in a democratic image of collaboration."[42] "Canción para Vieques," on the other hand, speaks from a position of subalternity; as a home-grown effort, its organizers appealed to the international music community for a demonstration of solidarity while controlling both the message and its dissemination locally. This local control allowed them to maintain the emphasis on the restoration of an agrarian community to its lands and its roots that had been echoed throughout all aspects of the campaign against the Navy in Vieques and had been instrumental in garnering international support for the movement. It was an argument, nonetheless, based on a community constructed, rather than imagined, from symbols of national identity invoked by both the left and the right in Puerto Rican political and intellectual life, chief among them that of the *jíbaro* or subsistence farmer from the island's interior who came to represent, as José Pedreira phrased it, the "steadiest branch" of the tree of Puerto Rico's society.[43] As José Luis González has argued, Puerto Rican intellectuals who lament the disappearance of an agrarian past in which the homegrown *hacendado* (landowning) class controlled the nation's political and economic destiny, do so by "consciously creating an ideology of things past and gone, i.e., *jíbarismo* or cult of the jíbaro, to oppose the imagined virtues of an idealized past to the real or imagined evils of a present, characterized (among other things) by the destruction of many of the traditional values of a now marginalized creole bourgeoisie."[44] Hence the recasting of the people of Vieques as *jíbaros-manqués*, as representatives of a constructed collectivity whose victory over the Navy would uphold the quest for sovereignty of the unfulfilled nation.

The *jíbaros* of Vieques, however, have been more myth than reality. Throughout the nineteenth century the island had been an efficient producer of sugar, averaging 8,000 tons of sugar a year in production. The history of the Vieques population was not that of subsistence agriculture but rather of a sustained struggle against the local sugar oligarchy which in 1915 led to a four-year strike that paralyzed the industry. The construction of the Navy base in 1941 ended sugar cultivation and led to the uprooting of about two-thirds of the island's population, many of whom moved to the neighboring island of St. Thomas. Ironically, Puerto Rican government efforts to re-establish an agricultural economy in the non-occupied sector of Vieques between 1945 and the early 1960s failed rather miserably. Since the late 1960s, manufacturing (primarily in the local General Electric plant) and the tourist sector have been the most consistent sources of employment on the island. Who the farmers of the newly liberated Vieques lands will be remains to be seen.

Indeed, who the farmers of the sustainable agrarian societies of the Caribbean region imagined by environmentalists, writers, and artists will be is less crucial a question than whether the land on which that sustainability will depend has retained its fertility despite the slow violence to which the islands have been subjected through centuries of unsustainable colonial exploitation. Haiti's despoiled land, as we have come to see, has lost its potential for productivity with the devastating loss of its topsoil. The vision of a post–Navy Vieques constructed during the campaign against the bombing, with its focus on decontamination, restoring public health, and fostering sustainable development on the island, responded to the quasi-utopian aim of environmental justice in which happy farmers would return to their "natural" role in agrarian production.

This sentiment was echoed by the editors of the journal *Cultura*, a publication of the Puerto Rican Institute of Culture, which dedicated a testimonial issue to the struggle for social and environmental justice in Vieques, inviting leading intellectual, literary, artistic, and musical figures to offer contributions that would incorporate the Vieques struggle into "our testimonial canon." The pieces contributed to the volume weave notions of social justice, political sovereignty, environmental restoration, and the dismal possibilities for a sustainable agrarian future into one thematic continuum that underscores the importance of the environmental focus to the struggle for Vieques. This was not the first effort of the journal to support the people of Vieques. The presence in its editorial board of prominent figures like Enrique Laguerre and art historian Osiris Delgado had translated into a firm focus on the defense of the environmental and cultural heritage of the small island. A resolution from the Board published in the December 2000 volume of the journal asked for an immediate stop to the bombings and "the protection of the environment, archeology, and cultural values" of Vieques. That issue includes a poem by Héctor H. Colón Atienza that underscores the environmental impact of the bombings by alluding to "the uranium deployed / which sickened and terrorized the people" and to the dangers posed by powerful antennas and radars.[45]

The journal's testimonial issue of 2003 includes an essay by singer/songwriter Danny Rivera and a "chronicle in two voices" that gathers the recollections of Tito Auger and Raúl Rosario about the "Canción para Vieques" project. It also includes a "Poema colectivo por Vieques" (Collective Poem for Vieques) written by six Puerto Rican poets representative of the generations of the 60s, 70s, and 80s.[46] The collective poem, which plays upon the name of David Sanes Rodríguez — the bombing victim whose death spearheaded the final thrust of the movement — through references to David and Goliath, is built on images of environmental deterioration and potential agrarian unsustainability that point to the collapse of the utopian dream of a sustainable agrarian community in the small island. Eric Landrón writes of how Vieques, under the umbrella of poetry, is transformed into the "hortaliza de Patria arada y plena" (garden of a Nation furrowed and bountiful), but his fellow writers are less sanguine (58). Elsa Tió describes the island as an "open wound / healed by the stars during the night" (herida abierta / que curan en la noche las estrellas), a "maternal island" (isla maternal) with a "fertile and courageous beach" (playa fértil y brava) whose "womb of sand / cannot be reached by nesting turtles" [a tu vientre de arena no llegan las Tortugas] (59). For Etnairis Rivera, the island had been invaded by "the demons of war" (los demonios de la guerra), who "usurp the island, the fish, the space / and in this intimate human territory spread bombs / cancer, mistreatment, the macabre number of death" [y usurparon la isla, los peces, el espacio / y en el íntimo territorio humano regaron bombas, / cáncer, maltrato, el macabro número de la muerte] (59).

Ironically, what was transformative about the successful Vieques struggle — in May 2003 the Navy withdrew from Vieques — was the ultimate defeat of the agrarian project. The lands held previously under U.S. Navy control were not returned to the people of Vieques but were instead designated a wildlife reserve under the control of the U. S. Fish and Wildlife Service and remain closed to the local population. The land in Vieques, as subsequent studies have demonstrated, is toxic, too contaminated for use without a costly cleanup project that may take years and still not result in soil suitable for agricultural use. The land's high level of toxicity renders the political victory meaningless, at least in so far as the aim of the protests was to restore/create a sustainable agrarian space. Like the land of Haiti, the potentially agrarian spaces of Vieques may never be suitable for cultivation. A study released in October 2008 found dangerous levels of toxic metals in produce grown on the island, as much as twenty times the acceptable levels of lead and cadmium. The findings underscore the illusive foundations of the agrarian project that was so prominent in the environmentalist arguments of the people of Vieques and the many activists — among them writers, artists, and musicians — who worked with them in solidarity.

The reality of Vieques's toxicity — like the growing infertility of the land of Haiti — signals the precarious condition of many of the Caribbean territories and underscores the urgency of the region's environmental quandary. Given their prominence in Caribbean societies, it has fallen to the lot of writers, artists, and musicians to articulate this predicament and to popularize the need for widespread community support in addressing what in many islands is an environmental emergency. As this discussion shows, writers, artists, and musicians across the Caribbean region accepted this challenge — both as activists and in their own creative endeavors. The loss of what Laguerre called an island's "most valuable patrimony" — the beauty and fertility of its land — is to Caribbean territories like that of Vieques more than just a pretext for poetic nostalgia, for bemoaning, like Edgardo Rodríguez Juliá does, the loss of childhood landscapes that sends shivers down his spine. It reminds us of the vulnerability of small island nations whose ability to restore and sustain their environments seems suspended between local action and global powers. Hence the growing apocalyptic strain in the region's environmental thought, born of fears of that day of which Walcott speaks when we may have to ask what happened not only to the trees or the land, but to the region's people.

NOTES

1. Rodríguez Juliá, *San Juan, ciudad soñada* (Madison: University of Wisconsin Press, 2005), 3. My translation.

2. *Ibid.*, 3–4.

3. Huggan, "Greening Postcolonialism," 702.

4. Jackson, "Fertility and the Age of Soils."

5. See pages 329–357 of Jared Diamond's study *Collapse.*

6. See Paravisini-Gebert, "He of the Trees: Nature, Environment, and Creole Religiosities in Caribbean Literature."

7. Quoted in Benson, "A Long Bilingual Conversation about Paradise Lost: Landscapes in Haitian Art," 108.

8. Adamson, "What Winning Looks Like," 1259.

9. Corretjer, "Pared de la soledad," and "Yerba bruja."

10. Ruiz Marrero, "The Poetry that Saved a Forest."

11. *Ibid.*

12. *Ibid.*

13. Colston, "Beyond Preservation: The Challenge of Ecological Restoration," 251.

14. Pattullo, *Last Resorts*, 1.

15. Walcott, "The Argument of the Outboard Motor," 129

16. *Ibid.*, 128

17. Quoted in Pattullo, *Last Resorts*, 4.

18. *Ibid.*

19. Walcott, "The Argument of the Outboard Motor," 129.

20. Walcott, "The Antilles: Fragments of Epic Memory," 83.

21. *Ibid.*

22. Alegre Barrios, "Enrique Laguerre: Prójimo y palabra (sus fundamentos)."

23. Huggan, "Greening Postcolonialism," 703.

24. Glissant, *Poetics of Relation*, 125, 146.

25. *Ibid.*, 146

26. Watts, "The 'Wounds of Locality,'" 114.

27. *Ibid.*, 125.

28. Confiant, "Cultural and Environmental Assimilation in Martinique," 144.

29. Watts, "Toutes ces eaux!" 900.

30. Confiant, "Cultural and Environmental Assimilation in Martinique," 145.

31. AUMA, "Convocatoria Acción Urgente Mail Art / Postales por Vieques."

32. *Ibid.*

33. *Ibid.*

34. "Vieques Libre."

35. "Acción de arte 'Creo en Vieques.'"

36. See López, "Las camisetas de Vieques: Mitología y militancia de una lucha popular."

37. See Cotto Morales, "Arte y Cultura con el pueblo," 23–25.

38. See Cumpiano, "Artistas levantan sus voces por la Paz para Vieques."

39. See Gurza, "New Bombings of Vieques Re-Energize Political Protest Songs."

40. *Ibid.*
41. Quoted in Luna, "All-Star Single Highlights Problem in Vieques."
42. Feld, "A Sweet Lullaby for World Music," 169.
43. See Guerra, *Popular Expression and National Identity in Puerto Rico*, 74.
44. Quoted in Guerra, 67.
45. Colón Atienza, "Isla nena," 49.
46. See Rodríguez Nietzche, Quiñones, Galib, Landrón, Rivera and Tió. "Poema colectivo por Vieques," 57–59.

Works Cited

"Acción de arte 'Creo en Vieques.'" http://www.heterogenesis.com/Heterogenesis-5/H-43/Cas/vieques.htm.

Adamson, Joni. "What Winning Looks Like: Critical Environmental Justice Studies and the Future of a Movement." *American Quarterly* 59.4 (2007): 1257–67.

Alegre Barrios, Mario. "Enrique Laguerre: Prójimo y palabra (sus fundamentos)." http://www.alternativabolivariana.org/modules.php?name=Content&pa=showpage&pid=1296.

AUMA. "Convocatoria Acción Urgente Mail Art/Postales por Vieques." http://www.boek861.com/hemeroteca/vieques.htm.

Benson, LeGrace. "A Long Bilingual Conversation about Paradise Lost: Landscapes in Haitian Art." In DeLoughrey, Gosson, and Handley. *Caribbean Literature and the Environment*, 99–109.

Colón Atienza, Héctor H. "Isla Nena." *Cultura*. 4.8 (July-December 2000): 49.

Colston, Adrian. "Beyond Preservation: The Challenge of Ecological Restoration." In *Decolonizing Nature: Strategies for Conservation in a Post-Colonial Era*. Edited by William M. Adams and Martin Mulligan, 247–67. London: Earthscan, 2003.

Confiant, Raphaël. "Cultural and Environmental Assimilation in Martinique: An Interview with Raphaël Confiant." By Renée K. Gosson. In DeLoughrey, Gosson, and Handley, *Caribbean Literature and the Environment*, 143–52.

Corretjer, Juan Antonio. "Pared de la soledad." http://www.ciudadseva.com/textos/poesia/esp/corret/pared.htm.

_____. "Yerba bruja." http://www.ciudadseva.com/textos/poesia/esp/corret/yerba.htm.

Cotto Morales, Liliana. "Arte y Cultura con el pueblo: Desarrollo sustentable para Vieques." *Cultura* 6.12 (2002): 23–25.

Cumpiano, Flavio. "Artistas levantan sus voces por la Paz para Vieques, Puerto Rico." *Kontra Ruta*, October, 11 2002. http://www25.brinkster.com/4kr/articles/vieques-10-11-02.asp.

DeLoughrey, Elizabeth M., Renée K. Gosson, and George B. Handley, eds. *Caribbean Literature and the Environment: Between Nature and Culture*. New World Studies. Charlottesville: University of Virginia Press, 2005.

Diamond, Jared. *Collapse: How Societies Choose to Fail or Succeed*. New York: Viking, 2005.

Feld, Steven. "A Sweet Lullaby for World Music." *Public Culture* 12.1 (Winter 2000): 145–71.

Gallagher, Mary. "Genre and the Self: Some Reflections on the Poetics and Politics of the 'Fils de Césaire.'" *International Journal of Francophone Studies* 10.1–2 (2007): 51–66.

Glissant, Édouard. *Poetics of Relation*. Translated by Betsy Wing. Ann Arbor: University of Michigan Press, 1997.

Gosson, Renée and Eric Faden. *Landscape and Memory: Martinican Land-People-History* [videorecording]. New York: Third World Reel, 2003.

Guerra, Lillian. *Popular Expression and National Identity in Puerto Rico: The Struggle for Self, Community, and Nation*. Gainesville: University Press of Florida, 1998.

Gurza, Agustín. "New Bombings of Vieques Re-Energize Political Protest Songs." *Los Angeles Times*, June 30, 2001.

Huggan, Graham. "Greening Postcolonialism: Ecocritical Perspectives." *Modern Fiction Studies* 50.3 (2004): 701–33.

Jackson, Wes. "Fertility and the Age of Soils." *The Land Institute*. 1 December 2000. http://www.landinstitute.org/vnews/display.v/ART/2000/12/01/3aa90b0d9.

López, Ramón. "Las camisetas de Vieques: Mitología y militancia de una lucha popular." *Centro* 18.1 (2006): 36–61.

Luna, Randy. "All-Star Single Highlights Problem in Vieques." *Billboard* August 18, 2001.

Paravisini-Gebert, Lizabeth. "He of the Trees: Nature, Environment, and Creole Religiosities in Caribbean Literature." In DeLoughrey, Gosson, and Handley, *Caribbean Literature and the Environment*, 182–98.

Pattullo, Polly. *Last Resorts: The Cost of Tourism in the Caribbean*. 2nd ed. New York: Monthly Review Press, 2004.

Regan, Jane. "Forest Lands in Haiti Fading Fast: Natural Resource Nudged to the Brink." *The Miami Herald*, August 5, 2003. http://www.latinamericanstudies.org/haiti/haiti-deforestation.htm.

Rodríguez Juliá, Edgardo. *San Juan, ciudad soñada*. Madison: University of Wisconsin Press, 2005.

Rodríguez Nietzsche, Vicente, Magaly Quiñones, Hamid Galib, Eric Landrón, Etnairis Rivera and Elsa Tió. "Poema colectivo por Vieques." *Cultura* 7.14 (July-December 2003): 57–59.

Ruiz Marrero, Carmelo. "The Poetry that Saved a Forest." *World Rainforest Movement Bulletin* 66 (January 2003). http://www.wrm.org.uy/bulletin/66/CA.html.

"Vieques Libre." http://www.peacehost.net/Vieques/latest.html.

Walcott, Derek. "The Antilles: Fragments of Epic Memory." In *What the Twilight Says: Essays*, 65–84. New York: Farrar, Straus and Giroux, 1998.

_____. "The Argument of the Outboard Motor: An Interview with Derek Walcott." By George B. Handley. In DeLoughrey, Gosson, and Handley, *Caribbean Literature and the Environment*, 127–41.

Watts, Richard. "'Toutes ces eaux!': Ecology and Empire in Patrick Chamoiseau's *Biblique des derniers gestes*." *MLN* 118 (2003): 895–910.

_____. "The 'Wounds of Locality': Living and Writing the Local in Patrick Chamoiseau's *Ecrire en pays dominé*." *French Forum* 28.1 (2003): 111–29.

Paradise Lost: A Reading of *Waslala* from the Perspectives of Feminist Utopianism and Ecofeminism

Marisa Pereyra

(Translated by Diane J. Forbes)

During the last decades of the twentieth century and the first years of the twenty-first, a series of novels written by women were published in Latin America, very different in theme, but which discuss in some form utopian ideas from a feminist perspective. Included among these novels, to name just a few, are *Antigua vida mía* (1995; *Antigua and My Life Before*) and *Lo que está en mi corazón* (2001; What is in My Heart) by Marcela Serrano, *El cielo dividido* (1996; Divided Heaven) by Reina Roffé and *La nave de los locos* (1984; *The Ship of Fools*) by Cristina Peri Rossi.[1] This is also the case of some of the works by Nicaraguan writer Gioconda Belli. The present essay is an analysis of Belli's novel *Waslala: Memorial del futuro* (1996; Waslala: Memorial of the Future) from a feminist perspective; the theories of utopianism and ecocriticism will also converge in order to facilitate a new reading of Belli's work.

Belli's first novel, *La mujer habitada* (1988; The Inhabited Woman), and her third, *Waslala: Memorial del futuro* have a profound utopian content. One finds in both not only formal elements of the genre (such as travel, stopped time, closed spaces, etc.), but also the characteristic functions of utopian discourse: transgression, criticism, and subversion. That is to say, they are utopian novels because of their form and content, but more than anything, because they utilize utopian discourse to criticize the existing order, interrogating and questioning the model of the moment by way of an alternative project. It is helpful to clarify here that the feminist utopia, unlike the traditional utopia, does not propose fixed and didactic blueprints for a perfect new society, but rather processes of transformation that facilitate new and flexible forms of being and living. I propose for this work an approach that fits under the theoretical umbrella of "utopianism," such as it is understood by the German philosopher Ernst Bloch and the British scholar Lucy Sargisson. This type of utopia moves away from the genre initiated by More, considering it a closed and unique model. In contrast, the concept of utopianism proffered by Bloch and Sargisson presents ideas that manifest desire through a different and better form of being and living.[2] Its principal function is to provoke changes in consciousness by imagining a variety of conceivable futures. For Bloch, man has an incredible capacity to imagine and to desire something so profoundly that those ideas are converted into "images of desire." These images carry within themselves the seeds of transformation and make us think about how things should be, instead of how they are in reality.[3] Utopia flourishes in a special way in art and literature, since in these fields man can conceive of questions about himself and explore his most intimate desires. According to Bloch, the artist is metaphorically like a midwife who facilitates what already exists in potentiality in our unconscious, to materialize in a concrete way in history. In other words, what exists in the collective unconscious is born.[4]

Hope, desire and nostalgia are the tools that help us to build these "landscapes of yearning."[5] These aesthetic and philosophic constructions show society how much there is yet to do in order to achieve a just and egalitarian world for all, independent of race, gender, sexual orientation, or the social or economic class of its members.

According to the literary critic Jean Pfaelzer, traditional masculine utopias present a solitary, individualist, isolated and conquering male hero. Feminine utopias, on the other hand, show a fragmented, multiple, imperfect and ordinary woman hero.[6] In *Waslala*, we see Melisandra, a female hero who does not dominate, but rather adopts a collective voice by seeking and accepting the cooperation of her peers. It is worth remembering, too, as sociologist Hilary Rose points out in "Dreaming the Future," that many masculine utopias are feminine dystopias, thus the importance of differentiating them.[7] All feminine utopias are to a certain extent political, since they are concerned with relationships of power, sexual power and exploitation relationships between patriarch and nature; either sexual groups or racial minorities.[8] Guatemalan literary critic and political activist Isabel Aguilar Umaña maintains that utopias develop certain ideas about power, order, justice, ecology and economy. At the same time, in agreement with Sargisson, Aguilar Umaña argues that: "Es igualmente inevitable que las utopías formulen visiones acerca del poder, especialmente el poder político, el social y el económico" (It is equally inevitable that utopias formulate visions about power, especially political, social and economic power).[9]

In Lucy Sargisson's terms, utopia is, as indicated above, a transgressive discursive construction that permits criticism and provokes changes of consciousness: "I have identified a new utopian function as being variously manifested but as having the effect of provoking a paradigm shift in consciousness."[10] For this reason, it is essentially subversive; its character is revolutionary, and its goal is to facilitate a humanism that would permit construction of more just and peaceful worlds. Ernst Bloch explains that history's prevalent utopian impulse is the human capacity to fantasize beyond our experience and to reorder the world around us.[11] Utopia is thus employed in the present essay as process, impulse, and method, more than its traditional meaning of a literary genre or work that unites certain characteristics. Gioconda Belli, in an interview with Margarita Krakusin, states that in her novels, "me gusta ver el proceso en el cual las mujeres recuperan la voz y el protagonismo de sus propias vidas, o son victimizadas a partir de esa apropiación de su poder. Éste ha sido el eje de mi narrativa" (I like to see the process in which women recover their voice and the protagonism of their own lives, or they become victimized from the moment of that appropriation of their power. This has been the crux of my narrative).[12] And later she adds: "[en mis obras propongo] procesos en desarrollo. Es la mujer en proceso" ([in my works I propose] processes in development. It is woman in process).[13] The inclusion of this process towards a better life as the crux of the narrative of her novels is one of the elements that allow their reading as feminist utopias. Aguilar Umaña recalls that Martin Buber as well as Ernst Bloch in their defense of utopian socialism have proposed "un proceso de continuidad en el cual el carácter revolucionario sea permanente, adquiriendo, por lo tanto, un carácter procesal. La meta y el camino son, entonces, igualmente importantes" (a process of continuity in which the revolutionary character would be permanent, acquiring, therefore, a processual character. The goal and the means are, then, equally important).[14]

The novel *Waslala*, like *La mujer habitada*, takes place in a fictitious country, Faguas, which represents Nicaragua. In both, the principal protagonists are strong women, self-assured, with unrelenting political convictions, who are in the process of finding their own identity while exploring their past. As Laura Barbas Rhoden well writes, these characters "lack a female tradition, a memory of their others or female antecedents, that will center them and enable their empowerment."[15] And she adds that in all of Belli's narratives, there is one theme that is recurrent: "the confrontation of women [with] their own lack of history and the subsequent search for empowerment through a connection with their past."[16] In the case of Lavinia, the protagonist of *La mujer habitada*, the ancestor who unites her with the past is Itzá, a mythological warrior woman from the time of the conquest, who lives in her and gives her the power and the motivation to fight. In contrast, in *Waslala*, Melisandra's ancestors are neither historical nor mythological characters, but rather her mother, lost since Melisandra's infancy, and her grandmother, who died long ago.

Besides the search for ancestral past and the recovery of one's own voice, Belli presents in *Waslala* her worries about the deterioration of the environment in Latin American countries. In the literary criticism of the last fifteen years, a body of theory has appeared that is deeply connected to ecology and feminism. Ecofeminism, as it is called, is a philosophy and a movement that believes that the oppression and domination of women by patriarchal society has its correlative in the abuse of the environment that this same society is committing.[17] It advocates just relationships between humans, animals, and the Earth. In a wide sense, it fights for the liberation of nature, women, and children, and imagines different models of coexistence, challenging all relationships of domination and power. Author and activist Starhawk points out that "Its goal is not just to change who wields power but to transform the structure of power itself."[18] Ecofeminism stems from the radical North American feminism of the '70s and '80s. Both blame patriarchal culture for the problems that afflict the environment. Some ecofeminists affirm that it is man who commits oppressive and destructive acts against nature and against women.

On the other hand, women have a "natural way" of relating to nature because of our ability to be mothers, our natural cycles, our experience of oppression and marginalization.[19] Adopting this posture without analyzing historical, mythological and religious aspects bears a strong dose of essentialism. The inequality created between the dualities man/woman, body/spirit, reason/feeling, has led to a false dichotomy between humans and culture. Anthropological studies show that the associations that we make between women and the Earth, sexuality, and sin; and those of men with culture, reason, and the oppression of women are ancient.[20]

Moreover, ecofeminism plunges its roots into mythology and spirituality and returns to ancestral archetypes, which precede the monolithic, masculine god of the Judeo-Christians, prior to the Sumerians, Hebrews, Greeks: the woman god as representation of the feminine divinity. During this time, the energy of life is permanently circulating; death does not exist in the way we know it today, but is rather a pure transformation as in nature.[21] Starhawk defines "the spiritual wing of ecofeminism in terms of it [...] being based on a goddess tradition, nature theology, indigenous spirituality, and immanence rather than transcendence."[22] The attitude towards work related to the land (for example, farming — historically a feminine activity, versus exploding a mine — associated with male engineers), and not the natural proximity to the land based on our biological condition, is what makes women more able to situate ourselves in a privileged ecological position.[23] These religious, philosophical and historical arguments have all contributed to the development of the concept of ecofeminism.

The goals of feminist utopianism and ecofeminism are very similar: respect for all, celebration of diversity and recovery of a paradisiacal land lost in the ancestral past, but possible in a desiderative future. Annalisa DeGrave argues in her article "Ecoliterature and Dystopia: Gardens and Topos in Modern Latin American Poetry," that: "[...] three components are found in utopian literature: a critique of the present, model time and model space. Certainly all three components are also present in ecoliterature, however, the main point of intersection between ecoliterature and utopia is the importance of nature/place."[24] It is pertinent to place ecofeminism under the conceptual umbrella of utopian studies, since both share not only goals as I have explained, but also a strong religious and mythological component.[25] In the words of theologian Mary Judith Ress, ecofeminism:

> [...] make(s) the connection that the oppression of women and people of color by a system controlled by ruling-class males and the devastation of the planet are two forms of violence that reinforce and feed upon each other. They both come from a misguided sense of the need to control, to dominate the other. From being the source of life, both women and the Earth have become resources to be used (and abused) as the power structures see fit. Ecofeminists join with all those searching for a more holistic world view that recognizes and celebrates the web of all life.[26]

Feminism, environmentalism and the struggles of the subaltern are compartmentalized perspectives that have in common the dissatisfaction with present reality, but do not present a unified social vision of total transformation.[27] Therefore, I advocate a utopianism that would comprehend all possibilities. Rather than a unitary utopia that would propose a radical, global and unidirectional project, this utopianism would consist of "multiple microutopias disseminated to the entire social body."[28] Given the similarities between feminist utopianism and ecofeminism, I intend to use in my analysis of *Waslala* the critical tools that these two theoretical approach offer.[29]

With respect to utopian discourse, Belli's novel contains several clues that inevitably lead to More's *Utopia*. For example, the two novels share the same name, Raphael, for the principal masculine protagonist, and the city of Waslala was planned from utopian texts,[30] precisely like More's.[31] Likewise, both allude to universal utopias — in *Waslala* the myths of the flood and of paradise lost, in *Utopia* the Earthly paradise. As Susanna Layh well notes: "Belli's text pays tribute to the origin of utopia in the Old World by relying on Thomas More's *Utopia* as a framework of motifs, ideas, and characters. In its essence it's a revision and rewriting of the early modern time's 'original' by the inclusion of a feminist, anti-capitalist and ecological perspective."[32]

The principal feminine character, Melisandra, lives with her grandfather and some workers on a farm that is described as paradisiacal, surrounded by a jungle that is a "templo de humedad, musgo, líquenes [y] criaturas escurridizas" [a temple of humidity, moss, lichens, (and) scurrying creatures] (303). She is from a family of strong women and she does not comply with the stereotype of femininity; she always wears overalls, doesn't care about her physical appearance, and is not vain (40–41, 14). Melisandra is an androgynous character who possesses beauty and sensuality.[33] The narrator describes her in this way:

> Melisandra se escupió las manos y se las frotó contra las caderas. Estaban ásperas de polvo, las uñas ennegrecidas por el trabajo. El abuelo la miró de reojo comprobando su falta de vanidad. En esto se parecía a su mujer, que jamás dio importancia a su apariencia. Igual que su antecesora, sin embargo, la nieta emanaba una vitalidad animal, sensual, de criatura recién inaugurada, libre, perfecta. Parecía la estatua de una Diana saliendo a la caza [22].

> [Melisandra spit on her hands and rubbed them against her hips. They were rough from dust, fingernails blackened by work. Grandfather looked at her out of the corner of his eye, confirming her lack of vanity. In this she was like his wife, who never gave any importance to her appearance. The same as her ancestor, nevertheless, the granddaughter emanated an animal, sensual vitality, like a newly initiated creature, free, perfect. She looked like a statue of Diana going out for the hunt.]

Her parents had disappeared in the jungle when they were searching for Waslala, a city founded by poets as a utopian project (30). Wishing to find her progenitors, and to prove the existence of Waslala, Melisandra embarks on a journey of utopian characteristics. According to Uruguayan literary critic Fernando Ainsa, someone who searches for a lost paradise "deberá partir siempre del movimiento como actitud vital original" (should always start off from movement as a vital, original attitude).[34] Beatriz Pastor Bodmer, in her study of Latin American utopias form the colonial period, also points out "la vivencia de la inevitabilidad del movimiento" (the experience of the inevitability of movement) in every search for the object of desire.[35] In tracing the etymology of the word utopia, a sense of movement (geographic or psychological) stands out. For readers of the seventeenth century, utopia was synonymous with imaginary travel; while for those of the following century it meant a figurative journey to imaginary places.[36]

In the case of Melisandra, the journey itself is transformed into the focus of her travel. That is to say, it is the impulse and the process, not the final destination, which matter most. The open destination and the road ahead shape this feminist utopia. The journey as *leitmotiv* of utopianism appears in the book with multiple symbology: "la búsqueda de Waslala [por parte de

Melisandra] constituye una búsqueda de su propia identidad, un viaje al centro y al origen" (The search for Waslala [by Melisandra] constitutes a search
for her own identity, a journey to the core and to the origin).[37] The journey
is identified, in a way, with what Ernst Bloch calls *novum*, the hopeful tendency of the story to take us out of a suffering present and place us in a desired
future. The *novum* takes the form of an unconsciousness that projects itself
into the future, since it has a precognition of the new (thus its name) and
urges us to action.

Melisandra's journey from her farm to the middle of the jungle where
Waslala is located is, according to Ainsa's classification, a journey that exhibits
centripetal motion.[38] That is, the journey searches for an integration of space
as a function of the core, which represents symbolically arriving at the heart
of the continent. When the hero shifts towards the center, he sheds his vices
and adopts a purer attitude, upon coming into contact with the natural elements: water, fire, earth. Ainsa correctly points out that this return to nature
many times hides a nostalgia for a lost paradise and also the fantasy or idealization of nature as element that transforms the human character.[39] In fact,
in Waslala "nunca hay guerra [porque] ellos han logrado domar los malos
instintos, [...], es un lugar de gente mansa" (there is never war [because] they
have succeeded in taming evil instincts, [...], it is a place of gentle people)
according to Florcita, a resident of Las Luces (102).

This core, represented by Waslala in the novel, is more a state of being
that permits restructuring the surrounding chaos, than a geographic place.
As the protagonist Hermann acknowledges, everyone in some way is searching for his "own" Waslala (74). Remembering the double etymology of the
word utopia, it can be said that Waslala is at the same time "el buen lugar"
(the good place), and "el lugar no existente" (the non-existent place); this last
expression could be interpreted not as the absence of place itself, but as the
"no posesión aún" (no possession yet) of such a territory.

The town of Waslala was built on "una ranura del tiempo-espacio"
(a time-space slot): "algo así como un traslapo en la curvatura del espacio.
Waslala quedó existiendo en un interregno, tras una especie de puerta
invisible..." [something like an overlap in the curvature of space. Waslala
remained existing in an interregnum, behind a sort of invisible door...]
(58, 106). Its function was to facilitate a physical and psychological space,
a time that would permit imagining and dreaming new forms of being and
of living in community. Melisandra discovered that the reason for Waslala
was:

> [...] la utopía, el lugar que no era, que no podía ser sin el tiempo y el espacio
> habitual, sino otra cosa, el laboratorio, quizás, la luz tal vez, el ideal constante-
> mente en movimiento, poblado, abandonado y vuelto a repoblar; creído,

descreído y vuelto a creer. Había quienes tenían la función de soñar, de hacer los memoriales del futuro [...] [331].

[(...) utopia, the place that was not, that could not be without the usual time and space, rather something else, the laboratory, maybe, light perhaps, the ideal constantly in motion, populated, abandoned and repopulated again; believing, unbelieving and believing again. There were those who had the function of dreaming, of making the memorials of the future (...).]

Melisandra's canoe trip towards "*la terra incognita*" (113), is utopian also because in it another time governs: "el mundo empezaba a moverse en cámara lenta" [the world was starting to move in slow motion] (290). Melisandra loses her sense of time, and all are possessed by one where sacred images of the past appear (96, 83). To frozen time, a challenging space is added, full of tests to dodge. Melisandra is seen as "una portadora de [sus] esperanzas, una suerte de personaje mitológico a punto de iniciar en nombre de todos una jornada heroica llena de pruebas, acertijos y trampas" [a bearer of their hopes, a type of mythological character on the verge of starting in the name of every-one a heroic workday of tests, riddles and tricks] (290). Similar to the hero of a bildungsroman, the protagonist comes out of the tests triumphant, hav-ing won wisdom, since one of the characteristics of feminine utopias is the process of apprenticeship to which the characters submit themselves volun-tarily. The coordinates of a space that is difficult to travel and alien to the quotidian, and of a time almost frozen in an eternal present, mark the path to the promised land, the paradise lost. Raphael explains the phenomenon:

La humedad del ambiente, la selva tropical y sus pájaros extraños eran quizás responsables de la sensación de irrealidad, de la perspectiva alterada. Hasta el tiempo padecía una metamorfosis líquida y por momentos tenía la necesidad de apretar algún objeto para convencer[me] de que las leyes de Newton seguían intactas [26].

[The humidity of the atmosphere, the tropical jungle and its strange birds were perhaps responsible for the sense of irreality, of altered perspective. Even time suffered a liquid metamorphosis and at times I needed to squeeze some object to convince myself that Newton's laws continued intact.]

Now, paradisiacal nature is opposed to another reality that is its counterpart: the dystopian cities of Cineria and Las Luces, which were built on top of Mayan ruins and are now completely abandoned, converted into "depósito[s] de chatarra" [junk yards] (99). Besides being the First World's lung, the function of Faguas is to be the container of all of the garbage that the North produces:

marcos de miles de puertas y ventanas, estructuras de [in]contables camas de hierro, pilas de colchones, montañas de aparatos sanitarios, llantas, rines de llantas, electrodomésticos computarizados, antiquísimas lavadoras, secadoras, refrigeradores, televisores, monitores de computadoras voluminosas, paneles de plasma de modelo en desuso, sillas de ruedas, toneladas de botellas de vidrio escapadas del reciclaje, mobiliario de oficina, carrocerías, exhibidores de mercancías, maquinaria industrial, calderas, purificadores de aire, candelabros, lámparas [134].

[thousands of door frames and window frames, innumerable iron bedframes, piles of mattresses, mountains of toilets, tires, wheel rims, computerized appliances, ancient washing machines, dryers, refrigerators, televisions, bulky computer monitors, outdated models of plasma panels, wheelchairs, tons of glass bottles that escaped recycling, office furniture, car bodies, merchandise display shelves, industrial machinery, boilers, air purifiers, candelabras, lamps.]

That is to say, everything that doesn't work, is broken or is simply outdated in the United States, ends up in the hands of Engracia, the owner of Cineria's recycling company. In Faguas, what has been thrown away gains new life, thanks to the ability and ingenuity of its residents. Belli uses geographic (north/south), economic (rich/poor) and social (doctors/people without formal education), to show the injustices of a patriarchal system that abuses the weakest in the name of globalization. These dichotomies are in no way an original idea. According to Aguilar Umaña, the narrative discourse since discovery and conquest generates:

una visión dialéctica que ha dado como resultado la presencia de dicotomías cuyas características aún no terminan de adscribirse de manera definitiva a uno u otro de los elementos que se analizan: civilización/barbarie; pureza/corrupción; viejo/nuevo mundo; naturaleza/organización social; exuberancia/escasez; pecado/salvación; realismo/utopismo...[40]

[a dialectic vision that has given as a result the presence of dichotomies whose characteristics in a conclusive way still subscribe to one or another of the elements being analyzed: civilization/barbarism; purity/corruption; old/new world; nature/social organization; exuberance/scarcity; sin/salvation; realism/utopianism...]

But in no way does Belli present the North as an ideal society, since in it "nadie cree en las utopías" [no one believes in utopias] (59). Barbas Rhoden comments correctly that: "In highlighting the gap between the developed and underdeveloped regions, Belli also signals the hypocrisy of an international community whose advocacy of environmental issues is linked purely to self interest."[41]

One of the projects of ecofeminism is to criticize the dualism of the Western world (culture/nature, white/non-white, human/animal) that constructs a white male identity that is separate and superior to the identity of people of color, animals and the natural world.[42] Because the North considers the residents of Faguas inferior, it can abuse their nature and their resources; because the Espadas — the feudal family that de facto governs Faguas — believe themselves to be superior to their compatriots, they can maintain a tyrannical regime of terror.[43] The abuse in the macrocosm (industrialized North/ impoverished South) is repeated mirror-like in the microcosm of Faguas. This nation, together with parts of Asia, Africa, South America and the Caribbean, has involuted in such a way that it is immersed in constant senseless wars; its lands are condemned to ostracism, to epidemics, to curses from all of the gods. Its residents have been excluded from any technological, scientific or economic advance (17–19, 29). Belli, in an interview with Krakusin, submits that the United States is converting the poor countries little by little into "países maquiladores" (assembly plant countries). She argues:

> La única manera en que vamos a poder tener empleo y salir de esta situación va a ser con la maquila y con la cantidad de gente que se traslada a los Estados Unidos y a otros países y que manda remesas [a] familiares. Vamos a ser países de servicio, países que venden mano de obra barata. Nos han asignado el rol de mano de obra barata.[44]

> [The only way in which we are going to be able to have employment and get out of this situation is going to be with the assembly plant and with the amount of people who move to the United States and to other countries and who send money back to relatives. We are going to be service countries, countries that sell cheap labor. They have assigned us the role of cheap labor.]

Utopia is strongly connected to very specific instances in the history of humanity. It is born in precarious moments of history when the human being is overcome by "un sentimiento de abandono [...] profundo, experimentado por el ser, de encontrarse arrojado a la existencia sin una verdadera necesidad" (a feeling of profound abandonment [...], experienced by the person, of finding oneself thrown into existence without any real need).[45] And, although utopia is accused of avoiding reality for wanting to escape from the historical moment, its intrinsically subversive and revolutionary essence ties it to the present. That is to say, while longing for another reality, utopia always signals the mistakes of the present, emphasizing the lack of what is desired. In the words of Brazilian psychoanalyst and cultural critic Edson Sousa, utopia is "an uneasiness of the present that is pursued for the responsibility with tomorrow."[46]

It is in this state of desperation and total misery that the moment of most dramatic tension of the novel occurs; the group of young people that work under the command of Engracia finds a metal cylinder containing a phosphorescent blue powder. Surprised by the novelty, the kids and Engracia paint their bodies, ignoring the fact that they are dealing with cesium 137, a lethal radioactive isotope. This episode of the novel is based on a true event that happened in Brazil in 1987, when two garbage pickers found a metal tube that they sold to a scrap metal dealer. When he hammered it open to sell the lead, inside it he found a phosphorescent blue powder, cesium 137, which he gave as a gift to his friends and relatives.[47] As a result of this incident, 129 people were contaminated, twenty were hospitalized with serious health problems, and seven died. Belli herself informs the reader of this event in a note that she adds at the end of the novel. The irresponsibility of the First World in not disposing of the radioactive material appropriately, this time not only contaminates the environment, it also kills innocent people. Space and place form part of the utopian discourse when the first ones are threatened by destruction. As DeGrave asserts:

> When humankind's natural home/place is threatened, place, and nature in particular, comes to the forefront in utopian letters. Interestingly, one of the ways in which Bloch defines utopia is by "what is missing." By extension, in ecoliterature, it [is] "the missing part"—a lack of an ideal natural space or the threat to the existence of nature—that is the focus of utopian discourse.[48]

But the tragic incident of the radioactive contamination in the novel becomes the salvation that frees the inhabitants of Cineria from the abuse of the Espada family, whose domination oppresses and terrorizes everyone. In order to avoid a senseless death, Engracia and her young workers decide to go to the Espada barracks, painted blue like ghosts from Wiwilí, and to light the explosives that they carry hidden on their bodies.[49] Morris, out of love for Engracia, covers himself with the powder, and like a Christ figure sacrifices himself together with the group: "Morris era diferente y había optado [...] por inmolarse, por la crucifixión en la compañía de los pobres ladrones de despojos" [Morris was different and had opted (...) to immolate himself as crucifixion in the company of the poor garbage thieves] (200).

The explosion multiplies when all the weapons, munitions and bombs that the Espada family kept in the basement of the barracks also explode. A rain of fire, stones, smoke and rubble filled the sky and ground of Cineria. The residents, who attributed such punishment to the ghosts, were confused and lost their bearings,

> [...] se habían quedado sin mandamás ni mandamenos; sin los Espada, sin Engracia, sin armas y sin chatarra porque bien pronto se corrió la voz de que algo había sucedido en el depósito de basura y que nadie debía acercarse allí [...] Para colmo, el gobierno, con todo su gabinete de oportunistas y vividores, desapareció como tragado por la tierra, temiendo represalias o que se les acusara de haber sido los causantes de la debacle [275].

> [(...) they were left without the bigwigs and without the little guys; without the Espadas, without Engracia, without weapons and without junk, because word spread pretty fast that something had happened at the garbage dump and that no one should go near there (...) To top it all off, the government with all of its

cabinet of opportunists, disappeared as if swallowed up by the earth, fearing retaliation or being accused of having been the cause of the debacle.]

It is in the middle of this vacuum of power where a new physical and psychological space is produced, where something new can be created. Motivated by the memory and nostalgia of Waslala, the residents of Cineria decide to reorganize their city, awarding command to Melisandra. Inspired by hope, they mobilize to concretize their own dream. Engracia, before dying, had written a letter to Melisandra in which she explained the reason for utopias:

> Por Waslala conocí lo inefable que es tener fe, creer en las inmensas posibilidades del ser humano y participar en la realización de sueños impracticables, tiernos y descomunales. [...] la vida me ha convencido de que la razón de ser de los ideales es mantener viva la aspiración, darle al ser humano un desafío, la esperanza que sólo puede venir si pensamos que somos capaces de cambiar nuestra realidad y alcanzar un mundo bienaventurado en donde ni Morris ni mis muchachos, ni yo, ni tantos y tantos tengan que morir y vivir entre los desechos y los despojos [286].

> [From Waslala, I learned how ineffable it is to have faith, to believe in the immense possibilities of human beings and to participate in the realization of impractical, tender and magnificent dreams. (...) life has convinced me that the *raison d'être* of ideals is to keep hope alive, to give humans a challenge, the hope that can only come if we think that we are capable of changing our reality and achieving a fortunate world where neither Morris nor my kids, nor I, nor so many others, have to die and live among rubbish and rubble.]

And she adds the following words that echo the philosophy of Ernst Bloch: "Más que nunca estoy convencida que en la capacidad de imaginar lo imposible estriba la grandeza, la única salvación de nuestra especie" [More than ever, I am convinced that greatness lies in the ability to imagine the impossible, the only salvation for our species] (287). Again, hope takes front stage and mobilizes the actors to act. According to Bloch:

> The most important expectant emotion, the most authentic emotion of longing and thus of self, always remains in all of this — hope. Hope, this expectant counter-emotion against anxiety and fear, is therefore the most human of all mental feelings and only accessible to men, and it also refers to the furthest and brightest horizon.[50]

That was and is the objective of Waslala, to make hope flourish. After the explosion, Melisandra finally finds it. To the reader's surprise, the paradise has almost disappeared, devoured by nature, and her mother is the only inhabitant, since all the rest have died or decided to return to life outside this experimental community because of not being able to reproduce. Her mother comments to her that Waslala "cumple la función de un sueño capaz de mobilizar los deseos y las aspiraciones de quienes ansiaban un destino colectivo más acorde con las mejores potencialidades humanas" [carries out the function of a dream able to mobilize the desires and aspirations of those who longed for a collective destiny more attuned to the greatest human potentials] (325). This commentary reaffirms what has been shown earlier in this essay: the idea of utopia as impulse, as motivating force and not as unique plan or geographic place. When Waslala starts to become bureaucratic with laws and to stop its regenerative impulse, is when it disappears — literally — from the face of the Earth; its houses begin to be devoured by implacable nature. Nature now, instead of functioning as a paradisiacal garden, becomes a green prison; proving in this way that, as Manuel and Manuel affirm, all utopias carry hidden inside themselves a dystopia, and all dystopias are pregnant with utopia.[51] In *Waslala* the function of memory is akin to Bloch's category of the "not-yet-conscious," which suggests that memory should not always refer to the past — as does Freud's regressive unconscious; rather, it should project towards the future, since "albergamos el recuerdo de lo que puede llegar a ser" [we harbor the memory of what can become] (329). Bloch criticizes Freud, maintaining that his theory is repressive. According to Freud, experiences of infancy, the so-called Oedipal complex, are the base of all complexes. The person who understands the cause of these gets cured, and psychoanalysis is the only means of help in this process of healing. The path to self-knowledge is the interpretation of dreams, since they express the individual's most intimate desires. Freud's unconscious, therefore, always leads us backwards, to infancy; it is "an element of regression instead of progression."[52] In contrast, Bloch substitutes for the category of unconscious, that of the "not-yet conscious" that reveals itself in day dreams. Through hope, as motivating force, we are projected towards the future. In Bloch's words: "And so the point is reached where hope itself, this authentic expectant emotion in the forward dream, no longer just appears as a merely self-based mental feeling, but in a *conscious-known* way as *utopian function*."[53]

In 1990, Gioconda Belli gave a presentation at the Congress of Latin American Literature at Montclair State University and said that as a Nicaraguan, she could not live without hope and without dreams. She added that although in the everyday world utopias seemed to be impossible:

> [...] en el mundo de la ficción, sí son posibles. Si la literatura logra rendirlas creíbles y posibles, convirtiéndolas en ficciones que pasen a vivir en las mentes de los hombres y mujeres, su existencia inmaterial puede convertirse en su medio de subsistencia real. [...] Hay que crear nuevos mundos, nuevas sociedades, nuevas relaciones humanas en la literatura, en la pintura, en todas las artes. Así los seres humanos de ésta y de las futuras generaciones, aunque vivan en un mundo de plástico, con máscaras de gas y pestes, sabrán que hay otra realidad posible y algún día se atreverán a lanzarse en su búsqueda.[54]

[(...) in the world of fiction, they are possible. If literature manages to convey them as credible and possible, converting them into fictions that come to live in the minds of men and women, their immaterial existence can be converted into real subsistence (...) New worlds, new societies, new human relationships must be created in literature, in painting, in all of the arts. Thus humans of this and future generations, even though they may live in a plastic world with gas masks and plagues, will know that there is another reality possible and some day they will dare to set off in search of it.]

Clearly, Belli expresses the possibility that art can help us to imagine new options for daily living. She identifies her literature as utopian, in the sense that I have explained above, identifying the potential that art possesses to move us into action, in the way that Bloch and Sargisson theorize.

By including the environment as a principal element in *Waslala*, Belli recognizes that ecological concerns must form part of society's utopian project. And by emphasizing the central role that women have in the construction of this new society, she overturns the power structure that has traditionally viewed Latin American women as passive objects of reception, converting them into active creators of their own destiny. Significantly, the same patriarchal power structure that is overturned in her narrative is one that has also systematically oppressed nature. True to Belli's belief in the utopian role of literature, *Waslala* offers multiple paths by which to advance, diverse options to consider, and worlds different from the present one to create. She allows the reader's imagination to take flight so that we may begin the work of constructing a more human world.

NOTES

1. See Pereyra in the bibliography for several articles that I have published regarding utopian discourse in this group of novels.
2. Sargisson, *Contemporary Feminist Utopianism*, 1.
3. Bloch, *The Principle of Hope*, 46.
4. Zipes, "Toward a Realization of Anticipatory Illumination," xix–xx.
5. *Ibid.*, xxxix.
6. Pfaelzer, "Response: What Happened to History," 197.
7. Hilary Rose indicates that the majority of masculine utopias, such as *The Republic*, *Utopia* (that of More and that of Wells), and *The New Atlantis*, to name a few, represent nightmares for women. It is not until the publication of *Herland* (1915) by Charlotte Perkins Gilman that utopia is represented in a positive form for women. "Dreaming the Future," 124.
8. Sargisson, *Contemporary Feminist Utopianism*, 17.
9. Aguilar Umaña, *La utopía posible*, 127.
10. Sargisson, *Contemporary Feminist Utopianism*, 229.
11. Bloch, *The Principle of Hope*, 27–34.
12. Belli, "Entrevista a Gioconda Belli," 139.
13. *Ibid.*, 143.

14. Aguilar Umaña, *La utopia posible,* 134.

15. Barbas Rhoden, "The Quest for the Mother in the Novels of Gioconda Belli," 81.

16. *Ibid.*

17. I have adopted Mary Judith Ress' definition of patriarchal society. She conceives that patriarchal society is all social construction of reality and thought that dominates women and groups it considers inferior for reasons of race, religion, sexual orientation, class, disability, etc. This domination is carried out by structures of social, economic, educational, political, and intellectual power that justify the unjust distribution of power and resources. *Ecofeminism in Latin America* (New York: Orbis Books, 2006), 79.

18. Starhawk, "Power, Authority and Mystery: Ecofeminism and Earth Based Spirituality," 76.

19. Ress, *Ecofeminism in Latin America*, 77.

20. *Ibid.*, 99.

21. *Ibid.*, 84–85.

22. Quoted in Gaard and Murphy, *Ecofeminist Literary Criticism*, 3.

23. Salleh, "The Ecofeminist/Deep Ecology Debate," 208–209.

24. DeGrave, "Ecoliterature and Dystopia," 90.

25. According to Krishan Kumar, utopia shares characteristics with the Christian paradise and millennium. The first, lost forever in the genesis of creation; the other, to come about when Christ returns with his chosen saints to establish his reign on Earth for a thousand years. *Utopianism*, 3–11. Mary Judith Ress, besides indicating ecology and the feminist movements as sources of ecofeminism, adds that indigenous cosmologies and mythologies contribute beliefs of the Earth as our mother, and of the interdependence of all its creatures. *Ecofeminism in Latin America*, 68.

26. Ress, *Ecofeminism in Latin America*, 110.

27. Aguilar Umaña, *La utopia posible*, 168.

28. Carretero Pasín, "Imaginario y utopias."

29. Isabel Aguilar Umaña differentiates utopia from utopianism in that the first "es un producto histórico concreto y objetivo que se obtiene a partir de una cierta forma de expresión" (is a concrete and objective historical product that comes from a particular form of expression), while utopianism "es una categoría de trabajo intelectual, un tipo específico de mentalidad, manera de pensar, enfoque de visión" (is a category of intellectual work, a specific type of mentality, way of thinking, focus of vision). *La utopía posible*, 22.

30. Belli, *Waslala: Memorial del Futuro* (Barcelona: Editorial Seix Barral S.A., 2006), 52. All subsequent in-text page references to the novel are from this edition. All translations of passages from *Waslala* are Diane J. Forbes's, the translator of this essay.

31. Bloch indicates that More's novel was the first book that started the genre but not the concept, which is philosophically much wider and older. *Principle of Hope*, 14–15.

32. Layh, "Hythlodaeus' Female Heir," Unpublished Manuscript.

33. Pérez Marín, "Habitar, presagiar, imaginar, erotizar," 133.

34. Ainsa, *Los buscadores de la utopía*, 136.

35. Pastor Bodmer, *El jardín y el peregrino*, ii.

36. Aguilar Umaña, *La utopía posible*, 20–21.

37. Pérez Marín, "Habitar, presagiar, imaginar, erotizar," 134.

38. Ainsa, *Los buscadores de la utopía*, 135–148.

39. Ainsa, *Necesidad de la utopía*, 27; Ainsa, *Los buscadores de la utopía*, 140.

40. Aguilar Umaña, *La utopía posible*, 60.

41. Barbas Rhoden, "Greening Central American Literature," 13.

42. Gaard and Murphy, *Ecofeminist Literary Criticism*, 9.

43. The similarity is clear between the Espada family and the Somoza family. Shawn William Miller indicates that: "The Somoza dynasty in Nicaragua raped nature for finan-

cial and political gains, and eagerly sold the same opportunity to foreign companies. Logging ventures, such as the Nicaraguan Long Leaf Pine Company, entirely U.S. owned, deforested massive tracts including nearly all the pines in Nicaragua's northeast by 1961. In the 1970s, 30 percent of Nicaragua's forests disappeared, and nearly all the commercial timber along the Pacific coast. Despite Somoza having signed the Convention on International Trade in Endangered Species (CITES) in 1973, Nicaragua was Central America's worst offender, exporting tropical birds, turtle meat and big cat pelts to consumer worldwide. [...] Nicaragua was also among the most polluted nations due to heavy pesticide use. Most rivers and aquifers were contaminated, and Nicaraguans suffered the highest number of pesticide poisoning of any nation per capita, 400 of which resulted in death each year. After Haiti, degraded Nicaragua was the poorest nation in Latin America." *An Environmental History of Latin America*, 208.

44. Belli, "Entrevista a Gioconda Belli," 142.

45. Servier, *La Utopía*, 103–104.

46. Edson Sousa, Unpublished Paper.

47. The story of this event appeared in the newspaper article "Tourism Springs from Toxic Waste" by James Brooke, in the *New York Times* (May 3, 1995): A6.

48. DeGrave, "Ecoliterature and Dystopia," 93.

49. Wiwilí is a town in the department of Jinotega in Nicaragua. The "fantasmas de Wiwilí" (the ghosts of Wiwilí) is a reference to a myth with a historical base. In 1934, the communist guerrilla Sandino was tricked by liberal president Juan Sacasa and assassinated by a member of his military Guard. The Guard surrounded the Sandinista camp in Wiwilí and killed the young followers of Sandino. In 1936, by way of popular elections, Somoza rose to power and became Chief of State and Commander of the Guard. Thus began the tyrannical and cruel dictatorship of the Somoza family. Many believe that the ghost of Sandino followed Somoza all the years of his government. See Joes, *America and Guerrilla Warfare*. Belli symbolically identifies Engracia and her youths with the followers of Sandino as defenders of Nicaragua against its enemies — historically the Somoza family, and in the novel the Espada family.

50. Bloch, *The Principle of Hope*, 75.

51. Manuel and Manuel, *Utopian Thought in the Western World*, 6.

52. Bloch, *The Principle of Hope*, 56.

53. *Ibid.*, 144. Emphasis added.

54. Belli, "Hacia un nuevo canon literario," 9.

Works Cited

Aguilar Umaña. *La utopía posible*. Guatemala: Armar Editores, 2006.

Ainsa, Fernando. *Los buscadores de la utopía*. Caracas: Monte Ávila Editores C.A., 1977.

_____. *Necesidad de la utopía*. Buenos Aires: Tupac Ediciones and Editorial Nordan-Comunidad, 1990.

Barbas Rhoden, Laura. "Greening Central American Literature." *Interdisciplinary Studies in Literature and Environment* 12.1 (Winter 2005): 1–17.

_____. "The Quest for the Mother in the Novels of Gioconda Belli." *Letras Femeninas* 26.1–2 (2000): 81–97.

Belli, Gioconda. "Entrevista a Gioconda Belli." By Margarita Krakusin. *Confluencia: Revista Hispánica de Literatura y Cultura* 22.2 (Spring 2007): 138–144.

_____. "Hacia un nuevo canon literario." In *Actas del XII Congreso de Literatura Latinoamericana Montclair State University*, 3–9. Montclair: Ediciones del Norte, 1995.

_____. *La mujer habitada*. 1988. Tafalla: Editorial Txalparta, 2004.

_____. *Waslala: Memorial del Futuro*. 1996. Barcelona: Editorial Seix Barral S.A., 2006.

Bloch, Ernst. *The Principle of Hope*. Oxford: Basil Blackwell, 1986.

_____. *The Utopian Function of Art and Literature: Selected Essays*. Translated by Jack Zipes and Frank Mecklenburg. Cambridge: The MIT Press, 1988.

Carretero Pasín, Enrique. "Imaginario y utopias." *Athenea Digital* 7 (Spring2005): 40–60.http://antalya.uab.es/athenea/num7/carretero.pdf.

DeGrave, Analisa. "Ecoliterature and Dystopia: Gardens and Topos in Modern Latin American Poetry." *Confluencia: Revista Hispánica de Cultura y Literatura* 22.2 (Spring 2007): 89–104.

Gaard, Greta, and Patrick D. Murphy, eds. *Ecofeminist Literary Criticism: Theory, Interpretation, Pedagogy*. Urbana: University of Illinois Press, 1988.

Joes, Anthony James. *America and Guerrilla Warfare*. Kentucky: University Press of Kentucky, 2000.

Jones, Libby Falk, and Sarah Webster Goodwin, eds. *Feminist Utopia and Narrative*. Knoxville: University of Tennessee Press, 1980.

Kumar, Krishman. *Utopianism*. Minneapolis: University of Minnesota Press, 1991.

Layh, Susana. "Hythlodaeus' Female Heir: Transformation of the Utopian/Dystopian Concept in Gioconda Belli's *Waslala: Memorial del Futuro*." Unpublished Manuscript.

Manuel, Frank E., and Fritzie Manuel. *Utopian Thought in the Western World*. Cambridge: The Belknap Press of Harvard University Press, 1979.

Miller, Shawn William. *An Environmental History of Latin America*. New Approaches to the Americas. New York: Cambridge University Press, 2007.

Pastor Bodmer, Beatriz. *El jardin y el peregrino: Ensayos sobre el pensamiento utópico Latinoamericano 1492–1695*. Amsterdam: Rodopi, 1996.

Pereyra, Marisa. "La alteridad y sus múltiples representaciones: El modo utópico como dinámica del deseo en *La nave de los locos* de Cristina Peri Rossi." *MACLAS: Latin American Essays* 17 (2004): 63–72.

_____. "El modo utópico en la narrativa de Marcela Serrano." *Chasqui* 34.2 (November 2005): 33–47

_____. "Recontar la historia desde la censura: El modo utópico como estrategia de la nostalgia en Reina Roffé y Alina Diaconú." *Ciberletras* 9 (July 2003): http://www.lehman.cuny.edu/ciberletras/v09/pereyram.html.

_____. "Utopías locales en nuestra distópica Latinoamérica: Una aproximación a *Lo que está en mi corazón* de Marcela Serrano." *Hispanic Journal* 28.1 (Spring 2007): 105–115.

Pérez Marín, Carmen Ivette. "Habitar, presagiar, imaginar, erotizar: La narrativa de Gioconda Belli." *Revista de Estudios Hispánicos* 24.1 (1997): 127–35.

Peri Rossi, Cristina. *La nave de los locos*. Barcelona: Seix Barral, 1984.

Pfaelzer, Jean. "Response: What Happened to History?" In *Feminism, Utopia, and Narrative*. Edited by Sarah Webster Goodwin and Libby Falk Jones, 191–199. Tennessee Studies in Literature 32. Knoxville: University of Tennessee Press, 1990.

Ress, Mary Judith. *Ecofeminism in Latin America*. Women from the Margins. New York: Orbis Books, 2006.

Roffé, Reina. *El cielo dividido*. Buenos Aires: Editorial Sudamericana, 1996.

Rose, Hilary. "Dreaming the Future." *Hypatia* 3.1 (Spring 1988): 119–137.

Salleh, Ariel. "The Ecofeminist/Deep Ecology Debate." *Environmental Ethics* 14.3 (1992): 195–216.

Sargisson, Lucy. *Contemporary Feminist Utopianism*. London: Routledge, 1996.

Serrano, Marcela. *Antigua vida mía*. México: Alfaguara, 1995.

_____. *Lo que está en mi corazón*. Buenos Aires: Grupo Editorial Planeta S.A.I.C., 2001.

Servier, Jean. *La Utopía*. México: Fondo de Cultura Económica, 1979.

Slicer, Deborah. "Towards an Ecofeminist Standpoint Theory: Bodies as Grounds." In Gaard and Murphy, 49–73.

Sousa, Edson. "An Invention of Utopia." Unpublished Manuscript.

Starhawk. "Power, Authority and Mystery: Ecofeminism and Earth-based Spirituality." In *Reweaving the World: The Emergence of Ecofeminism*, edited by Irene Diamond and Gloria Feman Orenstein, 73–86. San Francisco: Sierra Club Book, 1990.

Zipes, Jack. "Introduction: Toward a Realization of Anticipatory Illumination." In *The Utopian Function of Art and Literature: Selected Essays* by Ernst Bloch, vii–xliii. Translated by Jack Zipes and Frank Mecklenburg. Cambridge, MA: MIT Press, 1988.

Barbarian Civilization: Travel and Landscape in *Don Segundo Sombra* and the Contemporary Argentinean Novel

Martín Camps

Introduction

In his Nobel Prize acceptance speech, "In Search of the Present" Octavio Paz affirmed that "the concept of a process open to infinity and synonymous with endless progress has been called into question. I need hardly mention what everybody knows: natural resources are finite and will run out one day."[1] Paz further elaborates in an interview that the ecological conscience modifies our attitude toward nature to re-establish a "fraternidad cósmica" (cosmic fraternity) that the modern era fractured by desecrating nature and trying to govern it through science and technology.[2] The problem, according to the Mexican author, is that man forgot to "dominar su propia naturaleza" (govern his own nature).[3] For Paz, nature is at the same time a creative and a destructive force, like man himself who by abusing progress must contemplate his own obliteration.[4] Therefore, he finds in ecological discourse the end of modernity or a mutation into a new era that does not trust blindly in the future but rather in revisiting the past.

The first part of this essay studies the novel *Don Segundo Sombra* as an example of a somewhat romantic vision of nature that rejects the project of modernization (represented by the city) by elevating the figure of the gaucho. In this novel, Don Segundo Sombra educates a young man who is eager to learn the ways of the pampas. As discussed below, a close reading of this novel also reveals the influence of the British Empire on the meat industry in Argentina.

The second part of this essay examines four novels by contemporary Argentinean writers Héctor Tizón, Juan José Saer, Osvaldo Soriano, and

154

Mempo Giardinelli. These authors have different narrative projects and distinct voices, but converge on the topic of travel and the description of the vast territory of the provinces of Argentina in stories where a nomadic subject almost always appears in transit. Perhaps Giardinelli is the author who most clearly represents the ecological conscience in his precautionary tone and denouncement of ecological devastation. Through my reading of these authors' texts, this essay offers some examples of how the scenery of Argentina continues to be a fundamental part of the narrative universe but not as a menace that could "devour" the characters as in some telluric novels, but as a main character of the story.

Nature in Regionalist Novels and the "Invisible Empire"

Nature is an irremovable presence that defines most of Spanish America's regionalist or telluric novels ("novelas de la tierra" or of the land/earth). As discussed in the first essay of this anthology, for example, in *La vorágine* (1924; *The Vortex*), by José Eustacio Rivera, the Colombian jungle swallows the "civilized" Arturo Cova. In *Doña Bárbara* (1929) by Rómulo Gallegos, Santos Luzardo attempts to restore his family's overgrown *hacienda* on the Venezuelan plains to its former glory while clashing with his *femme fatale* neighbor who devours men and dominates the territory. In the case of *Don Segundo Sombra* (1926) the Argentinean pampas expand like a "mar verde" (green sea) where eyes become lost in the horizon and where the adventure of Fabio Cáceres takes place.[5] In the aforementioned novels, nature itself is a character that is often presented as being capable of devouring any character who strives to subjugate it.[6]

Jennifer French in *Nature, Neo-Colonialism and the Spanish American Regional Writers* studies the interrelation between the British Empire and the regionalist novel, particularly in the works by José Eustacio Rivera, Horacio Quiroga and Benito Lynch. She demonstrates that the British had an informal power over the Argentinean economy by controlling the natural resources with the help of the ruling class. By presenting a Marxist reading of these works, French studies how the tentacles of the Empire expanded by land through the pampas to pursue a modernization that would provide extraordinary profits for the British Empire in the long run. The regionalist novel, she argues, registered the economic and social framework that functioned at the heart of the growing meat, coffee, and lumber markets. In *Don Segundo Sombra* there are some allusions to what French calls the "Invisible empire," for example, when the protagonist Fabio describes the *estanciero* (landowner)

Don Galván as an "inglés acriollado" (acculturated Englishman). The English have had a strong influence in the Southern Cone since Darwin's explorations.[7] His scientific voyages also served as the eyes and ears of the Empire by reporting on the natural resources available for exploitation. Thus, these early voyages established the long tradition of foreign interventionism during the national period or, from a different perspective, the early stages of globalization in the Southern Cone. However, the profits from this development seldom remained in the producing countries but ended up in the coffers of outside governments.

French's study explains how economic interests markedly affected ecology. This is evident in *Don Segundo Sombra* in chapter XIV when the meat market expansion is mentioned along with the "barcos frigoríficos" (refrigerated boats):

> El rematador dijo un discurso lleno de palabras como "ganadería nacional," "porvenir magnífico," "grandes negocios" [...] Alrededor del carrito, a pie o montados en caballos de los peones de la feria, estaban los ingleses de los frigoríficos, afeitados, rojos y gordos como frailes bien comidos. Los invernadores, tostados por el sol, calculaban ganancias o pérdidas, tirándose del bigote o rascándose la barbilla [185].

> [He reeled off a spiel of words like "national breed," "matchless future," "big business," [...] Around the wagon, either on foot or horses borrowed from the herders, watched the Englishmen from the refrigeration plants: smooth-shaven, red-faced fellows, for the most part fat as friars. The breeders for the market, bronzed by the sun, were reckoning profit and loss nervously tugging their moustaches or scratching their chins (124).]

Through passages such as this, Güiraldes introduces the subject of the expansion of British interests in the Argentinean cattle industry. On the following page Fabio mentions another Englishman: "traiba yo unas vacas por cuenta de un inglés de Guales" (186) [I come this way driving steers for an Englishman from Wales] (125). These passages clearly evidence the presence and economic influence of England in the Southern Cone.

As French argues, economic development created the conditions for the emergence of the telluric novel:

> A sudden boom meant a frenzy to increase supply and, in consequence, to claim and conquer the land and people capable of producing it. As a result new territories were constantly being conquered and exploited: increased demand for Argentinean beef [...] resulted in the *Conquista del Desierto* [conquest of the desert] and the extermination of the pampas Indians during 1879–80; high coffee prices led to the white settlement of Sao Paulo, Brazil and Colombia's Cauca Valley; and the demand for natural rubber after the invention of vulcanization led to the horrors of the Amazonian *cauchería* [rubber industry].[8]

For French the economy was the basis for the historical development of Latin America, a region that basically functioned as a resource deposit that was exploited for centuries to construct European wealth, at the expense of the work and blood of local (often indigenous) communities, as Eduardo Galeano has shown in his book about the five centuries of pillage to the continent: *Las venas abiertas de América Latina* (1977; *The Open Veins of Latin America*). French proposes that literature produced from 1870 to 1930 should be studied as an example of international colonialist literature, that is, the primitive globalizing experience in Spanish America and the capitalist exploitation that established an extractive industry. In this sense, the regionalist novel depicts the beginning of a process of modernization that has led to the depredation of the environment and of local communities in Spanish America.

Representations of the Land: Revisiting *Don Segundo Sombra*

Don Segundo Sombra is composed of several dichotomies: city and country, childhood and adulthood, civilization and barbarism. These contrasts augment the progress and tension of the novel, for example, the restrictive space of his aunts' house, where Fabio lives in the first segment of the novel, is contrasted with the free and adventurous life of Don Segundo Sombra on the pampas. John Brushwood asserts that Fabio Cáceres is also the abstraction of the rural starving youngster hungry for excitement in the same way that Don Segundo is the idealization of the gaucho.[9] This is why, from the first time the two characters meet, Fabio sees Don Segundo as a ghost "más una idea que un ser" (79) [more a thought than a living thing] (12). Nevertheless, these two opposing characters allow us to analyze the novel through the contrast between civilization and barbarism, in which the city is a manifestation of modernity in opposition to the pampas as a symbol of liberty.

Don Segundo is the incarnation of the pampas; he encompasses the valor, audacity, and justice of a hero forged by work, and he becomes a guide and tutor to Fabio Cáceres who selects Don Segundo as his master. The *pampa* itself is also his tutor as it demands hard work, days under the rain and sun, and solitude. Therefore Fabio is educated by nature, in barbarism, and he will eventually choose the life of an *estanciero* (landowner). Don Segundo, in contrast, cannot distance himself from his gaucho identity. Ultimately, Fabio assumes the values of the gaucho that turned him from a *guacho* (bastard) into a gaucho.

In effect, the novel is a *bildungsroman*, or coming of age novel. Fabio wants to become a gaucho, which is to have an "alma de horizonte" (117) [a soul of the horizon] (51). He is aware that the change implies suffering and affliction to the body, "sufriendo sin quejas ni desmayos la brutalidad del sol, la mojadura de las lluvias, el frío tajante de las heladas y las cobardías del cansancio" (122) [the blister of the sun without complaint, the drench of the rain, the bite of the frost and the subtle treacheries of fatigue] (57). That is, exposure to nature is the key to his transformation.

The code of the gaucho is work. By making a content analysis of the most frequent words in the novel we find that the word "horse" is mentioned 117 times, in comparison to the word "love" that is only mentioned 23 times. "Work" is mentioned 50 times and "pampas" 29. Consequently, through this selection of words, we can infer that the horse is one of the most important elements that dominate the pampas. The horse is the symbol of individualism and dominion over the land. This animal, brought overseas by the Spanish, made it possible to travel across the vast territory of the pampas.

For Güiraldes the countryside is a motive for inspiration and reflection. In a 1920 letter he writes, "La ciudad en el fondo me es antipática [...] Culpe Ud. de este modo arbitrario de juzgar a mi costumbre y amor por la pampa, con su sol, su aire y la exaltación individual que crea" (The city is not appealing to me [...] Chalk up this arbitrary way of judging to my customs and love for the *pampa*, with its sun, air and individual exaltation that creates).[10] It was in France where Güiraldes began to evoke the memory and image of the *pampa* and recognize in it his own Argentinean identity.[11] Furthermore, Don Segundo is what Güiraldes would like to be and Fabio is what he cannot stop being, an educated young man, with an important last name, a "cajetilla" (upper-class citizen). Güiraldes himself was educated in Paris and wrote the novel to resemble a painting that nostalgically portrays the figure of the gaucho, on his horse, flanked by an infinite landscape.[12] This helps to explain the importance of the dedication of the novel: "Al gaucho que llevo en mí" (67) [To the gaucho I bear within me] (v).

Don Segundo Sombra is divided into three parts; each one marked by the image of the protagonist Fabio contemplating a river or a lake. As Michael Predmore has observed, "The image of moving water comes to give symbolic expression, too, to this perpetual motion of the cowboy."[13] The first part consists of Fabio's escape from his aunt's house and his desire to become a gaucho and the godson of Don Segundo. Fabio is excited about the trip and abandoning small-town boredom. He recalls: "Sobre la tierra, de pronto oscurecida, asomó un sol enorme y sentí que era yo un hombre gozoso de vida. Un hombre que tenía en sí una voluntad, los haberes necesarios del buen gaucho y hasta una chinita querendona que llorara su partida" (120) [Now an enormous sun rose on the earth, obscuring it: and I felt I was a man to whom life is good. A man with a will of his own, with everything the gaucho needs, even a loving halfbreed girl to mourn his going away] (54). Nevertheless, playing with the idea of becoming a cowboy turns into a rite of passage that is only achieved with sweat and work, with the routine of constant motion. His maturity comes by way of pain, "en el vientre, las ingles, los muslos, las paletas, las pantorrillas" (136) [my stomach, my groin, my thighs, my calves, and my shoulders] (71). It also comes in the contemplation of his surroundings: "Dos horas pasé, así, mirando en torno mío el campo hostil y bruñido" (141) [There were two hours of this. I gazed at the burnished, hostile field] (77).

In chapter X after five years have passed, Fabio recalls what he has learned from Don Segundo in addition to the manual labor: "También por él supe de la vida, la resistencia y la entereza en la lucha, el fatalismo en aceptar sin rezongos lo sucedido, la fuerza moral ante las aventuras sentimentales, la desconfianza para con las mujeres y la bebida, la prudencia entre los forasteros, la fe en los amigos" (145) [And he taught me how to live: courage and fairness in the fight, love of one's fate whatever it might be, strength of character in affairs of the heart, caution with women and liquor, reserve among strangers, faith to friends] (81). Hence, Don Segundo has taught Fabio to restrain himself, to be responsible for his own education and to become one with the pampas. Moreover, he has taught him how to have fun, tell stories, be cautious and economical with words, and respect the value system of the gaucho. Chapter XVI underscores how the *pampa* also tames the gaucho: "Los sanos y jóvenes [...] eran los más, porque la pampa al que anda trastabillando muy pronto se lo traga" (208) [The young and healthy ([were] in the majority, of course, because the *pampa* soon gets rid of the laggard] (150). At the end of chapter XVII — when his process of becoming a gaucho is almost complete and this rite of passage, as any other, is sealed with blood, in this case the blood of the bull he kills after a struggle that brakes his clavicle — the bull and Fabio remain immobile "en un gran silencio de campo y cielo" (222) [in the silence of earth and sky] (166). And after this rite, when he is recuperating on Galván's farm, Galván says to Fabio as he places his hand on his shoulder: "-Ya has corrido mundo y te has hecho hombre, mejor que hombre, gaucho. El que sabe los males de esta tierra por haberlos vivido, se ha templado para domarlos" (224) [You've seen the world, now, my lad, and you've become a man — better than a man, a gaucho. The one who knows the world's evils because he has lived through them is tempered to overcome them] (167). Thus, his process of acquiring knowledge and wisdom has come to an end; he has become what he wanted to be.

In the second part of *Don Segundo Sombra*, which consists primarily of episodes in Fabio's apprenticeship and gaucho adventures, Fabio has been offered a job on an *estancia* (ranch), but he decides not to take it because it will mean detaching himself from Don Segundo. Shortly thereafter, Pedro Barrales informs him that he has inherited land on an *estancia* of his own and advises him that he should go to take possession of it. Fabio, who earlier in the novel had declared "no soy hijo más que del rigor" [I am only a son of rigor] (273) feels betrayed by this event that requires him to abandon his life as a gaucho, even though he had been weighing the risks and rewards of the pampas life and its "ley fatal" [fatal law] (284) after witnessing his friend Antenor Barragán kill a stranger with his fast knife. Prior to discovering that he had a name and a surname, Fabio had enjoyed the sense of freedom that accompanied this lack of identity. The thought of trading his gaucho life and identity seems to him "algo así como cambiar el destino de una nube por el de un árbol" (303) [something like changing from a cloud into a tree] (255). Nevertheless, he decides to confront his past and assume his destiny as a landowner. Don Segundo accompanies him for the first three years of his new life, but soon after decides to leave because he cannot live without movement.

In the third and final part of the novel, having readjusted to sedentary life, Fabio contemplates a lake and summarizes his life in the following manner:

> Está visto que en mi vida el agua es como un espejo en que desfilan las imágenes del pasado. A orillas de un arroyo resumí antaño mi niñez. Dando de beber a mi caballo en la picada de un río, revisé cinco años de andanzas gauchas. Por último, sentado sobre la pequeña barranca de una laguna, en mis posesiones, consultaba mentalmente mi diario de patrón [309].

> [You have seen how, in my life, water is a mirror for all the images of what has been. At the edge of a brook, long ago, I had gone over my childhood. At the ford of a river where I was watering my pony, I had checked up the five years of learning to how to be a gaucho. And now, by the margin of a pool on my own land, I studied my diary as an owner (262).]

Don Segundo bids farewell on the hill and disappears into the horizon "como si lo cortaran de abajo en repetidos tajos" (314) [as if he were being whittled away from below] (267). Fabio stays at the *estancia* having chosen his life as rancher and knowing that his education as a gaucho will be useful to him. He says "Me fui como quien se desangra" (315) [My going was like life-blood flowing away] (267), a phrase that in addition to describing the sadness of his final separation from Don Segundo, marks, again with blood, the end of his rite of passage and his final maturation. If Don Segundo is the embodiment of the pampas, then he must return to his place, and Fabio should fulfill his mission as a "civilized man" but one who has been educated on the pampas, and can dominate his own nature.

Theoretical Discussions on Nature in Latin America

For Christiane Laffite *Don Segundo Sombra's* message is that "la educación y la cultura son imprescindibles para una evolución en la que el hombre se encontrará en armonía con el medio" (education and culture are essential for an evolution in which man will find himself in harmony with the environment).[14] The ecological novel invites knowledge of the means and remedies of coexisting harmoniously with the world; not a savage modernization but a harmonization that seeks the meeting point between nature and civilization. The analysis of ecology in literature leads to asking new questions of the text and to breaking disciplinary boundaries to look for short and long-term solutions to redefining our place in the world and our responsibility to the next generation that will inherit the earth. In the words of Barbara Ward and Renee Dubos, it means to look for a balance between "the biosphere which we inherit, and the technosphere, which we create."[15]

The novelists of the Latin American Boom felt the need to shake off the rural dust breathed into the novels of the beginning of the twentieth century and chose to create works in which the settings are the nascent Latin American cities of Cortázar (Buenos Aires), Vargas Llosa (Lima), Fuentes (Mexico City), and García Márquez (Bogotá). In the dichotomy created by Sarmiento, twentieth-century civilization would triumph over barbarism and the development of the land would be seen as a necessary means for economic growth. In this framework, barbarism is personified by nature that must be controlled and subdued to pave the way to a form of civilization that is not questioned because it embodies the modernizing desire of progress. Nevertheless, in the first decade of the twenty-first century, the devastating effects wrought by this civilization have become one of the central concerns about the future of Latin America. Thus, the need for conservation and the creation of renewable sources of energy have gained significance in cultural discourse. Although the regionalist writers strove to distance their work from the rural flavor of earlier literature, they understood the danger of moving away from nature completely and looked suspiciously upon the intense growth of cities to an extreme in which civilization would become barbaric, and like their fictitious characters, civilization would finally devour them. Güiraldes looks at the city with scorn and rebels against the attraction that the city exercises on the avant-garde poets who try to imitate its sounds and movement as well as its culture of coffeehouses, automobiles and cinematography. He preferred to return to the pampas, to tranquility, to what he perceived to be essentially Argentinean. He had already seen the big metropolis, Paris, and knew that Buenos Aires was heading in the direction of becoming a major urban center. This is also why in the novel he does not call attention to the railroad, the telegraph, or the fencing that was already dividing the pampas and preventing the free and easy transit of the gauchos that his novel portrays.[16] Thus, *Don Segundo Sombra* finds itself at the intersection between nostalgia for nature and technological advances that threaten the countryside. Therefore it is feasible to read *Don Segundo Sombra* as a novel that was not seduced by the city but rather by the open spaces and the simplicity of the gauchos, and, in this way, rejects the industrialization of the beginning of the century.[17] Ironically, however, the novel is unable to fully escape Sarmiento's notion of civilization, as Fabio's education is ultimately founded on his mastery over the natural world.

This early resistance to industrialization might have been an important intuition of Güiraldes. Edwina Campbell (1990) rescues the reflections of Octavio Paz on ecology and progress when discussing the European debate on ecology. Campbell reminds us that the opposition between man and nature begins in the Christian tradition, in which man must conquer nature or risk the reverse. Octavio Paz, immersed in the midst of the Cold War, warns of a philosophical problem that had not been considered until the twentieth century — the complete annihilation of man: "The destruction of the planet Earth is an event that neither Marx nor Nietzche nor any other of the philosophers who have pondered the theme of decadence envisioned in their writings on the subject."[18] The race for progress by economic powers such as China and the United States could potentially only be stopped by a form of destruction of nature that would have global implications. Many natural resources are reaching the point of exhaustion. This poses a global problem that requires us to re-conceptualize the human relationship with the natural world and our place as immersed organisms in varied ecosystems.

Therefore, it is imperative to rescue the regionalist novel as an example of a literary genre in which nature is at the fore, as in *Don Segundo Sombra* where Fabio receives his education from the pampas by "governing his own nature" as Paz reminds us in his Nobel acceptance speech. The regionalist novel is not only an inventory of the tensions between civilization and barbarism, it also portrays the historical origins of the development of natural spaces driven by foreign interests. In many cases, the regional economic development that was seen optimistically at the beginning of the nineteenth century led to the depletion of natural resources by the end of the twentieth. Consequently, as environmentalists and ecocritics have argued, it is essential to reconsider the relation between man and environment. The protection of ecosystems ultimately means the protection of human surroundings and the subsistence not only of local economies and regions, but of the planet.

Nature in Contemporary Argentinean Novels

The second part of this essay concentrates on the use of landscape in contemporary Argentinean novels to offer a contrast to *Don Segundo Sombra* and to present a panorama of both poles of the twentieth century. *Don Segundo Sombra* is a novel that is opposed to the city. For a major part of the twentieth century, Buenos Aires was the center of literary gravity in Argentinean literature; one needs only to remember Borges's first book of poetry *Fervor de Buenos Aires* (1923; Fervour of Buenos Aires) as an example of the interest in the city as metaphorical space. Buenos Aires is a city that virtually cancels out natural scenery; it buries the sea and the pampas. In a sense, Buenos Aires is the anti-*pampa*, the desire to move away from the natural order and impose human order. Interestingly, the ecological reserve in Buenos Aires was created by debris of buildings and highways destroyed in the 1970s and thrown into the river. The original project was to expand the prestigious and prosperous zone of Puerto Madero with its high rise condominiums, but after years of not using this newly formed terrain, the project was canceled and the flora and fauna took over. It is also near the reserve that groups of socially displaced citizens live in tents, the underprivileged pushed back from the city, as captured by Juan Martini in his novel *Puerto Apache* (2002).

The immensity of the pampas territory imposes a silence upon it. As Fuentes has suggested, Buenos Aires lies in between two silences: "el silencio de la pampa y el silencio del mar" (the silence of the pampas and the silence of the sea) yet, as evidenced in the production of several generations of outstanding authors, this city was created to speak.[19] Although an analysis of the urban space of Buenos Aires is beyond the scope of this essay, it is noteworthy that in contemporary Argentinean fiction there appears to be a renewed interest in the less inhabited spaces of the provinces with their varied landscapes. This stands in contrast to the dominance of the city in the texts of other twentieth-century Argentinean authors such as Arlt, Borges, Cortázar, and Puig, but provides an opportunity for fruitful comparison with earlier regional novels such as *Don Segundo Sombra*. Celina Manzoni reflects on this newer regional literature's integration into Argentinean literature:

> Alrededor de los años setenta, en parte debido a la circulación de criterios más audaces y de nuevas revistas [...] algunos poetas y narradores alcanzaron el todavía esquivo reconocimiento nacional de su obra. Antonio di Benedetto, Daniel Moyano, Héctor Tizón, Juan José Saer, aún antes de las circunstancias del exilio, fueron editados, estudiados y también incorporados a la literatura nacional casi sin la marca regionalista.[20]

> [Around the seventies, partly due to the circulation of bolder criteria and new journals [...] some poets and narrators achieved the still reticent national recog-

nition of their work. Antonio di Benedetto, Daniel Moyano, Héctor Tizón, Juan José Saer, even before the circumstances of exile, were published, studied and also incorporated into the national literature almost without the regionalist mark.]

These and other authors discussed below offer a different perspective on the Argentinean nation that incorporates the incisive presence of the territory that was so frequented by telluric novelists, but they return to nature with an interest that is not purely ecological in the sense of protecting ecosystems (with the possible exception of Mempo Giardinelli). For these authors, natural landscapes create a narrative space for contemplating the solitude and neglect of the more remote Argentinean territories.

The demonstration of the geographical immensity of Argentina finds its maximum expression in travel narrative. As Héctor Tizón suggests: "El del viaje, ya sea real o imaginario, es una de las más grandes metáforas de la vida" (Travel, real or imaginary, is one of the biggest metaphors for life).[21] In *Luz de las crueles provincias* (1995), Héctor Tizón (Yala, Jujuy, 1929) narrates the desolation of exile in the Argentinean northeast. This is apparent in the story of Giovanni and Rossana, Italian immigrants who arrive in Argentina in search of a land of "milk and honey" in the country's expansive territory, immense "como un océano, donde millones de vacas, caballos, corderos y gallinas vagabundeaban por sus pampas" (like an ocean, where millions of cows, horses, lambs, and chickens wander around the pampas).[22] However they are forced to move to the northeast of the country to find work, recognizing that, "En este país nadie te dice sí y nadie te dice no, pero al menos es ancho y cabemos todos" [In this country no one tells you yes or no, but at least it is wide and we all fit in it] (72). Giovanni, the husband of this young Italian immigrant couple, dies prematurely and his wife remarries a landowner to survive. Her son Juan, who was conceived with Giovanni, is able to attend the University of Buenos Aires and returns changed from the city. Antonio, the coachman, commenting on the profound change that the south has had on Juan, declares: "Aquí está y no está" [He's here but not here] (170).

The novel presents some similarities with *Don Segundo Sombra*; for example, the inheritance that Fabio receives is similar to the one that is delegated to Juan. Another similarity between the two novels is the insistence on describing the immensity of the territory. Furthermore, both novels are replete with wise sayings. This novel, although written in 1995, is set historically near the time of Güiraldes's story when the lines of the railway system were spreading throughout the pampas. An example of this in Tizón's novel is when the governor reminds Juan: "¿te das cuenta, acaso, de cómo se valorizarán esas tierras si el ferrocarril las atraviesa? [do you even realize how these lands will be valued if the railroad crosses them?] (207). The cruel provinces are marked by the light and solitude of exile and the adaptation to a new place, to a new language and to the conditions of a new country.[23] In *Luz de las crueles provincias* there are certain thematic aspects also present in *Don Segundo Sombra*. If Güiraldes provides a vision of a gaucho that dominates the land, Tizón introduces us to the universe of the Italian exiles that deeply modify Argentinean culture and are a fundamental part of the development of the cities of the coast. He also introduces the topic of solitude that relates to the scenery and the tension between center and periphery that can be perceived in the oppressive presence of the bishop, or the customs of a rapidly aging people.[24] The universe of Tizón, in this sense, is similar to that of the Mexican writer Juan Rulfo in presenting lost villages of the provinces inhabited by ghosts of flesh and bone.

Juan José Saer[25] (Santa Fé, 1937–2005), on the other hand, in his novel *Las nubes* (1997; Clouds) tells the story of a psychiatrist who transports five madmen in caravans along with soldiers and prostitutes across the flatness of the pampas in an effort to evade the chief Josecito. The psychiatrist, who recalls the journey thirty years later, in August, 1804, is described as "doctor Real, especialista de las enfermedades que desquician no el cuerpo sino el alma" (Dr. Real, specialist in the illnesses that upset not the body but the soul).[26] Throughout the story the narrator offers reflections about what madness means, for example: "ya es sabido que la locura, cuando no hace reír, suele generar la incomodidad y más que nada el espanto" [it is already known that madness, when it does not make you laugh, usually generates discomfort and, most of all, fright] (39). The character of the nun, Teresita, is the most unusual for her apparent mental illness that drives her to speak obscenely and behave promiscuously. Frantically inclined to fornication, she has written a *Manual de amores* (Manual of love) because, according to the psychiatrist: "los enfermos mentales, cuando poseen cierta educación, tienen casi siempre la tendencia irresistible a expresarse por escrito, intentando disciplinar sus divagaciones en el molde de un tratado filosófico o de una composición literaria" [mental patients, when they possess a certain level of education, almost always have the irresistible tendency to express themselves in writing, trying to discipline their digressions in the mold of a philosophical treatise or a literary composition] (106). This passage offers the reader a clue that the doctor could also be suffering from dementia, given his need to "discipline his digressions" through his own writing.

The trip across the flatness of the pampas consists primarily of attempting to overcome the isolation of the seemingly infinite distances separating the towns: "dispersos en esos desiertos inacabables y salvajes, obligaba a sus habitantes a estar todo el tiempo alerta para enfrentar los peligros más variados" [dispersed in those interminable and wild deserts, the desolation obligated its inhabitants to be always alert to face the most varied dangers] (114). This fear of solitude is also apparent when the doctor writes: "tuve la impresión, más triste que aterradora, de que era al centro mismo de la soledad que habíamos llegado" [I had the impression, more sad than frightening, that it was the very center of solitude to which we had arrived] (152). The soporific monotony that marks the desert is akin to dementia; the doctor continues: "si este lugar extraño no le hace perder a un hombre la razón, o no es hombre, o ya está loco, porque es la razón lo que engendra la locura" [if this strange place does not make a man lose his reason, either he is not a man, or he is already crazy, because it is reason that engenders madness] (161). For the narrator, dementia is a contagious disease: "los que lo rodean adquieren sus mismos síntomas" [those who surround it acquire its same symptoms] (171). In this novel, the scenery serves to dismantle reason. As the text suggests, crossing the barren land "destruye en nosotros todo lo que, antes de entrar en ella, aceptábamos como familiar" [destroys in us everything that, before entering it, we accepted as familiar] (176). As the convoy advances, the travelers begin to assume an air of madness and wildness. For example, the women walk around naked, because the trip: "nos había incitado, de un modo imperceptible, a crear nuestras propias normas de vida, y los caprichos del clima" [had incited us, in an imperceptible way, to create our own norms of life, and the caprices of the climate] (191). At the end of the journey when they arrive at their destination, the travelers are seen as strange beings "sucios y ennegrecidos por el sol y también por el fuego, el humo y la ceniza" [dirty and blackened by the sun and also by fire, smoke and ash] (206). This novel is written, to use the doctor's own words, with the "ductilidad elegante de su pensamiento" [elegant ductility of his thought] where the limits of reason and insanity are dispelled the same way they are projected onto a territory of outrageous proportions (46). Indeed, the extension of the pampas is appropriate for bedlam, the solitude and isolation of the vast plains disturb not only the body, but the mind.

The narrative universe of Osvaldo Soriano (Mar del Plata, 1943–1997), our third contemporary novelist, has also been marked by the travel experience since his first novel *Triste, solitario y final* (1974), which narrates a trip to the United States.[27] His other well-known novel *Una sombra ya pronto serás* (1990, A Shadow soon you will be) tells of a man wandering the pampas with no ultimate goal who encounters along the way a banker, an astrologist and other singular characters. In the words of one of the main character's friends, the protagonist is "nada más que una sombra que va por ahí" (nothing more than a shadow that drifts around), going nowhere and driven only by chance.[28] In his final novel, *La hora sin sombra* (1995; The hour without shadow), Soriano tells the story of a man who loses the manuscript of a novel he is writing, so he recounts the novel but is interrupted by the search for his father who has escaped from the hospital. When his father was younger, he worked for Paramount Pictures traveling around the Argentinean provinces to ensure that this company's movies were well exhibited. The narrator says: "En esa época yo soñaba con escribir relatos de viajes a la manera de Jack London y Ambrose Bierce y empecé a acompañarlo en sus giras" [Back then I wanted to write travel stories in the way of Jack London and Ambrose Bierce so I started accompanying him on his tours.][29] *La hora sin sombra* is also a novel about travel in which the author briefly evokes novels by Melville, Kafka, Borges, and Güiraldes (as a seminal Argentinean novel), and also describes the process of writing and the story of his father. In an interview included after the end of the novel, Soriano acknowledges the symbolism of the novel's setting on the plains: "El pibe siempre está solo, por más que coincida a veces con alguien en algún trayecto de su viaje. Siempre hay una soledad que acentúa al situar la historia en zonas de la llanura" [The kid is always alone, as much as he encounters people on his trip. There is always an accentuated solitude by situating the story in the plains.][30] The plains constitute a metaphor for solitude and the search for identity in the characters of *Una sombra ya pronto serás* and *La hora sin sombra*. This metaphor might also be extended to Soriano's own identity as an exiled Argentine in Brussels and Paris when he escaped Argentina's military dictatorship from 1976–1984.[31]

The loneliness of travel and the immensity of the plains are also recurring motifs in the work of Mempo Giardinelli (Resistencia, Chaco, 1947), in particular in his novel *Final de novela en Patagonia* (2000; End of novel in Patagonia) in which the narrator (who takes on the persona of the author Giardinelli) and a Professor from Virginia go on a trip to Patagonia to see this region for the first time and to allow Giardinelli to finish his novel. The narrator recalls novels and movies that have fed the Patagonian imaginary. The text consists of fragments of the novel that the author hopes to finish as well as some poems, comments, descriptions of encounters and inserted notes that ultimately create a travel narrative that attempts to move away from other works such as *En la Patagonia* [In Patagonia] by Bruce Chatwin in which the European gaze still persists, ready to severely judge Latin America. *Final de novela en Patagonia* is a road novel in which the author/narrator seeks to explore the vast Patagonian territory in order to retell the story from an Argentinean perspective (through his own experience and vast cultural knowledge of the region) and thus move away from the imperial gaze of other works by nineteenth-century European explorers that had an interest in documenting exploitable resources. Moreover, the author/narrator reflects on the long roads and apparent quietude of this land, registering multiple encounters with diverse individuals, such as an English cyclist with a wasted body after traveling for eleven years; heroic teachers preoccupied with the education of children in these remote regions who are fighting to get resources from the government; inhabitants with a strong need to talk; tourists in the glacier Perito Moreno; and the various encounters with the image of Gaucho Gil, a popular saint who protects travelers. In several parts of the novel, the author manifests his preoccupation with the ineffectiveness of the government to create an ecologically conscious tourist industry based on the natural wonders of the country:

> Mientras caminamos sobre el glaciar Perito Moreno, pienso también en las posibilidades turísticas de este país privilegiado que tiene — entre sus muchas maravillas — las cataratas del Iguazú en el Norte, una docena de glaciares como éste en el Sur y esa indolencia feroz en varios millones de sus habitantes.[32]

> [As we walk on the Perito Moreno glacier, I think also about the tourism possibilities of this privileged country that has — among its many marvels — the Iguazú falls in the North, a dozen glaciers like this one in the South and this fierce indolence in several million of his inhabitants.]

Giardinelli judges harshly the lack of protection of Argentinean natural wonders by criticizing the open garbage dumps exposed to wind and emphasizing the need to protect the glacier that "sólo pudo construir los siglos y el silencio" [only centuries and silence could form] (150). *Final de novela en Patagonia* is composed of several genres including poems, notes, transcriptions of dreams, chronicles, memoirs, and historical information. This structure presents the air of freedom and exploration that the novelistic genre allows. Giardinelli describes the text's organization as "quien camina al azar: en apariencia distraído, lo que encuentre me hará feliz, sobre todo si me abre los ojos aún más" [one who walks at random: in appearance distracted, what I find will make me happy, especially if it opens my eyes more] (111). Despite the levity of the structure, when it comes to environmental issues, the text always acquires a tone of admonition. For example, when the narrative voice speaks about a petroleum company that plans to construct a gas pipeline with the authorization of the government, he criticizes the apathy of the people and their lack of will to prevent the project. He thus confirms the assertion of one of the characters on the trip: "No es lo peor el deterioro sino el desgano" [The worst is not deterioration but apathy] (139). Giardinelli reads and interprets the history of his country in the landscape, as an open jail where "uno está en libertad pero no se puede mover" [one is in liberty but cannot move] (93) or long roads "como el latigazo de un dios desesperado" [like the whip of a desperate god] (57). Throughout his journey through the arid region of almost 800,000 square kilometers, the narrator is constantly accompanied by the evocations of books and movies and by the story of Victorio and Clelia, characters who appear in Giardinelli's previous novel *Imposible equilibrio*, which is also constructed of long journeys and presents an environmental theme.[33] Immensity and movement are the axes that carry the narrator of *Final de novela en Patagonia* throughout his multiple fortuitous meetings with lost cyclists, walkers, talkative inhabitants, and Nazis sheltered in the Patagonian quietude, but he always returns to the topic of the lack of use of the natural resources, such as the abundant wind energy in this territory, or the water. However, he concludes that to accomplish this, we need to "educar y pavimentar... y mantener un control férreo sobre ese enemigo feroz de la naturaleza que es el ser humano" [educate and pave... and to maintain a strong control over that fierce enemy of nature, the human being] (229). This travel narrative is told through the eyes of an Argentinean citizen who finds government apathy and ignorance a main cause in preventing national progress in this province. However, he does not advocate a civilization that destroys or violates the scenery of Patagonia but, rather, a sustainable development that also benefits the inhabitants of this region.

In sum, the enormity of the Argentinean territory invites an exploration of travel narrative and scenery. In contrast to the telluric novels of the early twentieth century that present humans in constant struggle with the forces of nature, in the contemporary novels analyzed above, the pronounced interest in reflecting nature's scenery appears as a possible reaction to or rejection of globalization, which attempts to erase the borders between countries and ignores the characteristics that define a nation and are a source of local pride. As Doris Sommer writes, "Pride of place may again be working, as it did in the nineteenth century, to safeguard a sense of personal and collective autonomy."[34] It is possible that we are witnessing a resurgence of regionalism as a response to the global modernization that attempts to group broadly and erase particularities rather than recognize the heterogeneity of Latin American histories. The city that for much of the nineteenth and twentieth centuries was the place of civilization and modernity is being replaced in a new generation of novels in which the landscape becomes a character that represents a region and is also the only patrimony of the inhabitants of these lands.

NOTES

1. Paz, "In Search of the Present."
2. Paz, *Itinerario*, 155.
3. Ibid, 158.
4. María Eugenia Petit-Breuilh's *Naturaleza y desastres en Hispanoamérica* is a well documented study of the destructive element of nature in Spanish America based on indigenous perspective, myths, legends and sacred places or "guacas." Juan Ramón Naranjo presents a similar perspective based on mystical nature in the *Popol Vuh* in his article "La ecología profunda y el Popol Vuh."

5. Güiraldes, *Don Segundo Sombra*, ed. Sara Parkinson de Saz. (Madrid: Cátedra, 2004), 30. All subsequent in-text page references to the novel are from this edition. Page references to English translations are from *Don Segundo Sombra: Shadows on the Pampas* translated by Harriet de Onís (New York: Farrar and Rinehart, 1935).

6. The Amazonian novel is part of this group of novels that is commonly represented as an "infierno verde" or green hell. See Marcone, "De retorno a lo natural: La serpiente de oro, la 'novela de la selva' y la crítica ecológica."

7. Darwin traveled on the Beagle for five years starting when he was 23 years old. One eventual result of this trip to the Southern Cone and the Galápagos Islands was *The Origin of the Species* published in 1859. For an insightful article about this topic see Dame Gillian Beer "Darwin in South America: Geology, Imagination and Encounter." The British have long had an interest in Argentina; in 1806 and 1807 British troops tried to conquer the region but were stopped by Argentinean troops. In other words, the British that had dominated the Spaniards were defeated by the colonies. See also "Metaphors and Metamorphosis: Naturalists in La Plata" by Fermín Rodríguez.

8. French, *Nature, Neo-Colonialism, and the Spanish American Regional Writers*, 22.

9. Brushwood, *La novela hispanoamericana del siglo XX*, 56–59.

10. Quoted in Blasi, "La escritura de *Don Segundo Sombra*," 469.

11. Parkinson de Saz, Introduction to Güiraldes, *Don Segundo Sombra*, 36.

12. Güiraldes had a strong fascination with painting; in her introduction to the novel, Parkinson writes that Ricardo "dibujaba escenas campestres y realizaba pinturas al óleo. En una ocasión su fervor artístico llegó a tal extremo que su mujer, Adelina del Carril, escribió al amigo de ambos, Valéry Larbaud, escritor francés, quejándose de que Güiraldes pintaba más que escribía" [he drew country scenes and oil paintings. On one occasion his artistic fervor was so extreme that his wife Adelina del Carril wrote to their mutual friend, Valéry Larbaud, a French writer, complaining that her husband painted more than wrote] (12).

13. Predmore, "The Function and Symbolism of Water Imagery in *Don Segundo*," 429.

14. Laffite, "La ecología humana en América Latina," 97.

15. Ward and Dubos, *Only One Earth*, 47.

16. Michelsen, "Don Segundo Sombra y la historia de la Argentina rural," 195–203.

17. Leo Pollmann (1987), in a study of narrative positions in the Argentinean novel, coincides with this premise and adds: "Todos nuestros autores de novelas de la pampa son porteños. Van hacia la pampa con su conciencia de porteños, de hombres altamente civilizados, cargados de expectativas literarias e idealistas" [All our novelists who write about the pampa are from the port. They go to the pampas with their conscience of very civilized city people, filled with literary and idealistic perspectives] (286). Therefore the *pampa* becomes a nostalgic promise of an alternative natural way of life. Another similar study is the one by Weiss (1958), which concludes that the man of the pampa "is bound to his surroundings in a wedlock that cannot be suddenly broken without fatal consequences" (152) and adds that "The Man of the Pampa must not give up his vigorous way of life, for it is in this life, not in commercial activity [...] that the health of the individual and the nation lies" (152).

18. Campbell, "Ecological Crisis and Faith in Progress," 451.

19. Fuentes, *El espejo enterrado: The Price of Freedom*.

20. Manzoni, "Migración y frontera en la escritura de Héctor Tizón," 30.

21. Rey, "La voz inconfundible del viajero," 2.

22. Tizón, *La luz de las crueles provincias* (Buenos Aires: Alfaguara, 1995), 25. All subsequent in-text page references to this novel are from this edition.

23. For a study about the subaltern representation in this novel see Bolikowska, "La representación de lo subalterno en *Luz de las crueles provincias* de Héctor Tizón."

24. See Benites, "Centro y periferia en *Luz de las crueles provincias* de Héctor Tizón."

25. Juan José Saer's most famous novel is *El entenado*, the story of a failed expedition to Argentina, led by Juan Díaz de Solís, who died in an ambush by native tribes. The only survivor, a cook, has to live with a cannibalistic tribe, the Colastiné. He recalls his experience many years later in Europe.

26. Saer, *Las nubes* (Argentina: Emecé, 2006), 20. All subsequent in-text page references to this novel are from this edition.

27. See María Inés Zaldívar's essay about Soriano's trip to Los Angeles, "El viaje *Triste, solitario y final* del periodista argentino Osvaldo Soriano a la ciudad de Los Angeles en Estados Unidos de Norteamérica."

28. Soriano, *Una sombra ya pronto serás* (Madrid: Mondadoria, 1990), 59.

29. Soriano, *La hora sin sombra* (Buenos Aires: Seix Barral, 1995), 16.

30. Ibid, 235.

31. For the theme of solitude in Soriano's work see Giacomimo's interview "Espacios de soledad, entrevista con Osvaldo Soriano." For the importance of exile in his work, see Devesa, "La imagen del extranjero y el exilio en los cuentos de Osvaldo Soriano."

32. Giardinelli, *Final de novela en Patagonia* (Barcelona: Grandes viajeros, 2000), 154. All subsequent in-text page references to this novel are from this edition.

33. The plot of this novel is an initiative by the Chaco authorities to import a pair of hippopotami so they can consume a plague of "camalotes" (water lily) that threaten the water resources contaminated by floods. But the animals are kidnapped by a group of friends who escape to the north of Argentina. The chase ends with the escape of the characters in a hot air balloon and their entry into fiction.

34. Sommer, *The Places of History: Regionalism Revisited in Latin America*, 1.

WORKS CITED

Beer, Dame Gillian. "Darwin in South America: Geology, Imagination and Encounter." In *Science and the Creative Imagination in Latin America*, edited by Evelyn Fishburn and Eduardo L. Ortiz, 13–23. London: Institute for the Study of the Americas, 2005.

Benites, María Jesús. "Centro y periferia en *Luz de las crueles provincias* de Héctor Tizón." *Revista interamericana de bibliografía* 49.1–2 (1999): 241–248.

Blasi, Alberto. "La escritura de *Don Segundo Sombra*." In *Actas del IX Congreso de la Asociación Internacional de Hispanistas, I & II*, edited by Sebastian Neumeister, 469–74. Frankfurt: Vervuert, 1989.

Bolikowska, Agnieszka. "La representación de lo subalterno en *Luz de las crueles provincias* de Héctor Tizón." *Rio de la Plata: Culturas* 29.1 (2004): 463–474.

Borges, Jorge Luis. *Fervor de Buenos Aires*. Buenos Aires: Emecé, 1925.

Campbell, Edwina S. "Ecological Crisis and Faith in Progress: Octavio Paz's 'Reflections on Contemporary History.'" *History of European Ideas* 12.4 (1990): 443–457.

Devesa, Patricia G. "La imagen del extranjero y el exilio en los cuentos de Osvaldo Soriano." In *II Coloquio Internacional de Literatura Comparada: 'El cuento,' I–II*, 181–85. Buenos Aires: Fundación María Teresa Maiorana, 1995.

French, Jennifer. *Nature, Neo-Colonialism, and the Spanish American Regional Writers*. Hanover, NH: Dartmouth College Press, 2005.

Fuentes, Carlos. *El espejo enterrado: The Price of Freedom*. Directed by Christopher Ralling. VHS. Public Media Video, 1991.

Galeano, Eduardo. *Las venas abiertas de América Latina*. Bogotá: Siglo XXI, 1977.

Giacomimo, Marta. "Espacios de soledad, entrevista con Osvaldo Soriano." *Quimera* 89.5 (1980): 45–57.

Giardinelli, Mempo. *Final de novela en Patagonia*. Barcelona: Grandes viajeros, 2000.

_____. *Imposible equilibrio*. Argentina: Planeta, 1995.

Güiraldes, Ricardo. *Don Segundo Sombra*. Edited with an introduction by Sara Parkinson de Saz. Madrid: Cátedra, 2004. Translated by Harriet de Onís as *Don Segundo Sombra: Shadows on the Pampas*. New York: Farrar and Rinehart, 1935.

Laffite, Christiane. "La ecología humana en América Latina, en la literatura y en los medios de comunicación." *Cuadernos Americanos* 73 (1999): 90–106.

Manzoni, Celina. "Migración y frontera en la escritura de Héctor Tizón." *Hispamérica: Revista de Literatura* 26.78 (December 1997): 29–37.

Marcone, Jorge. "De retorno a lo natural: La serpiente de oro, la 'novela de la selva' y la crítica ecológica." *Hispania* 81 (1998): 299–308.

Martini, Juan. *Puerto apache*. Buenos Aires: Sudamericana, 2002.

Michelsen, Jytte. "Don Segundo Sombra y la historia de la Argentina rural." *Río de la Plata: Culturas* 11–12 (1991): 195–203.

Naranjo, Juan Ramón. "La ecología profunda y el Popol Vuh." *Anales de literatura hispanoamericana* 33 (2004): 85–100.

Paz, Octavio. "In Search of the Present." Nobel Lecture. 1990. http://nobelprize.org/nobel_prizes/literature/laureates/1990/paz-lecture-s.html.

_____. *Itinerario*. Mexico City: Fondo de cultura económica, 1993.

Pettit-Breuilh Sepúlveda, María Eugenia. *Naturaleza y desastres en Hispanoamérica*. Madrid: Sílex, 2006.

Pollmann, Leo. "Situaciones y posiciones narrativas en la novela argentina. La pampa en *Amalia, Sin rumbo, El inglés de los guesos, Don Segundo Sombra y Zogobi*." *Río de la plata: Culturas* 4–6 (1987): 255–72.

Predmore, P. Michael. "The Function and Symbolism of Water Imagery in *Don Segundo Sombra*." *Hispania* 44.3 (1961): 428–30.

Rey, Pedro. "La voz inconfundible del viajero." *Suplemento Cultural La Nación*, April 25, 2004: 1–4.

Rodríguez, Fermín. "Metaphors and Metamorphosis: Naturalists in La Plata." *Journal of Latin American Cultural Studies* 16.3 (2007): 241–60.

Saer, Juan José. *El entenado*. Argentina: Planeta, 2005.

_____. *Las nubes*. Argentina: Emecé, 2006.

Sommer, Doris. *The Places of History: Regionalism Revisited in Latin America*. Durham: Duke University Press, 1999.

Soriano, Osvaldo. *La hora sin sombra*. Buenos Aires: Seix Barral, 1995.

_____. *Una sombra ya pronto serás*. Madrid: Mondadori, 1990.

Tizón, Héctor. *Luz de las crueles provincias*. Buenos Aires: Alfaguara, 1995.

Ward, Barbara and Renee Dubos. *Only One Earth: The Care and Maintenance of a Small Planet*. London: André Deutsch, 1972.

Weiss, G.H. "Argentina, the Ideal of Ricardo Güiraldes." *Hispania* 41.2 (1958): 149–53.

Zaldívar, María Inés. "El viaje *Triste, solitario y final* del periodista argentino Osvaldo Soriano a la ciudad de Los Ángeles en Estados Unidos de Norteamérica." *Hispamérica* 28.83 (1999): 17–31.

III. ECOLOGY AND THE SUBALTERN

Dissecting Environmental Racism: Redirecting the "Toxic" in Alicia Gaspar de Alba's *Desert Blood* and Helena María Viramontes's *Under the Feet of Jesus*

Dora Ramírez-Dhoore

Through Alicia Gaspar de Alba's *Desert Blood: The Juárez Murders* (2005) and Helena María Viramontes's *Under the Feet of Jesus* (1995), this essay proposes to connect the transnational perspectives of the material migrations of maquiladora and migrant workers to the greater contexts of social justice concerns. In particular, the socially constructed use of myth in literature is used to identify how the language of "difference" in the literary, media and governmental texts (such as NAFTA) influence environmental policy and action surrounding Latina/o communities. By doing this, the term "toxic" can be redirected towards those that instigate environmental racism on minority communities with their use of rhetoric.[1] Chicana authors Gaspar de Alba and Viramontes employ story as resistance to the societal structures that define and enclose immigrant and migrant workers in definitions of depravity — both social and ecological. These definitions are what have allowed for "three of every four toxic waste sites in the United States" to be "located in low-income communities of color" and for "75 percent of Latinas/os in southwestern states" to be "drinking pesticide-tainted water."[2] *Desert Blood* and *Under the Feet of Jesus* delve into sociological and ecological matters by connecting the labored female body to the social, physical, and metaphorical environments of the borderland. In particular, Gaspar de Alba's characters hone in on the potent environments and national mythologies that make up the U.S./Mexican border (most specifically El Paso, Texas and Ciudad Juárez, Chihuahua, Mexico), while Viramontes's characters embody the migrant farmworker experience within the confines of pesticides and poverty and whose locality is undetermined and can thus be placed in any rural U.S. location. By drawing on the construction of myth to contrast the rhetoric of difference, these authors are able to add to the larger ecological discussion and give voice to the concerns of the disenfranchised working Mexican and Mexican American populations.

The definition of "difference" is a socially constructed phenomenon that inserts wedges between populations in order to create dissimilarity among groups. Chicana theorist Chela Sandoval explicates how the rhetoric of difference works within this framework in *Methodology of the Oppressed*:

> It is through the figure [Roland] Barthes calls inoculation that consciousness surrounds, limits, and protects itself against invasion by difference. The inoculation works homeopathically; it provides cautious injections — in modest doses only — of dissimilarity (the affirmative action approach). The outcome is that, by incorporating a small, tidy portion of difference, the good citizen-subject does not have to accept its depth or enormity, and thus s/he can remain as is.[3]

Inoculation protects the subject-citizen from disruption. Disruption is what Gloria Anzaldúa understood as being, "exactly what propel(s) the soul to do its work: make soul, increase consciousness of itself."[4] Disruption is not normally well-received, but persuasion to maintain oneself "as is" or in-line with the dominant status quo is amenable to the general public, and this is what difference rests on in order to survive.

Habitually, in making the topic of the environment amenable to the general public, difference is engaged by the mainstream media when defining immigrant and migrant workers and their relationship to the environment and the corporate sector. In "Public Opinion, the Media, and Environmental Issues," Glenn Sussman, Byron W. Dayness and Jonathan P. West discuss the use of media in regards to its "agenda-setting function, the problem of science and risk as it relates to media coverage of the environment, and what factors might account for how journalists cover environmental issues, given the structure of and norms of mass media."[5] This focus on the media's influence in constructing public opinion about the environment brings to attention the fluidity of news and its passing nature. Sussman et al. write, "The mass media constitute an important means by which to disseminate public service messages about the environment. Corporate America has also used the media to respond to criticisms that it is more interested in making profits than in environmental protection."[6] In addition, Sussman et al. understand that the journalists covering stories concerning the environment may have only limited knowledge of the subject and are still required to educate the public and maintain the entertainment value found in television programming. These subjects all account for the way information is disseminated to the public and can be referred to in relation to how race and the environment are married in the media. These factors create a broad knowledge base for the general public.

When including race in this discussion, it is easy to find news entertainment channels that employ the rhetoric of difference as a mechanism for environmental change through fear and ignorance. The media's use of environmental racist rhetoric is made apparent when the term "illegal alien" is used to refer to undocumented workers in the United States without apology, especially in reference to the "invasion" of land — land that the general public is told they need to save from environmental degradation (which often alludes to immigration). By giving the ownership of land to the "American" population and referencing Mexican and Mexican Americans as invaders, the ecology of the subject becomes grounded in difference.

The rhetoric of difference then is a construct of power used to create national mythologies that define groups of people. In respect to Mexican and Mexican Americans, their connection to land has been portrayed in literature by the use of territory as a central character in Chicano political movements, often referencing the 1848 Treaty of Guadalupe-Hidalgo. In "From the Homeland to the Borderlands, the Reformation of Aztlán," Rafael Pérez-Torres references Aztlán as a place, not of reclamation, but of affirmation:

> Although the introduction to the fine critical collection of *Aztlán: Essays on the Chicano Homeland* argues for the primacy of Aztlán as the completion of Chicano identity, I suggest that the notion of Aztlán — highly influential in the articulation of Chicano identity — marks less the wholeness than the heterogeneity evident in the subject position Chicano. It is impossible, for example, to ignore the role that the Chicanos and Mexican migrant workers play within a diasporic history. One can no longer assert the wholeness of a Chicano subject when the very discourses that go into identity formation are themselves contradictory. It is illusory to deny the nomadic quality of the Chicano community, a community in flux that yet survives and, through survival, affirms its own self.[7]

I add that the Chicano community continues to wrestle with the collision of identity and place, and agree with Pérez-Torres in that the diasporic nature of migrant workers is privy to the economic, socio-political pressures of a global world — this is what sustains survival. Myth is an inroad to the sharing and collection of this knowledge. Thus, Aztlán maintains its primacy because it is continually being re-defined by those who embody the understanding and theorize about the land — historically, economically, and ecologically. Thus, how land is viewed through broken treaties, the toiling of the land after losing it to squatters or untranslated laws, and/or understanding land through a lens of violence focuses the attention to ecological democracy.

The term invader, illegal, or alien references an oppositional force which places the Mexican and Mexican American worker in the position of a foreign body. This position, then, sets up an interesting quandary where the way in which the land is defined depends on how the person is socially constructed. This is what makes the myth of Aztlán especially venerated. In line with Pérez-Torres, Devon G. Peña discusses the concept of "resistance identities" in "Identity, Place and Communities of Resistance." He focuses on La Sierra in Colorado and defines the community members' resistance identities as revolving "around the place-based memories and oppositional narratives of the multigenerational acequia farming families. 'Sin agua, no hay vida' is the local aphorism — 'Without water, there is no life.' Another *dicho* (aphorism) is 'La tierra es familia' or 'The land is family.' These are expressions of a land ethic and deeply felt 'memory maps' that farmers and other local residents have developed over generations."[8] Peña continues to explicate why he ties resistance to identity by explaining that this concept "extend(s) deep into local subaltern history [...] derives from lifelong experiences with racial discrimination and racist ideology [...] [and has] been used by locals to mobilize widespread opposition to development projects."[9] Consequently, there is an understanding that the "farmer's ethnoecological knowledge of the land, water, plants and animals remains an enduring source of moral authority" and that is why land is an integral part of a worker's identity and life.[10]

Identity is a theoretical concept, but one that has its roots in resistance and life experience. The migrant/maquiladora worker and the land they work are facing ecological degradation because of the intersections of the environment, ethics and economics in a transnational era. Thus, the "memory maps" Peña references are being altered. Viramontes and Gaspar de Alba ask what is the relationship between the identities of migrant and maquiladora laborers, the land and their work? In referencing the forgotten worker, this is an especially important question to ask in view of the invisibility of these two populations. This question is also complicated because the issue of immigration is tightly bound by the national mythologies of land ownership (Aztlán/U.S./ Mexico), the American dream, corporate America, and democracy. Within these mythologies lie the humanity of the workers and the health of the environment which is where story/myth finds its place within the novels this essay examines.

The need for ecological democracy arises when economics overpower a situation. I.G. Simmons elucidates the connections between economics, technology, and our environment by making it clear that technology has affected our ethics, and influences how we discuss what we can do with or to our environment in order to sustain the economy. In *Interpreting Nature: Cultural Constructions of the Environment*, Simmons elucidates:

A second major idea proposes that science shows us how we ought to behave, i.e. that ethical principles can be derived directly from the findings of natural science [...]. Science becomes a kind of fundamentalist knowledge and like any fundamentalism [it] needs questioning [...]. Economics is said to be neutral between ends and is thus simply a study of means and so is separated from Ethics. In everyday life, a market-oriented version of economics is now the most important mediator between humans and their environments: the question, 'is it economic?' is the significant one in most projects.[11]

Ethics are left unquestioned when the neutrality of economics is maintained. Consequently, myth becomes relevant in that it questions this neutrality outside of the scientific sector. Novels such as *Under the Feet of Jesus* and *Desert Blood* raise the question of whether the environmental degradation of the Mexican and Mexican American worker and the land they work on is economic or racial — and with what consequences. Also inherently important in this discussion are Laura Pulido's ideas from "Ecological Legitimacy and Cultural Essentialism," where she ties cultural essentialism to the cause of some environmental practices. She writes:

Cultural essentialism denies or obfuscates the whole problem of social or historical agency, obscuring dominant power dynamics such as the struggles between rich and poor landowners and tenants, thus reifying cultural differences. Instead of examining how and why various constellations of wealth and power result in different environmental practices, cultural essentialism tends to view variations in environmental practices as originating in 'natural' ethnic or cultural differences.[12]

An example she gives is that of the racism inherent in laying blame on the inhabitants of the Chama Valley in New Mexico for the overgrazing of the area, while exonerating the "Anglos and capitalism for the region's deep poverty."[13] She makes note of the historically polarized racial and economic past of that area, illustrating how the Hispano population's use of resources and over-grazing of the area should not be essentialized through a cultural lens. This is inline with blaming the migrant/maquiladora workers in *Desert Blood* or *Under the Feet of Jesus* for their lack of education regarding their own health and/or job security. Viramontes's protagonist illustrates this polarization when she experiences racial discrimination at the health clinic. Estrella's anger at the nurse's essentialist definition of her is a pivotal moment in the text, illustrating the effects of everyday cultural essentialism. Viramontes writes, "Estrella stared at the nurse an extra second. How easily [the nurse] put herself in a position to judge."[14] Then, Estrella reads and stares at the "memory map" of Perfecto's tired face. "The wrinkles on his face etched deeper with the sweat and soil and jagged sun" and her mother's map of "resentfulness, at whom, what, she didn't know" (147). This moment illustrates the connection between the "memory maps" and Estrella's and Alejo's (her friend and fellow farmworker whose exposure to pesticides is central to the narrative) futures which are clearly drawn by the inherent racism of the healthcare system and its long history with fieldworkers in the United States. Estrella is able to break through the nurse's cultural essentialism when she slams a crowbar down on the desk. What is taken to task in this moment is the illusion of the dutiful and ignorant farm worker. The nurse's tears, though, can either reinforce the reader's essentialism or raise awareness of the relationships difference creates, because as Estrella states, "They make you that way, she sighed with resignation. She tried to understand what happened herself. You talk and talk and talk to them and they ignore you. But you pick up a crowbar and break the pictures of their children, and all of a sudden they listen real fast" (151).

Consequently, modifying myths within a larger national imagination that incorporates cultural essentialism gives literary authors access to the realm of difference and to disrupt it with story. Fiction, particularly myth, presents Viramontes and Gaspar de Alba a forum to work with and tell a story. Myth is constructed through the lens of national memory, thus connecting material knowledge with nature. To make this connection, I reference Simmons who makes a case for the possibility of a "different type of 'knowing' altogether," as a way to move beyond language, which "may, it seems, impose a reality rather than simply attach labels to what is 'there.'"[15] Simmons references the Garden of Eden in Genesis (pastoralism and agriculture) to illustrate that moving beyond language involves myth.[16]

In order to understand this through the way environmental degradation is explained in Latino/a mythology—it is important to focus on the overarching myth of La Llorona found in *Desert Blood* and in *Under the Feet of Jesus* (including Viramontes's extension of this myth, the harelip boy). Ray John De Aragon's website, "The Legend of La Llorona," defines this archetype: "In ancient American Indian mythology one can find accounts of a weeping woman of death in search of her loved ones. The Aztecs themselves related the story of Ciuacoatl, a weeping goddess, in their ancient myths. She would capture infants from their cradles, and after killing them would roam the streets of Tenochtitlán at night with a mournful wail, foreshadowing wars and misery."[17] In *Massacre of the Dreamers*, Ana Castillo references the nationalist version of the myth which "prefers to see her as an Indian woman who is lamenting over the lost race after the Conquest. In fact, as the snake goddess, Cihuacóatl, she appeared as the sixth omen predicting the fall of the Empire of Tenochtitlán when she was heard wailing in the night, 'O my children, you are lost; where shall I hide you?'"[18] Largely, La Llorona references the colonization of the indigenous because the myth is a reminder that the underclass or oppressed class exists. Ana María Carbonell describes La Llorona as having descended from Cihuacóatl, the patron of midwives, who descended from Coatlicue. She writes, "Coatlicue brings suffering to the forefront of consciousness, providing a clearer vision as to whom or what to confront."[19] *Under the Feet of Jesus* and *Desert Blood*, then, articulate an empowered intellectual metaphor of migration by recuperating the concept for the scholarly purpose of insinuating an epistemological shift from the place of understanding hegemonic, white rhetoric as normative to understanding and empowering multiple sites for Chicana/o rhetorical agency. La Llorona's wail and inaccessible voice connects colonization to the individual. Estrella's insistence that you "talk and talk and talk" (151) but it is the crowbar they listen to suggests how it is that La Llorona foreshadows wars and misery.

In many ways, myth shifts or migrates the hegemonic meaning of rhetoric to give meaning to socio-economic events that affect the Latino population — even when the oppressed group does not have a consistent political voice. Simmons writes:

> Myths about the environment may be one of the inputs to our construction of it, whether at an individual level or in the shape of a national (or indeed transnational) ideology. The pervasive idea of the frontier rolling forward into the wilderness is still alive in North America, for example, in the land use policies for 'wilderness areas' or in the designation of outer space as the 'high frontier' during the Kennedy administration.[20]

Other examples Simmons employs juxtapose people who live in the country or outback versus the city, as well as the way these either/or ideas or caricatures resonate in our world-views and political and "environmental meanings."[21] Thus, in Gaspar de Alba and Viramontes's works, written characters are formulated with national mythological archetypes in mind as a method of examining these world views.

In particular, *Desert Blood*'s framework connects the population and the landscape while in contrast also repeatedly referencing la Llorona — which alludes to the forgotten worker disconnected from the landscape and references the oppositional structure of city/wealth/life or desert/poverty/death. One example comes from Gaspar de Alba's focus on the paradox created by contrasting world views and those constructed by the rhetoric of difference. She writes, "At the top of the bridge, sitting between the two flags, was one of Ivon's favorite views of downtown El Paso: tall bank buildings against the slate gray mountains and a bluebonnet sky. She loved this place. She hated this place. Always, the same contradictions."[22] The character's relationship to the landscape of the city is revealed when it is juxtaposed to the barren desert landscape of Juárez. This relationship is imbedded in the text and represents the way characters perceive themselves and others and the way they interact with one another in the story. Ivon's reasons for leaving El Paso are revealed in her thoughts:

> "I've always said that people lie to themselves in this town," Ivon said. That's one of the things that had driven her away. People like to pretend they can cover the sun with one finger, while the truth is shining all over the place. People forget things in El Paso [...]. Denial is not a river in Egypt, her father used to say. But nobody gets it. Nobody gets anything in El Paso. That's why Ivon had it in mind to take her little sister away from this lithium-loaded city where nothing and nobody ever changed [31].

The setting also influences the duality of the characters' decisions to disconnect themselves from the landscape emotionally (while sensing their strong connection to the landscape), thus reflecting how the population is equated to the landscape's degradation.

Gaspar de Alba considers the socio-ecological matters of NAFTA and the U.S./Mexican border, and gives voice to the protagonist Ivon, who faces the disappearance of her sister, as a possible victim of the Ciudad Juárez murders. The events in this text occur on the Mexican border and focus on how difference in mainstream rhetoric has defined the general public's understanding of the murders and the environmental degradation happening along both sides of the border. As a writer and researcher working on her dissertation, Ivon weaves her way through a labyrinth of information, trying to decipher how knowledge of these murders is presented to the public in the Juárez/El Paso region and the rest of the United States. By bringing the media aspect into her novel, Gaspar de Alba elucidates how the rhetoric of difference allows for the disassociation from and ignoring of a large group of oppressed women by the general public.

In *Desert Blood*, Ivon becomes conscious of the murders of hundreds of Mexican women in Juárez, Mexico during her visit to El Paso. During Ivon's research of the maquiladora murders, she encounters a website, titled *Borderlines*, which provides

> typical tourist information on the region, but also promote[s] prostitution by informing the potential and obvious male tourists that [...] Every week hundreds of young Mexican girls arrive in Juárez from all over Mexico. Most of these young ladies are looking for work that will be a primary source of income for their families back home. While many will begin their careers in one of the various maquiladora factories in the area, often they end up in the many bars and brothels [117].

Women workers are often defined as illegal aliens or cheap, expendable, surplus labor. These types of definitions are made global through the use of the internet and carry various debasing meanings. Ivon continues her web search and discovers "a link called Those Sexy Latin Ladies [...]. Pictures of young women in bikinis and high heels illustrated the page, and the words Prostitution is legal here and You will not find a place with more beautiful, available, hot-blooded young ladies flashed in yellow letters" (117). These sexual references allude to the historical consequences La Llorona suffered for having relations with a Spaniard and because of the death of her children. Difference defines these women as their bodies are used purely for the pleasure of the tourist society. Ivon's response to this rhetoric is: "'Shit,' she said aloud, 'No wonder there's so many freaks here. They're selling women online'" (117). It's an honest response that deserves attention as it is situated in the realities of the border, especially after the creation of NAFTA.

For those women who work in the maquiladoras created by NAFTA, labor conditions are below the standards set by this same policy. In *The Children of NAFTA,* journalist David Bacon interviews Rosario Acosta, mother of one of the missing women and a leader in Nuestras Hijas de Regreso a Casa. Her words illustrate the state of the border at present: "It has to do with the opening of the big door, which is our border to the U.S., in order to allow big multinationals — more than four hundred of them to settle in our city [...]. We gave them a permit to do absolutely everything. They don't guarantee the most elementary security measures to their female workers who commute back and forth from their homes."[23] Bacon continues by adding that Acosta "also cites poverty and the lack of elementary social services, such as running water and electricity in their homes."[24] Both agree that because these women are positioned in poverty and lack the most basic effects, it makes them blind to their rights. The women in *Desert Blood* face these hardships, including being kidnapped, raped, mutilated, dismembered, used as pure labor, and have their reproductive capabilities controlled by the maquiladora company. In addition to what is occurring to these women, Gaspar de Alba also examines why and how these atrocities are being perpetuated along the border to women who are powerless against small and large corporate and government systems. Thematically, powerlessness is tied to corporations with Gaspar de Alba's reference to the pennies and nickels placed in the dead women's bodies by the murderers — pennies for the Mexican women and nickels for the American women. The cost of life is differentiated by the police officers (in the novel) working along the border and responsible for the murders.

In tying the novel to the reality it mirrors, female workers in the United States and on the border face conditions similar to Third World individuals. Edna Acosta-Belén and Christine E. Bose explicate, "The concerns of third-world feminists vary considerably and are not always obvious to those of us in core countries. For peasant, poor, and working class women, the primary concern is survival: escaping war and violence or having ready access to shelter, food, and pot-able water for their families."[25] These are transnational concerns that transgress boundaries, and it is becoming more and more apparent as statistics continue to surface that reflect working and living conditions in the border region that are significantly below poverty level and national standards. Devon G. Peña's research *Mexican Americans and the Environment* furthers this knowledge and reveals that "Rates for infectious and chronic diseases, malnutrition, and infant and maternal mortality by far exceed U.S. averages and are closer to patterns in Third World nations. The EPA receives at least 300,000 reports of pesticide poisoning each year, far less than the actual number."[26] These conditions are compounded by rural poverty, sub-standard housing, malnutrition, child labor, living conditions, health hazards, and economic pay.[27] Peña pushes for the "Environmental justice movement (EJM) activists [to] illustrate the significance of the direct lived experience of poverty, discrimination, and violence at the hands of the dominant white power structure."[28] He writes, "I once heard a maquiladora worker in Juárez explain that the managers 'kill us in wretched factories.' She was referring to the hundreds of workers killed every year in factories on both sides of the border. Occupational segregation by race and gender affects workers' experiences with workplace environmental risks."[29] His research shows that Mexican Americans are disproportionately concentrated in occupations that "pose greater risks of work-related injuries, unsafe working conditions, and environmental hazards."[30]

The lack of the regulation of labor laws defines the maquiladora workers in *Desert Blood* by focusing on the actual lived connections these women face with environmental dangers and the dangers of the dominant societal structures that surround them. The rhetoric of difference which allows for this style of environmental and social degradation is a focus in Chicana literature. A passage from Deborah Owen Moore's, "Art, Imagination, and Violence: An interview with Helena María Viramontes" can move ideas to a more complex understanding by furthering our understanding of Chela Sandoval's idea of "love as an hermeneutic," the connection to La Llorona's need to wail for her children in a conquered place, and Ivon's striving to move out of her privilege and find empathy for the poverty-stricken people of Juárez. Viramontes states:

> My signature story, "The Moths" was inspired by a photograph taken in 1971 by W. Eugene Smith for *Life Magazine*, I believe, and I think the title of it is "Minamata." Like all wonderful photographs, this one has a story to tell. It was taken to document a village struggle against mercury pollution that caused a number of birth defects. In this black and white photograph, a Japanese mother bathes her nineteen year-old child. I was overpowered by the love I saw between this mother and her severely deformed daughter. While her child looks into

space with a certain expression of contentment, the mother sees her with such love and compassion as she's holding her. It moved me to see such strength of bonding, of love and trust between the two. It's a very powerful photograph. I was fascinated with that photograph and just wanted to write about that love, that wonderful, powerful, infinite beautiful love — existing even in the worst of circumstances.[31]

The love found in this photograph as well as in Gaspar de Alba's novel, illustrates the inability discourse has to fully rationalize lived realities; it lives within the Coatlicue state, a state which represents duality and the contradictory in life,[32] while situating itself within the very real consequences of ecological and sociological issues. This photograph does not dismiss the various forms of violence imposed on people, or the ecological degradation at work, but what Viramontes alludes to in this pictorial representation is how to survive oppressions outside of the dualistic paradigm that is often offered. Viramontes's strength against oppression is present in this passage. Gaspar de Alba draws on such empathy when Ivon struggles with the idea of adopting the unborn child of Cecilia, a young poverty-stricken mother living in Juárez.

As globalization makes immigrant and migrant labor necessary, the price paid are intimate relationships between the self and the environment, the self and others, and within one's self. Gaspar de Alba examines how transnational globalization physically assaults the psychological, political, and socio-ecological self when she begins the novel with the murder of Cecilia, a young maquiladora worker and her unborn child, whom Ivon was to adopt. Unfortunately, both the child and mother are mysteriously killed, and like many of the other women in the text, they disappear without anyone's knowledge or concern. The only reason anyone even knows of her murder is because her child was to be adopted by Ivon. Without this connection, her murder would have gone unnoticed. This murder continues to haunt Ivon throughout the narrative because of her connection to the child and these other reasons. Ivon's dream of the unborn child saying "Mapi, come supervise me in the kid's section" (340) haunts her with the knowledge that the violence in the area is only justified because poverty and those that fall within that category are criminalized. This text clearly defines violence as social control, thus drawing on the use of La Llorona's presence to foreshadow wars and misery.

Ivon then looks for another child to adopt, and finds Jorgito, a young boy who suffers from physical and social abuse by his grandmother and whose mother, Elsa, was artificially inseminated by "The Egyptian," or Dr. Amen — the character arrested for conducting experiments on women in the maquiladoras for his own profit. The struggle with empathy is apparent in the text as Ivon works through the "what ifs" or the socially acceptable definitions of what a child should look like or be like at the point of conception or adoption. La Llorona makes an appearance in this section as the young pregnant women of Juárez look towards women in the United States, across the river, to adopt their children. These women must sacrifice their children in order to survive in the world of their oppressor. When Elsa tells Ximena and Ivon who it was that artificially inseminated her at the factory, "Elsa start(s) to cry again. Deep sobs that shook the bed" (92). She fears that Jorgito would not be adopted if it were known how he was conceived. La Llorona's inability to voice her experience is referenced in this moment, as well as creating a crossroads where two sides must comprehend one another.

Elsa's fear is not unfounded. The idea of perfection *is* in Ivon's mind, when she questions her sister: "'Is he okay?' Ivon asked Ximena. 'I mean, there's nothing wrong with him, is there? His mother's not like a big boozer or an addict, right?'" (82). Ivon visits Jorgito's home and finds an abusive grandmother and the mother, Elsa, who was artificially inseminated at the maquiladora by the Egyptian Hassan and is dying from cancer. Elsa recalls, "They took my temperature in my mouth and ... you know ... back there. And then he put something else inside me, something different. I don't know what it was, but it was sharp, almost like a needle. It hurt so bad, I could feel myself bleeding. And then he told me I had to lie with my legs up for fifteen minutes. The nurse watched me to make sure I didn't put my legs down" (91). This knowledge puts the focus on the environmental and social consequences of economic racism on the child, Jorgito. Much like the children drowned in the river by the experiences of La Llorona, the child once again embodies the consequences. Ivon argues with her sister Ximena about adopting a child that "came from the sperm of a pervert and possible serial killer" (91). The mother, Elsa, becomes the victim of what Ximena understands as the normal treatment of maquiladora workers. Ximena explicates:

> "Listen, you have no idea the kinds of things they do to women at some of those maquilas. They give them birth control shots, they make them show their sanitary napkins every month, they pass around amphetamines to speed up their productivity. Hell, they've even got Planned Parenthood coming over to insert Norplant, which basically sterilizes the women for months. What's to prevent some sick fuck from raping them during a so-called pregnancy test?" [90].

In this case, the mother and child are the victims of economic gains set forth by NAFTA as globalization disintegrates intimate relationships between individuals and as society continues to maintain a consumerist stronghold on the imagination.

Language also plays a role in this relationship as Ivon turns her fears into action when at the beginning of the novel Cecilia and her unborn child are murdered, and then when her own younger sister, Irene is kidnapped. Ivon examines the laws governing the maquiladoras, including NAFTA, and represents them as a driving force in that landscape. She also makes it obvious that the maquiladoras deliberately refrain from sharing this knowledge with the workers. This is symbolized by the environmental degradation in the text and by making La Llorona's river too dark and polluted to even make the discovery of her children possible. Before her disappearance, Irene was last seen and reported as swimming in a river next to a party house, so Ivon visits that area. "The river stunk of sewer. Beer cans and human feces floated in the black water. 'I can't believe Irene was swimming in this shit. There is actual shit here. Look at this!'" (141) Later, Ivon encounters the maquiladoras's backyard where she finds a sign reading, "To promote and expand world trade and tourism" (269). She continues:

> The putrid stench of petroleum, wafted into the car's air vents. She noticed the yellow warning signs posted at 10-yard intervals up and down the park that prohibited digging in the ground or building fires, a skull-and-bones image to warn off those who couldn't read that this verdant oasis was not a safe place for picnics and barbeques. She knew where she was now. On the other side of the river, just past midtown El Paso, sprawled the Chevron Oil Refinery. The stench was emanating out of the ground of this idyllic community constructed between Chevron and Pemex back in the days of the OPEC crisis. Made sense that this place was called the Elysian Fields, the name in Greek mythology for heaven, which was just another place for the dead [270].

At this point, she hears the voice of the baby again, representing the fears of a community. The fears of the effects of pesticides are justified and realistic. Hearkening back to Upton Sinclair's vision of the labor class as animals in his socialist muckraking novel *The Jungle*, *Desert Blood* offers the words of Paula Del Río, a guest on Rubí Reyna's show *Mujeres sin fronteras*:

> The majority of the victims are very poor women from villages and ranchos in the interior. They are also very young women, hired with false papers. In a society in which women are second-class citizens and in which the poor are no better than animals, a society where cows and cars are worth more than the lives of women, we are talking about the complete devaluation of the feminine gender, as well as the utter depreciation of the female laboring class [323].

Paula Del Río continues by stating that "Were these crimes happening to men [...] we would already know the answers to the questions 'Who is Killing the Women of Juárez?'" (323). The women in *Desert Blood* understand that their lives are defined by a stronger force they cannot see or understand. Regardless of class or what side of the border they live on, it is ruled by frustration, silence, anger, and fear. NAFTA and the lack of enforcement of the laws stated in the policy rule the lives of these women and the rivers they roam.

Patrick Novotny encourages a move towards environmental social justice as a way to raise public awareness and education. In "Popular Epidemiology and the Struggle for Community Health in the Environmental Justice Movement" he points to the importance of clearly illustrating "the interconnections among environmental destruction, occupational hazards, racial and socioeconomic inequities, access to health care, and medical research appropriate to the diagnosis and treatment of health problems in communities impacted by environmentally hazardous facilities."[33] The photograph Viramontes describes of the woman and her child and Gaspar de Alba's novel focus on the various forms of violence imposed on people and the ecological degradation at work. Viramontes continues to draw on such moments in her novel, *Under the Feet of Jesus*, and focuses on the love between Petra (the mother), the child growing in her belly, Estrella (her daughter of 14 years), Perfecto (her partner), and Alejo (a friend of the family who is victim to pesticide poisoning). Viramontes focuses on the actual lived connections migrant workers face with the dangers of the earth and dominant societal structures that surround them.

I also draw on the idea of the way La Llorona represents the health of our intimate relationships, including how an individual perceives themselves and others, and the environment. Are children the cost of these perceptions? Ester R. Shapiro connects globalization to the lack of intimate relationships between individuals in "Because Words Are Not Enough: Latina Re-Visionings of Transnational Collaborations Using Health Promotion for Gender Justice and Social Change," when she states, "I also discovered how as immigrants we are encouraged to drink the U.S. Milk of Amnesia [Tropicana 2000] and forsake our collective responsibilities as engaged citizens fighting for justice; as immigrants this was the price of admission to a fragmenting, isolating consumer culture in which everything is for sale including our intimate relationships."[34]

Viramontes understands how transnational globalization assaults sociological and ecological matters when she records, "Petra thought of the lima bean in her, the bean floating in the night of her belly, bursting a root with each breath. Would the child be born without a mouth, would the poisons of the fields harden in its tiny little veins?" (125). The thought of giving birth to a deformed child haunts Petra throughout her pregnancy. Language plays a role in this relationship as Petra turns her fears into a story to teach her daughter Estrella about reproduction, sexuality, and the realities of their work and daily existence. In one scene, Estrella shares a bottle of cola with Alejo and quickly realizes her attraction to him. In this moment Estrella recalls that,

> The mother had yelled No and Estrella should have been safely tucked away like the other women of the camp because the moon and earth and sun's alignment was a powerful thing. Unborn children lurking in their bodies were in danger of having their lips bitten just like the hare on the moon if nothing was done to

protect them. Is that what you want, the mother yelled, a child born sin labios? Without a mouth? [69].

In this seemingly innocent scene of teenage infatuation, intimate relationships are compromised as the pesticides used to spray the fields become a prominent character in the novel. Petra's fears are taught to her daughter. The "harelip" child appears throughout the novel, haunting the characters by reminding them of their environmental surroundings.

Estrella understands her mother's warning in a variety of ways. Petra senses that Estrella is working through the dangers lurking in the world and finds that they are interconnected through story. In a pivotal scene in the novel, Estrella runs from the baseball field sensing that someone is after her. When Petra asks her daughter, "¿Qué diablos te' ta pasando?" and "¿Por qué corres?" her response is that she is "Gonna teach someone a lesson" and "Someone's trying to get me" (60–61). Petra's interpretation of this moment is illuminating when she replies, "It's La Migra" (61), and follows her statement with "Yo ya no voy a corer. No puedo más [...] No sense telling La Migra you've lived here all your life, the mother continued [...] Do we carry proof around like belly buttons?" (62). Petra connects Estrella's fears to her lived reality of encounters with Immigration and Naturalization Services. She states:

> Don't run scared. You stay there and look them in the eye. Don't let them make you feel you did a crime for picking the vegetables they'll be eating for dinner. If they stop you, if they try to pull you into the green vans, you tell them the birth certificates are under the feet of Jesus, just tell them [...] The mother raised her voice [...] — Tell them que tienes una madre aquí. You are not an orphan, and she pointed a red finger to the earth, Aquí [63].

Estrella hears her mother's message, but also senses that "Something's out there" (62). Petra tells her, "Ya cállate before you spook the kids," knowing that *La Migra* is not the only danger affecting her family (62). The myth of La Llorona is used here to represent and teach the caution migrant families have towards government-associated authorities and those in power in general. It is the scene that follows this one which defines how family, community, and migration intersect for these farm workers from el Valle del Río Grande. Viramontes describes familial disconnections, community connections, and draws on pesticides as a character in the novel.

The effects of pesticides are seen in this novel, and in addition to the findings of *Toxic Wastes and Race* referred to at the beginning of this essay, Peña understands that, "Compared to the older hydrocarbon pesticides, however, organophosphates are hundreds or even thousands of times more acutely toxic at the point of production. What may be safer for consumers is more dangerous to farmworkers and wildlife who face immediate exposure in the fields."[35] Once again, the landscape is degraded and La Llorona is unable to see through her environment.

Intimate relationships, specifically those of mother and child, are again compromised when Viramontes introduces pesticides as a character. The harelip boy is referenced when Petra and Perfecto realize "there was no wind today" and "the silence of the birds in the quiet trees" made it known that "the plane had stopped its fumigation" (75). This was their forewarning because the fumigation was not supposed to occur for another week. But this knowledge is not shared with the workers. The harelip boy reminds Perfecto that this knowledge has never been shared with workers and that pesticides, miscommunication, and unspoken laws have always been a part of that landscape. Perfecto's desire to tear down the barn is pushed by his knowledge that some-one died there — that someone being the harelip boy. This is the reason "peo-ple stay away" (75). His need to tear the barn down is also economically driven, giving him the means to return home before the tumor "lodged under the muscle of Perfecto's heart and getting larger with every passing day" ended his life. Viramontes writes, "Perfecto lived a travesty of laws. He knew noth-ing of their source but it seemed his very existence contradicted the laws of others, so that everything he did like eat and sleep and work and love was prohibited" (83). Perfecto reads the world by using the memory maps that offer him his knowledge.

Viramontes illustrates the severity of the disconnection between the laws Perfecto doesn't understand and the community of people and the living envi-ronment that feed this country. Alongside Perfecto, who adopted Petra's fam-ily as his own, the reader is given the young character of Alejo, who works in the U.S., sends his money to his grandmother, and is alone except when he works alongside his cousin Gumecindo, who finds his family in the farm-working community. Alejo's poisoning and hospitalization epitomize how dualistic thinking allows for subjugation. Viramontes writes, "Alejo's head spun and he shut his stinging eyes tighter to regain balance. But a hole ripped in his stomach like a match to paper, spreading into a deeper and bigger black hole that wanted to swallow him completely. He knew he would vomit, then the sheet of his skin absorbed the chemical and his whole body began to cramp from the shrinking pull of his skin squeezing against his bones" (77). When Estrella and Perfecto attempt to get medical care for Alejo, they visit a doctor's office, where they pay $9.07 to be told that they need to go a hos-pital. Estrella's anger wells up when she doesn't understand how a person could take someone's last penny just to tell them they will die without med-ical care. When she uses violence to make her voice heard, Alejo meekly protests by saying, "No. No. No.... Can't you see, they want us to act like that?" Estrella replies, "Can't you see they want to take your heart?" (153). Slowly, their hearts are taken by the consumer-driven necessity for pesticide spraying, the medical system, and the authorities who as Perfecto recalls "would pull their hearts inside out like empty pockets" to check for residency (163). After they leave Alejo at the hospital as a "John Doe" so he can get the medical attention he deserves, Estrella thanks Perfecto for taking them to the hospital. Viramontes writes, Perfecto "had given this country his all, and in this land that used his bones for kindling, in this land that never once in the thirty years he lived and worked, never once said thank you, this young woman who could be his granddaughter had said the words with such honest gratitude, he was struck by how deeply these words touched him" (155).

The emergency room scene is two-fold. The first issue represents the disintegration of family structures in the migrant farmworking community. Although the ties within the community are forced to be strong, the immediate family structure is severely strained. Whether it is because of distance from relatives or economic depravity, the strains on the familial structure suffer. In addition, there are also great "disparities in health mortality for low-income persons and persons of color," which have to "do with the fact that there is little in the way of early detection or preventative screening for these problems [...] Many times, these groups also tend to rely on emergency medical services or inadequate health facilities and public hospitals."[36] It is unfortunate to see the absence of the mother figure for Alejo as well as the undue stress Petra must endure at times when health is concerned.

The second issue is the use of the maternal figure in representing the health of the community. Viramontes draws on the notion of maternal responsibility in this scene. Carbonell notices that, "Within folkloric literature on the La Llorona legend, La Llorona emerges as both a figure of maternal betrayal and maternal resistance."[37] She goes on to describe "ethnographic accounts dating back to the colonial period," where "La Llorona and her antecedent, Cihuacóatl, repeatedly emerge as dangerous and destructive figures."[38] Carbonell also moves into another important avenue of interpretation for the figure of La Llorona. She writes:

> In these Llorona tales of resistance, maternal identity resembles feminist psychoanalytic definitions of the female "self-in-relation," an *interdependent* versus a *dependent* or *independent* self. Yet, whereas the female self's community consists of other interdependent adults, the "community" to which the maternal self belongs is comprised of dependent children. Therefore, the maternal self is responsible for defending her own welfare as well as that of her children. Consequently, La Llorona's actions in these tales of resistance constitute a necessary, if extreme, response to domination that allows her to continue to enact her motherlove — to protect and nurture *both* herself and her children.[39]

Thus, within the various interpretations of the myth of La Llorona, the children's survival is dependent on the mother's response to subjugation/oppression. This essay has laid out some of the complexities of the decisions farmworkers and maquiladora workers have to make in order to survive a daily existence. The strategies involved in making these decisions are complicated as well; therefore, pinpointing why certain decisions are made by the female characters in these texts and why certain beliefs are held is even more difficult. Basic to these texts is the tenet that the choices a mother makes regarding her children are based on the community's trust of the societal structures that surround them.

In Laura Pulido's discussion of the UFWOC's pursuit of unionization, she explains, "Some have suggested that the farmworkers' pesticide struggle is not an environmental issue but an economic struggle with an environmental component."[40] Is it a struggle within a movement, or with identity and quality of life? This is where the "knowledge" of the subaltern group is questioned. Is it a movement about environmental justice or is it more specifically essentializing a large group of people and placing responsibility on the individual's capability to survive a difficult life? Relevant to both of the examples I have discussed above (Petra's understanding that she is pregnant and working with pesticides and her mistrust of *La Migra*, and Perfecto's knowledge that the U.S. government keeps information from the workers), is the level of mistrust migrant farm workers have of governmental authority in the United States.

Political scientists María L. Chávez, Brian Wampler, and Ross E. Burkart's study, "Left Out: Trust and Social Capital Among Migrant Seasonal Farmworkers," illustrates that migrant seasonal farm workers "are less trusting of others than Hispanics nationally; this is a significant finding because MSFWs of today will likely be the 'Mexican Americans,' or Hispanic citizens and voters of tomorrow [...] With the increase in immigration, especially of Mexicans, we may be creating a rural underclass that is not connected to American society."[41] Social capital is an avenue in which to gain trust for a system and this is not present in the communities of migrant farmworkers or maquiladora workers on the border. Towards the end of Viramontes's novel, we see the mother, Petra, embracing "Estrella so firmly, Estrella felt as if the mother was trying to hide her back in her body" (171). The rhetoric of difference causes mistrust of governmental systems and this is present at a very basic level in *Under the Feet of Jesus* and *Desert Blood*. In addition, these issues of mistrust fall upon the child. Petra's only recourse to the rhetoric of difference is her understanding of her ever-present need to protect her children from that of the experience of the harelip boy.

The need to engulf the child can be explained through Chela Sandoval's discussion of the idea that excess and madness lead to truth and strength, and it is through this process that a Coatlicue state can be achieved.[42] Petra's fear, parental control, and love — as well as Ivon's fear, anger, and silence fall into this idea, and this is also where love is considered — beyond the physical — beyond language, which often adheres to the rhetoric of difference. This process is understood by examining the characters in *Under the Feet of Jesus* and *Desert Blood* as these authors draw on the strength of women who remain powerless but whose experiences reflect a large population on the border and in the interior. In many ways, the rhetoric that defines the Mexico/U.S. border defines these women regardless of and because of their physical location.

In conclusion, by discussing how discourse can move beyond power structures, binaries, and dualisms in interpreting texts, the environment that United States social structures create must also be questioned. Simmons asks what surroundings need to be changed if humanity is to be realized.[43] In light of current immigration policies, it is easy to understand how Third World workers and the land itself are encased in globalization movements of which they are defined by the rhetoric of difference. Thus, landscape defines groups of people as well as societal attitudes towards these populations. This essay moves toward an understanding of language and myth as discourse that blurs oppositional discourse and the rhetoric of difference and moves towards a coalitional consciousness that values human dignity and rights above cultural essentialism. The rhetoric of difference creates and at times leads to toxic action for populations that are anti-immigrant; but as the rhetoric shifts it will lead to the rhetoric of social change for those who write to share knowledge otherwise hidden.

NOTES

1. Lawrence Buell discusses and gives definition to the term "toxic discourse" in chapter 1 of *Writing for an Endangered World*, 30–54.
2. Peña, "Identity, Place and Communities of Resistance," 141.
3. Sandoval, *Methodology of the Oppressed*, 119.
4. Anzaldúa, *Borderlands/La Frontera*, 46.
5. Sussman, Daynes, and West, "Public Opinion, the Media, and Environmental Issues," 69.
6. *Ibid.*, 81.
7. Pérez-Torres, "From the Homeland to the Borderlands, the Reformation of Aztlán," 61.
8. Peña, "Identity, Place and Communities of Resistance," 153. He describes memory maps as local people who "have constructed their positions of resistance through the recollection of multigenerational narratives of place [...] Resistance identities extend deep into local subaltern history."
9. *Ibid.*
10. *Ibid.*
11. Simmons, *Interpreting Nature*, 6–7.

12. Pulido, "Ecological Legitimacy and Cultural Essentialism," 294.
13. *Ibid.*, 296.
14. Viramontes, *Under the Feet of Jesus* (New York: Plume Books, 1995), 144. All subsequent in-text page references to the novel are from this edition.
15. Simmons, *Interpreting Nature*, 2–3.
16. *Ibid.*, 15.
17. Aragón, "Excerpt from The Legend of La Llorona."
18. Castillo, *Massacre of the Dreamers: Essays on Xicanisma*, 109.
19. Carbonell, "From Llorona to Gritona," 53.
20. Simmons, *Interpreting Nature*, 15.
21. *Ibid.*, 15.
22. Gaspar de Alba, *Desert Blood: The Juárez Murders* (Houston: Arte Público, 2005), 57. All subsequent in-text references to the novel are from this edition.
23. Bacon, *The Children of NAFTA*, 314.
24. *Ibid.*
25. Acosta-Belén and Bose, "U.S. Latina and Latin American Feminisms," 1118.
26. Peña, *Mexican Americans and the Environment*, 157.
27. *Ibid.*
28. *Ibid.*, 134.
29. *Ibid.*, 159.
30. *Ibid.*, 160.
31. Viramontes, "Art, Imagination, and Violence," 54.
32. Anzaldúa, *Borderlands/La Frontera*, 46.
33. Novotny, "Popular Epidemiology," 155.
34. Shapiro, "Because Words Are Not Enough," 144.
35. Peña, "Identity, Place and Communities of Resistance," 157.
36. Novotny, "Popular Epidemiology," 152.
37. Carbonell, "From Llorona to Gritona," 54.
38. *Ibid.*
39. *Ibid.*, 57.
40. Pulido, "*Environmentalism and Economic Justice*," 58.
41. Chávez, Wampler, and Burkhart, "Left Out," 1026.
42. Sandoval, *Methodology of the Oppressed*, 142.
43. Simmons, *Interpreting Nature*, 100.

WORKS CITED

Acosta-Belén, Edna and Christine E. Bose. "U.S. Latina and Latin American Feminisms: Hemispheric Encounters." *Signs: Journal of Women in Culture and Society* 25.41 (2000): 1113–19.

Anzaldúa, Gloria. *Borderlands/La Frontera: The New Mestiza.* San Francisco: Aunt Lute Books, 1987.

Aragon, Ray John De. "Excerpt from The Legend of La Llorona." *The Cry: La Llorona, the Film and the Ten Year Search for La Llorona.* 1980. http://www.lallorona.com/1cultures.html.

Bacon, David. *The Children of NAFTA: Labor Wars on the U.S./Mexico Border.* Berkeley: University of California Press, 2004.

Carbonell, Ana María. "From Llorona to Gritona: Coatlicue In Feminist Tales by Viramontes and Cisneros." *MELUS* 24.2 (Summer 1999): 53–74.

Castillo, Ana. *Massacre of the Dreamers: Essays on Xicanisma.* Albuquerque: University of New Mexico Press, 1994.

Chávez, María L., Brian Wampler, and Ross E. Burkhart. "Left Out: Trust and Social Capital Among Migrant Seasonal Farmworkers." *Social Science Quarterly* 87.5 (Dec. 2006): 1012–29.

Faber, Daniel, ed. *The Struggle for Ecological Democracy: Environmental Justice Movements in the United States*. New York: The Guilford Press, 1998.

Gaspar de Alba, Alicia. *Desert Blood: The Juárez Murders*. Houston: Arte Público, 2005.

Hovey, Joseph D. and Cristina G. Magaña. "Exploring the Mental Health of Mexican Migrant Farm Workers in the Midwest: Psychosocial Predictors of Psychological Distress and Suggestions for Prevention and Treatment." *The Journal of Psychology* 136.5 (2002): 493–513.

Novotny, Patrick. "Popular Epidemiology and the Struggle for Community Health in the Environmental Justice Movement." In Faber, *The Struggle for Ecological Democracy*, 137–58.

Ortega, Mariana. "Being Lovingly, Knowingly Ignorant: White Feminism and Women of Color." *Hypatia* 21.3 (Summer 2006): 56–74.

Peña, Devon G. "Identity, Place and Communities of Resistance." In *Just Sustainabilities: Development in an Unequal World*, edited by Julian Agyeman, Robert D. Bullard, and Bob Evans, 146–67. London: Earthscan Publications, 2003.

_____. *Mexican Americans and the Environment: Tierra y Vida*. Tucson: University of Arizona Press, 2005.

Pérez-Torres, Rafael. *Movements in Chicano Poetry: Against Myth, Against Margins*. New York: Cambridge University Press, 1995.

Pulido, Laura. "Ecological Legitimacy and Cultural Essentialism: Hispano Grazing in the Southwest." In Faber, *The Struggle for Ecological Democracy*, 293–311.

_____. *Environmentalism and Economic Justice: Two Chicano Struggles in the Southwest*. Tucson: University of Arizona Press, 1996.

Sandoval, Chela. *Methodology of the Oppressed*. Theory Out of Bounds 18. Minneapolis: University of Minnesota Press, 2000.

Shapiro, Ester R. "Because Words Are Not Enough: Latina Re-Visionings of Transnational Collaborations Using Health Promotion for Gender Justice and Social Change." *NWSA Journal* 17.1 (Spring 2005): 141–172.

Simmons, I.G. *Interpreting Nature: Cultural Constructions of the Environment*. New York: Routledge, 1993.

Sussman, Glen, Byron W. Daynes, and Jonathan P. West. *American Politics and the Environment*. New York: Longman, 2002.

Viramontes, Helena María. "Art, Imagination, and Violence: An Interview with Helena María Viramontes." By Deborah Owen Moore. *Interdisciplinary Humanities* 22.2 (2005): 53–60.

_____. *Under the Feet of Jesus*. New York: Plume Books, 1995.

Nature as Articulate and Inspirited in *Oficio de tinieblas* by Rosario Castellanos

Traci Roberts-Camps

In Rosario Castellanos's *Oficio de tinieblas* (1962; *The Book of Lamentations*) nature is both articulate and inspirited.[1] This is most evident in the passages that describe the Tzotzil relationship with nature. Curiously, this idea is also problematized by two female characters, Catalina Díaz Puiljá and Teresa Entzin López, who seem to communicate with nature but manipulate the outcomes of this relationship to their own purposes. This chapter will examine the representations of nature and its relationship to humans in *Oficio de tinieblas* by Rosario Castellanos. Furthermore, it will compare these images to those found in the Mayan "libro de consejos" (book of advice), *Popol Vuh*. Essays from the following will inform my observations: Glotfelty and Fromm's *The Ecocriticism Reader: Landmarks in Literary Ecology* (1996), Gaard's *Ecofeminism: Women, Animals, Nature* (1993), Phillips's *The Truth of Ecology: Nature, Culture, and Literature in America* (2003), and Greg Garrard's *Ecocriticism* (2004) among others. I will specifically draw upon the ideas of Christopher Manes in his 1992 essay "Nature and Silence" to discuss the concept of nature as articulate and inspirited.

While Castellanos's work has been examined from the feminist perspective as well as that of literature that addresses indigenous communities, the current study seeks to create a new connection in her work between the feminist, indigenous, and ecocritical points of view. Within mainstream ecocriticism itself the connection between feminist theory and indigenous cultures has been made and this study will observe what Castellanos can add to this conversation. As Glen A. Love states: "American literature is not unique in its ecological perspective and [...] we need to recognize our kinship with nature-oriented writers in New England, in Canada, in Europe, in South and Central America, in Africa, in Australia, everywhere."[2] As a novel written by

196

a Mexican woman who spent much of her life in Chiapas, *Oficio de tinieblas* can greatly enrich the discussion on ecocriticism.

At first glance, *Oficio de tinieblas* is not a "nature-oriented" novel; however, nature plays a key role in the narrative because of the Mayan relationship to the natural world. This novel fictionalizes a Mayan uprising in Chiapas, Mexico that occurred in the mid-nineteenth century. Although Castellanos sets her novel in the 1930s, in many other ways it is true to the original historical event. According to Alma Guillermoprieto, whose introduction appears in the English translation *The Book of Lamentations* (1996):

> The novel is faithful to the known facts in many respects, including the character who sparks the rebellion when she hears miraculous voices issuing from three "talking rocks"—a woman called Catalina Díaz Puiljá in the book, Agustina Gómez Checheb in real life—and the ritual crucifixion of her foster child, called Domingo in both fact and fiction.[3]

Furthermore, the novel calls to mind other indigenous uprisings that have taken place in the last two centuries in Southern Mexico, most recently that of the Zapatista National Liberation Army (started on January 1, 1994). Finally, this novel is one of the first examples of a more realistic, less-romantic view of the indigenous community partly due to the fact that Castellanos spent much of her youth in Chiapas, although as a landowner.[4] She is one of the earliest Mexican writers to reveal the uniqueness of the Mayan world view as opposed to the mestizo and Spanish world views.

Oficio de tinieblas begins in the valley of Chamula, in Chiapas, introducing Catalina Díaz Puiljá, a Tzotzil *ilol* (shaman or seer), and her husband, Pedro González Winiktón, a Tzotzil judge. The narrator then introduces Marcela, a young indigenous woman, who travels to Ciudad Real, also known as San Cristóbal de Las Casas.[5] In Ciudad Real, Leonardo Cifuentes, an important mestizo leader, rapes Marcela. After this, Marcela's mother Felipa disowns her and the childless Catalina takes her in as her own daughter. Throughout the remainder of this novel, the narrator weaves back and forth between the Tzotzil inhabitants of Chamula and the mestizo (or ladino) inhabitants of Ciudad Real. The climaxes occur when these two worlds collide. Some of the most striking events that lead up to and encompass this collision include: the birth of Marcela's son, Domingo, known as "el que nació cuando el eclipse" (the one born at the eclipse); Winikton's job on La Constancia, the land owned by the German Don Adolfo Homel; the arrival of Fernando Ulloa, who eventually plays a large part in the Tzotzil uprising; the moment when Teresa, the nanny of Leonardo's daughter Idolina, reveals to Idolina that she can see the future in the ashes from a fire; when Catalina hears the three stones speaking to her in the cave near Tzajal-hemel; the trial of Catalina and other Tzotzil women for attempting to start an uprising; the crucifixion of

Domingo and the Tzotzil uprising against Ciudad Real; and the eventual dispersing and hiding of the Tzotzil tribe in the mountains surrounding Chamula.

Two of these events have special significance for the current reflections on *Oficio de tinieblas*: Teresa reading the ashes and Catalina hearing the stones. In both cases, the women are supposedly able to hear nature and they are both perceived as having power over that nature, and thus over human lives. Within the Tzotzil world view, nature is articulate, or able to communicate. In "Nature and Silence," Christopher Manes observes that while nature is silent in Occidental culture:

> In contrast, for animistic cultures, those that see the natural world as inspirited, not just people, but also animals, plants, and even "inert" entities such as stones and rivers are perceived as being articulate and at times intelligible subjects, able to communicate and interact with humans for good or ill. In addition to human language, there is also the language of birds, the wind, earthworms, wolves, and waterfalls — a world of autonomous speakers whose intents (especially for hunter-gatherer peoples) one ignores at one's peril.[6]

This is not unlike the pre–Christian belief in an inspirited world: "In Antiquity every tree, every spring, every stream, every hill had its own *genius loci*, its guardian spirit. These spirits were accessible to men, but were very unlike men [...]. Before one cut a tree, mined a mountain, or dammed a brook, it was important to placate the spirit in charge of that particular situation, and to keep it placated."[7] Castellanos's novel presents a very similar relationship with nature where the Tzotzil community is animistic, believing that objects in nature have spirits just as humans do. As Manes sustains, such cultures believe that all entities in nature are able to communicate and even interact with human beings. Teresa and Catalina both hear nature speaking to them and believe, or project, the idea that human lives depend on this reciprocal communication.

In *Oficio de tinieblas*, one of the first examples of nature's articulateness is Teresa's reading of the ashes. Weeks before Teresa reveals her power to Idolina, the narrator explains that the girl thought her nanny might be "una 'canán,' la poseedora de un nahual de fuego, dotada del poder suficiente para convertirse en este elemento y para dictarle sus mandatos"[8] (a canán, possessor of a fire nahual, endowed with the power to transform herself into fire and dictate her commands to the flames).[9] First of all, this quote reveals a belief in a strong connection between nature and human beings. As Esther Allen explains in the glossary of her English translation *The Book of Lamentations*, a *nahual* is "[t]he animal that is the double or alter ego of a human soul" (380). Each member of the indigenous tribe possesses a *nahual*, which determines certain characteristics of its human counterpart. Thus, Idolina believes that Teresa has a special relationship with fire and is able to communicate with this element. She later asks her nanny what the ashes tell her, to which Teresa replies: "La ceniza dice que se va a quemar esta casa. Dice que el marido y la mujer van a morir" (87) [The ashes say this house will burn. They say the husband and wife will die] (79). The husband and wife refer to Idolina's mother, Isabel, and her step-father, Leonardo Cifuentes, whom Idolina suspects of murdering her father. The narrator describes Teresa's surprise at the omens of her own vision: "no podían haber brotado de sí misma sino que forzosamente tuvo que haberlas recibido por medios sobrenaturales" (87) [(They) could not have sprung up inside her of their own accord, but must have been received by supernatural means] (79). Thus, Teresa, a Tzotzil woman who had been living with a mestizo family for years, manifests a kinship with nature and even Idolina, born and raised in a mestizo family, believes in her power. This example is indicative of the representations of nature throughout *Oficio de tinieblas*; more specifically, the sections that describe the Tzotzil community.

This passage is akin to the diviner of Part One of the Mayan creation story *Popol Vuh* "whose hand is moved over the corn kernels, over the coral seeds, the days, the lots" and who says "'Just let it be found, just let it be discovered, / say it, our ear is listening, / may you talk, may you speak.'"[10] In his introduction to the text, Tedlock explains that this divination process is still in use today and practiced "on top of the mountain called Tohil's Place" (33). Just as the Quiché diviners "read" the corn kernels, Teresa "reads" the future in the ashes of the fire. Thus, nature is articulate; nature is able to communicate with humans within the Mayan world view of both the *Popol Vuh* and the Tzotzil tribe in *Oficio de tinieblas*.

The second example of nature's articulateness is when Catalina rediscovers the inspirited stones that she and her brother, Lorenzo, had encountered as children. Catalina and Lorenzo had found the stones in a cave when they were little and, according to Catalina, her brother's spirit had then been taken by a *pukuj*, or demon, inhabiting the cave. Catalina decides to search for the cave and finds it near another village, Tzajal-hemel. In the cave she seems to hear the stones communicating with her. She prophesies about a significant event to the other Tzotzils: "Está madurando el tiempo; se acercan los grandes días, los días nuestros. El hacha del leñador está derrumbando el árbol que ha de caer para destruir a muchos. Te lo digo a ti y a ti. Que lo que se acerca no te coja desprevenido. Alístate, prepárate. Porque se aproxima un gran riesgo" (195) [The time is growing ripe; the great days are approaching, our days. The woodcutter's ax is chopping the tree which must fall in order to destroy many people. I am telling you and you. Do not let what is coming catch you off guard. Get ready. Be prepared. Because a great peril is coming soon] (189). Just as Teresa receives information from nature about the future of humans, Catalina also sees the future of the Tzotzils. In fact, both women are actually receivers of information; the active party in both conversations is nature itself. The fire tells Teresa of Isabel and Leonardo's future and the stones tell Catalina of the Tzotzils' future. This last foretelling will eventually lead to the Mayan uprising described in *Oficio de tinieblas* because Catalina's fellow tribe members begin to believe her prophecies and their own power against the mestizos of Ciudad Real. Although they eventually call upon the gods of Chamula, principally San Juan, el Fiador (the Guarantor), they only begin to believe in their strength after Catalina's prophecies. Thus, nature is a powerful force that directs the lives of the characters in *Oficio de tinieblas*.

The stones that Catalina finds in *Oficio de tinieblas* recall Part Four of the *Popol Vuh* where humans enter the Mayan creation story. In this section, the narrators describe the original four fathers and mothers of the descendent tribes "including the Mexican people."[11] The tribes congregate at the mountain they call "Tulan Zuyua, Seven Caves, Seven Canyons"; "those who were to receive the gods arrived there."[12] The narrators then describe the tribes taking away their gods and hiding them in a canyon, mountain, and forest and later seeking them out, similar to how Catalina found the inspirited stones in the cave at Tzajal-hemel: "And when they went before Tohil and Auilix [Quiché gods], they went to visit them and keep their day. Now they gave thanks before them for the dawning, and now they bowed low before their stones, there in the forest."[13] The narrators' description of the tribes' sacrifices to their gods also resembles later scenes of Catalina drawing the other members of her village to the stones in the caves:

> And when they got hold of the birds and fawns, they would then go to anoint the mouth of the stone of Tohil or Auilix with the blood of the deer or bird. And the bloody drink was drunk by the gods. The stone would speak at once when the penitents and sacrificers arrived, when they went to make their burnt offerings.
> [...]
> And when they went before Tohil, Auilix, and Hacauitz, they took stitches in their ears and their elbows in front of the gods. They spilled their blood, they poured gourdfuls into the mouths of the stones. But these weren't really stones: each one became like a boy when they arrived, happy once again over the blood.[14]

The first segment is analogous to the Tzotzil community visiting the stones at Tzajal-hemel where Catalina found them; the stones in *Oficio de tinieblas* also speak through Catalina. The second segment foreshadows the gods' thirst for human blood in the *Popol Vuh*; it also relates to Domingo's sacrificial crucifixion in Castellanos's novel. The fictional Tzotzil sacrifice in this Mexican novel is rooted in the Mayan creation story the community shares with the Quiché peoples of neighboring Guatemala. In both instances, nature wields power over humans and calls for human sacrifice.

Nature is central to the Tzotzil's stories of their past and present, as in the story of the cave where Catalina and her brother find the animate stones and then, later, when Catalina rediscovers the stones. Examining the Pueblo world view of the American Southwest, in "Landscape, History, and Pueblo Imagination," Leslie Marmon Silko describes a similar perception of reality: "Location, or 'place,' nearly always plays a central role in the Pueblo oral narratives. Indeed, stories are most frequently recalled as people are passing by a specific geographical feature or the exact place where a story takes place. [...] Often [...] the turning point in the narrative involved a peculiarity or special quality of a rock or tree or plant found only at that place."[15] Later, Marmom Silko clarifies of the Pueblo world view: "Each ant, each lizard, each lark is imbued with great value simply because the creature is there, simply because the creature is alive in a place where any life at all is precious."[16] The desert of the American southwest is a harsh environment thus making survival difficult. This is similar to the harsh terrain surrounding Chamula in *Oficio de tinieblas*; an environment in which the Tzotzils must respect the land in order to survive.

Others theorists further describe this interrelated existence with nature seen in communities such as the American Indian tribes. For example, Paula Gunn Allen declares that "tribal people allow all animals, vegetables, and minerals (the entire biota, in short) the same or even greater privileges than humans."[17] Later she explains:

> The notion that nature is somewhere over there while humanity is over here or that a great hierarchical ladder of being exists on which ground and trees occupy a very low rung, animals a slightly higher one, and man (never woman)— especially "civilized" man — a very high one indeed is antithetical to tribal thought. The American Indian sees all creatures as relatives (and in tribal systems relationship is central), as offspring of the Great Mystery, as cocreators, as children of our mother, and as necessary parts of an ordered, balanced, and living whole.[18]

This view of nature as an equal is evident in *Oficio de tinieblas* and the *Popol Vuh*, as well. As illustrated in previous examples, the Tzotzils in Castellanos's novel turn to nature for answers to their questions and see natural elements such as the moon and sun as "cocreators" of their existence. Furthermore, the Mayan beliefs set forth in the *Popol Vuh* mirror the American Indian principle that all creatures are relatives and necessary parts of the whole of existence. To avoid romanticizing the image of the American Indian, Gunn Allen clarifies:

In a sense, the American Indian perceives all that exists as symbolic. This outlook has given currency to the concept of the Indian as one who is close to the
earth, but the closeness is actual, not a quaint result of savagism or childlike
naiveté. An Indian, at the deepest level of being, assumes that the earth is alive
in the same sense that human beings are alive.[19]

This conceit is analogous to the Tzotzil view of nature as represented by Castellanos, in which the Tzotzils view the earth as alive just as they are alive.
Moreover, Castellanos avoids the romanticizing view of the indigenous community by showing that this relationship is born of necessity, not "savagism
or childlike naiveté."[20]

Interestingly, Teresa and Catalina's experiences with nature also prob-
lematize the assertion that nature is articulate and inspirited. As is typical of
Castellanos's style in *Oficio de tinieblas*, nothing is an absolute certainty;
everything has shades of uncertainty and the narrative presents events from
different perspectives. For example, the narrator casts a shadow of doubt on
Teresa and Catalina's abilities to communicate with nature. When Idolina
reminds Teresa of what she foresaw, Idolina replies: "Era juego, niña" (81) [It
was a game, niña] (73). The reader is left to wonder whether Idolina really
did foresee something in the ashes of the fire. In the case of Catalina, after
her tribe ceases to believe in her prophecies and the stones are taken from the
cave, she creates new stones from clay. This act implies that she created the
stones out of desperation from not hearing more prophecies and insinuates
that Catalina possibly imagined the earlier prophecies. Again, as with other
situations in *Oficio de tinieblas*, Castellanos presents different views on the same
situation. This particular style avoids the typical Occidental romantic view
of Mayan culture by evading an idealized indigenous image.

Whether the reader eventually believes in Teresa and Catalina's communication with nature, the Tzotzil characters accept this relationship and feel
that their lives depend as much on the whims of nature as of man. This worldview differs from the Occidental belief that man is more important than
nature. In "Nature and Silence," Manes discusses the evolution of the concept of *scala naturae*, the "Great Chain of Being."[21] According to Manes, in
the Middle Ages this scale was "a depiction of the world as a vast filigree of
lower and higher forms, from zoophytes to Godhead, with humankind's place
higher than beasts and a little less than angels" and where "nature was a symbol for the glory and orderliness of God."[22] During the Renaissance, "humanism converted it [*scala naturae*] from a symbol of human restraint in the face
of a perfect order to an emblem of human superiority over the natural
world."[23] Thus, man replaced God at the top of the list. Post-Enlightenment
belief "made the human subject the expectant ground of all possible knowledge."[24] It was not until postmodernism, Manes argues, that the subject is

"fragmented and decentered in the social realm" which "set the stage for the reevaluation of the silence of nature imposed by the human subject."[25] In other words, it is not until humans question their own centrality that they return to the concept of a reciprocal relationship with nature. Manes states that animistic cultures, as opposed to Occidental culture, see humans and the natural world as inhabiting the same plane, no higher or lower than the other. The examples in *Oficio de tinieblas* of nature speaking to Teresa and Catalina are emblematic of this world view, where humans and nature communicate. Marmon Silko clarifies that:

> The land, the sky, and all that is within them — the landscape — includes human beings. Interrelationships in the Pueblo landscape are complex and fragile. The unpredictability of the weather, the aridity and harshness of much of the terrain in the high plateau country explain in large part the relentless attention the ancient Pueblo people gave the sky and the earth around them. Survival depended upon harmony and cooperation not only among human beings, but among all things — the animate and the less animate, since rocks and mountains were known to move, to travel occasionally.[26]

In this quote, it is apparent that the landscape is central to the Pueblo world view rather than the Occidental *scala naturae*. Seeing the world as landscape places humans and nature visually at the same level. Furthermore, human beings and nature are on the same imaginary plane in the Pueblo landscape, or world view. The Pueblo awareness of nature is comparable to the Tzotzil observation of the natural world in *Oficio de tinieblas*, where even an eclipse is an augury, as with the birth of Domingo during the solar eclipse. The scene of Domingo's birth represents the significance of nature for the Tzotzil world view: "Y cuando llegó el día no fue como todos los días sino que se mostró oscurecido de presagios. El sol y la luna luchaban en el cielo. La tribu de los tzotziles asistía, aterrorizada, a esta lucha, procurando con gritos, con ensordecedor resonar de tambores, con estrepitoso voltear de campanas, el triunfo del más fuerte" (48) [And when the day came it was not like other days; it revealed itself to be overshadowed with omens. The sun and the moon were doing battle in the sky. The tribe of the Tzotzils witnessed this battle in terror, striving with screams, a deafening beating of drums, a frantic clanging of bells, to ensure the triumph of the strongest] (39). In this quote, nature's power to communicate to human beings is apparent; if humans are able to understand the message, nature is able to communicate the future to them. Moreover, as Manes posits: "In addition to human language, there is also the language of birds, the wind, earthworms, wolves, and waterfalls — a world of autonomous speakers whose intents (especially for hunter-gatherer peoples) one ignores at one's peril."[27] The Tzotzils believe that they must listen to nature in order to survive and that any great natural event directly affects their lives.

As is evident in the two examples being discussed — Teresa and Catalina's communication with nature — the relationship between women and nature is paramount in Castellanos's *Oficio de tinieblas*. One branch of ecocriticism that will shed light on these examples which has not been discussed hitherto is ecofeminism. Cheryll Glotfelty, in the introduction to her volume of eco-critical essays defines the term as follows: "a theoretical discourse whose theme is the link between the oppression of women and the domination of nature."[28] *Oficio de tinieblas* presents a well-established relationship between women and nature; more specifically, between the Tzotzil women and nature. Analyzing Castellanos's work, Keefe Ugalde affirms: "en el contexto del discurso feme-nino, la significación de la naturaleza se multiplica, sugiriendo una relación recíproca entre las mujeres y la Tierra" (in the context of feminine discourse, the signification of nature multiplies, suggesting a reciprocal relationship between women and Earth).[29] Glotfelty also clarifies that ecofeminism stud-ies the link between the subjugation of women and the subjugation of nature. Greta Gaard explains this link: "Drawing on the insights of ecology, femi-nism, and socialism, ecofeminism's basic premise is that the ideology which authorizes oppressions such as those based on race, class, gender, sexuality, physical abilities, and species is the same ideology which sanctions the oppres-sion of nature."[30] This is evident in *Oficio de tinieblas* in the treatment of nature and women by the mestizo community.

The socio-historical backdrop of Castellanos's novel is Southern Mex-ico in the 1930s, a place where the Spanish Conquest of Mexico still has res-onances. This is apparent in *Oficio de tinieblas*, where the Mayan population of the region suffers subjugation at the hands of the mestizo and European inhabitants of Ciudad Real. More specifically, the Tzotzil women are victims of the suppression of men such as Leonardo Cifuentes, as is the case in the rape of Marcela. The Tzotzil women are not the only victims; the descen-dents of the Spanish conquerors continue to oppress the land in Southern Mexico.[31] Following the Mayan uprising:

> El valle de Chamula — de niebla, de regatos — ahora es el valle de las humaredas. Humo es lo que antes fue paraje, sembradío, pueblo. Humo: tierra sollamada, aire envilecido, arrasamiento y aniquilación.
> [...]
> A manos de sus enemigos perecieron los rebeldes y los mansos fueron hechos cautivos por los vencedores. Éstos también violaron a las mujeres y pusieron la marca de la esclavitud en el anca de los recién nacidos [362].

> [The valley of Chamula — once a place of mists and brooks — is now dense with smoke. What once was village, sown field, town is now smoke. Smoke: scorched earth, tainted air, ruin and annihilation.
> ....

The rebels perished at the hands of their enemies and the meek were taken captive by the victors, who raped the women and put the mark of slavery on the rumps of newborn babies (360).]

First, a valley of "mists and brooks" is reduced to "scorched earth"; the mestizos led by Cifuentes destroy the land the Tzotzils were living on, driving them to scatter in the surrounding mountains. Second, mirroring the rape of Marcela by Cifuentes, the men of Ciudad Real rape the Tzotzil women and brand their children. There is a strong link here between the domination of women and nature. Furthermore, as Jennifer H. Bain points out, "women are the most adversely affected by the degradation of their immediate environment" in regions such as Southern Mexico because they are largely in charge of family sustenance.[32] The domination of the Tzotzils in *Oficio de tinieblas* is so complete that: "Solos, estos hombres olvidan su linaje, la dignidad que ostentaban, su pasado. Aprenden de los animales cobardes las ciencias de la furtividad. [...] Siempre el amo que no se aplaca con la obediencia más abyecta ni con la humildad más servil. Siempre el látigo cayendo sobre la espalda sumisa" (362) [Alone, these men forget their lineage, the dignity they once displayed, their past. They learn the sciences of furtiveness from fearful animals. ... Always the master who is not appeased by the most abject obedience or the most servile humility. Always the whip falling onto the submissive back] (360). As evidenced in this passage, the Tzotzils are oppressed so much that they are comparable to animals, from which they learn survival tactics. In this sense, the indigenous relationship with nature is not the romanticized vision of man communing with the earth, but the reality of an oppressed people driven to hide in the mountains and live in inhumane conditions.

In conclusion, Rosario Castellanos presents a close relationship between humans and nature in *Oficio de tinieblas*; more specifically, between Tzotzil women and nature in Southern Mexico. As seen in the examples studied from this novel, the Tzotzils believe in nature's power over human lives and pay heed to its messages; their everyday lives encompass a close relationship to nature that is meant to ensure their survival. When compared to the belief systems of other autochthonous populations of the Americas, it is apparent that this affiliation with nature is part of a uniquely indigenous world view that challenges the idea that the natural world is silent. Finally, Castellanos's novel as well as the *Popol Vuh* offer ecocriticism a unique perspective on the human relationship to nature — a decidedly non–Western perspective that affirms the belief that nature is both articulate and inspirited.

NOTES

1. Rosario Castellanos (1925–1974) "grew up on the family ranch on the Jataté River near the Guatemalan border, and later in the town of Comitán, Chiapas. [...] In 1941,

when the land reform program launched by President Lázaro Cárdenas stripped the provincial elite of their properties, the Castellanos family moved to Mexico City" (Ahern, 140). For an extensive bibliography of the author's published work as well as work published on Castellanos, see Ahern's bio-bibliographical entry on Castellanos in *Spanish American Women Writers: A Bio-Bibliographical Source Book.*

2. Love, "Revaluing Nature: Toward an Ecological Criticism," 237.

3. Guillermoprieto, "Introduction," in *The Book of Lamentations*, Rosario Castellanos, trans. Esther Allen (New York: Penguin, 1998), xi.

4. In *An Introduction to Spanish-American Literature* (1994), Jean Franco explains that Rosario Castellanos's novels are part of the last stage of Indianist literature, which attempts to "comprehend the Indian mind through his mythology, poetry, and legend" (242). According to Franco, this is a more realistic view than earlier novels, such as *El indio* by Gregorio López y Fuentes, which tend to idealize the indigenous figure.

5. Esther Allen's English translation of *The Book of Lamentations* defines Ciudad Real as "[t]he colonial name of San Cristóbal de Las Casas which was restored during the 1920s and 1930s when the Mexican government attempted to ban saints' names as part of its persecution of the Catholic Church. Ciudad Real is the name of the Spanish city to the south of Toledo in Castilla-La Mancha that was the home of the conquistador of the Chiapas highlands," 379–80.

6. Manes, "Nature and Silence," 15.

7. White, "The Historical Roots of Our Ecologic Crisis," 10.

8. Castellanos, *Oficio de tinieblas* (1962; Mexico City: Joaquín Mortiz, 1988), 86.

9. Castellanos, *The Book of Lamentations*, trans. Esther Allen (New York: Penguin, 1998), 78. All subsequent in-text page references to English translations of *Oficio de tinieblas* are from this edition.

10. *Popol Vuh: The Definitive Edition of the Mayan Book of the Dawn of Life and the Glories of Gods and Kings*, 70.

11. *Ibid.*, 151

12. *Ibid.*

13. *Ibid.*, 163.

14. *Ibid.*, 164–65.

15. Marmom Silko, "Landscape, History, and Pueblo Imagination," 270.

16. *Ibid.*, 275.

17. Gunn Allen, "The Sacred Hoop: A Contemporary Perspective," 243.

18. *Ibid.*, 246.

19. *Ibid.*, 256.

20. For further examination of the avoidance of romanticizing the relationship between indigenous cultures and nature, see Greg Garrard's chapter "Dwelling" on the 'Ecological Indian' in *Ecocriticism*, 120–27; as well as Dana Phillips' discussion of the writings of Richard Nelson and Barry Lopez in *The Truth of Ecology*, 223–29.

21. Manes, "Nature and Silence," 20.

22. *Ibid.*

23. *Ibid.*

24. *Ibid.*, 22.

25. *Ibid.*

26. Marmom Silko, "Landscape, History, and Pueblo Imagination," 267.

27. Manes, "Nature and Silence," 15.

28. Glotfelty, "Introduction," xxiv.

29. Keefe Ugalde, "Hilos y palabras: Diseños de una ginotradición (Rosario Castellanos, Pat Mora y Cecilia Vicuña)," 51.

30. Gaard, "Living Interconnections with Animals and Nature," 1.

31. In her introduction to *Mujer y sociedad en América Latina* (1980), Lucía Guerra Cunningham discusses the origins of the differences of the sexes and their social roles in light of indigenous and Spanish cultures. She discusses some of the roles taken on by men after the Conquest of the Americas: "El estereotipo de Don Juan, bajo las condiciones de un nuevo ambiente natural y social, adquirió nuevas dimensiones que dieron origen al fenómeno del Machismo con dos características básicas: a) el poder para seducir al sexo femenino y b) la capacidad para ser agresivo y violento frente a la naturaleza y a los otros hombres" [The stereotype of Don Juan, under the conditions of a new natural and social ambience, acquired new dimensions that caused the phenomenon of Machismo with two basic characteristics: a) the power to seduce females and b) the capacity to be aggressive and violent towards nature and other men] (14).

32. Bain, "Mexican Rural Women's Knowledge of the Environment," 263.

WORKS CITED

Ahern, Maureen. "Rosario Castellanos (1925–1974) Mexico." In Marting, *Spanish American Women Writers*, 140–55.

Bain, Jennifer H. "Mexican Rural Women's Knowledge of the Environment." *Mexican Studies/Estudios Mexicanos* 9.2 (Summer 1993): 259–74.

Castellanos, Rosario. *Oficio de tinieblas.* Mexico City: Joaquín Mortiz, 1988. Translated by Esther Allen as *The Book of Lamentations.* New York: Penguin, 1998.

Cortés, Eladio, ed. *Dictionary of Mexican Literature.* Westport, CT: Greenwood Press, 1992.

Franco, Jean. *An Introduction to Spanish-American Literature.* Third Edition. Cambridge: Cambridge University Press, 1994.

Gaard, Greta. "Living Interconnections with Animals and Nature." In *Ecofeminism: Women, Animals, Nature,* edited by Gaard, 1–12. Philadelphia: Temple University Press, 1993.

Garrard, Greg. *Ecocriticism.* London and New York: Routledge, 2004.

Glotfelty, Cheryll, and Harold Fromm, eds. *The Ecocriticism Reader: Landmarks in Literary Ecology.* Athens: University of Georgia Press, 1996.

Guillermoprieto, Alma. "Introduction." In Castellanos, *The Book of Lamentations* translated by Esther Allen, vii–xiii.

Gunn Allen, Paula. "The Sacred Hoop: A Contemporary Perspective." In Glotfelty and Fromm, *The Ecocriticism Reader*, 241–63.

Keefe Ugalde, Sharon. "Hilos y palabras: Diseños de una ginotradición (Rosario Castellanos, Pat Mora y Cecilia Vicuña)." *Inti: Revista de Literatura Hispánica* 51 (Spring 2000): 50–67.

Love, Glen A. "Revaluing Nature: Toward an Ecological Criticism." In Glotfelty and Fromm, *The Ecocriticism Reader*, 225–40.

Manes, Christopher. "Nature and Silence." In Glotfelty and Fromm, *The Ecocriticism Reader*, 25–29.

Marmon Silko, Leslie. "Landscape, History, and the Pueblo Imagination." In Glotfelty and Fromm, *The Ecocriticism Reader*, 264–75.

Marting, Diane E., ed. *Spanish American Women Writers: A Bio-Biographical Source Book.* Westport, CT: Greenwood Press, 1990.

Phillips, Dana. *The Truth of Ecology: Nature, Culture, and Literature in America.* Oxford: Oxford University Press, 2003.

Popol Vuh: The Definitive Edition of the Mayan Book of the Dawn of Life and the Glories of Gods and Kings. Revised Edition. Translated by Dennis Tedlock. New York: Simon and Schuster, 1996.

White, Lynn, Jr. "The Historical Roots of Our Ecologic Crisis." In Glotfelty and Fromm, *The Ecocriticism Reader*, 3–14.

National Nature and Ecologies
of Abjection in Brazilian Literature
at the Turn of the Twentieth Century

Mark D. Anderson

Nada de Brasil verde, nada de Brasil aquático, nada de Brasil de jardins e
pássaros amáveis... Só as exacerbações do sol. As alegorias das árvores desfeitas.

[None of that green Brazil, none of that aquatic Brazil, that Brazil of gardens and
amenable birds... Just the sun's exacerbations. The allegories of trees undone.][1]

— José Américo de Almeida, *Os coiteiros*

E o sertão de todo se impropriou à vida...

[And the *sertão* became entirely inappropriate for life...]

— Euclides da Cunha, *Os sertões*

Brazil is paradise; everyone knows that. The earliest descriptions of European travelers to the region gushed the praises of its exuberant greenery, tem-
perate climate, and natural abundance. Taking their cue from the unabashed
nudity and rumored superhuman longevity of the natives as well as a variety
of climactic and geographic indicators borrowed from classical thought and
medieval cosmology, explorers from Christopher Columbus to Jesuit missionary Simão de Vasconcelos imagined themselves to be honing in on the
Garden of Eden.[2] Analogical thinking prevailed: they looked for parallels in
Western culture to explain the novelties that they encountered in the "New
World." Even relatively pragmatic Amerigo Vespucci could not resist comparing the coast of what is now Northern Brazil to the fabled "Earthly Paradise," though he used the reference in a more symbolic way than his fanciful
colleagues.[3] In the febrile European imagination, the new lands were only a
stone's throw from heaven.

As Brazilian historian Sérgio Buarque de Holanda argued in his seminal

Visão do paraíso (1957; *Visions of Paradise*), however, the Portuguese colonizers seemed to have a more practical take on things. Not given to the flights
of fancy and mystical transport of their Spanish and Italian counterparts, perhaps due to prior contact with cultural and environmental difference in their
colonial enterprises in Africa and India, they typically limited themselves to
describing "mechanically" the curiosities that diverged from the classical "natural order."[4] They nevertheless entertained a vision of Brazil as the utopian
future of the Portuguese empire, where a new Portugal would be founded,
leaving behind the historical problems and sense of decadence and exhaustion that they associated with the "Old World."[5] For most Portuguese, Brazil
embodied paradise only in function of its possibilities for colonization. To
this end, sixteenth-century soldier Ambrósio Fernandes de Brandônio penned
his iconic *Diálogo das grandezas do Brasil* (1618; *Dialogue on the Greatness of
Brazil*), which described the colony squarely in terms of its utility to the
metropole, particularly in its potential for agricultural development using
Old World species.[6] From early on, the Portuguese viewed their colony as a
prime site for the construction of what Alfred Crosby has called a "Neo-
Europe," where the biota of Mediterranean flora and fauna with which the
Europeans traveled could easily prosper and expand, serving as a base for the
transplanting of Portuguese society to the new lands.[7] The implication was
that Brazil could be a more perfect Europe than Europe itself: far from the
strife-torn Iberian Peninsula, but nearer than the ethereal colonies in Asia,
nourished by the incredible natural abundance of eternal spring, Brazil represented the future of Portugal.

Colonial idealizations of the Brazilian climate and nature were soon complemented by homegrown utopian texts such as Sebastião da Rocha Pita's
História da América portuguesa (1724; *History of Portuguese America*), which
scholars recognize as the first history of Brazil written by a Brazilian. A foundational text of Brazilian nationalism, this book's author freely admitted to
allowing himself to be carried away by patriotic zeal in his repetition of the
tropes of paradise employed by his Portuguese precursors.[8] In any case, the
uncritical reiteration of the paradise motif created what Buarque de Holanda
called a "mythical geography" of Brazil based on indigenous oral accounts
and legends and the superimposition of European fantasies and desires on the
landscape (72). As mythical as these representations may have been, however,
they had very concrete political uses, from extolling Portuguese geographical
knowledge as greater than that of the ancients to attracting European immigrants for colonization.[9]

The cultural politics of paradise became all the more prevalent during
Brazilian independence. Murilo de Carvalho describes a literary pamphlet
war between Brazilians, who championed their land armed with the tropes

of paradise, and Portuguese authors, who belittled it using the classical cosmology of the Torrid Zone and racist arguments comparing Brazilians to Africans. At issue was whether Dom João VI, who had been exiled to the colony during Napoleon Bonaparte's invasion of Portugal, would return home to the Iberian Peninsula or remain in Brazil.[10] As ephemeral as these pamphlets may have been, their patriotic fervor did not recede with independence in 1822. The tropes of paradise experienced a resurgence when romantic authors such as Antonio Gonçalves Dias and José de Alencar used descriptions of an abundant Brazilian nature to foment national pride and assert cultural independence through environmental difference. In this national imaginary, the natural bounty promised to translate into economic opulence, while cultural abundance would clear the path for the insertion of Brazilian culture into the "universal," Western canon. Both nature and culture would play their role in transforming Brazil into a modern, Westernized nation state. The patriotic sublimation of the national landscape culminated in the late nineteenth-century trend of "ufanismo" (literally "pride-ism"), which took its title from Count Afonso Celso's unmistakable *Porque me ufano do meu país* (1901; *Why I Am Proud of My Country*).

Gonçalves Dias was not particularly known for his involvement in politics, and, a true romantic, he died a youthful death in a shipwreck in 1864, before the political tensions between centralists and federalists, monarchists and republicans, and abolitionists and apologists of slavery acquired the violent tenor of the final decades of the nineteenth century. In contrast, both Alencar and Celso were avowed monarchists, combating in word and deed the rising tide of republican sentiment. Perhaps due to their political affiliations, their idealized literary depictions of Brazilian nature came under harsh criticism from liberal opponents, who took them as examples of a monarchist mentality out of touch with the social and cultural realities of Brazil.

In point of fact, the "practice of paradise," as Elaine Freedgood has shown in her studies of English colonial literature, often serves to mitigate misgivings about risks inherent in colonial (whether external or internal) enterprises and to garner support for their undertaking.[11] In the case of the Brazilian romantics, it certainly seems feasible that the presentation of an idealized, generally uniform Brazilian nature and ethnicity was aimed at assuaging fears about the success of the project to integrate marginalized groups and regions into a concept of national citizenship rooted in homogeneity. Tellingly, Alencar's books by and large reframe the issues of cultural and racial difference that were on many Brazilian intellectuals' minds at the time as *mestiço* homogeneity and regional variations on a single theme: essential Brazilian-ness. The only stark differences between characters and environments in his works are their geographic coordinates. In this way, he reduced the problem of difference to distance, which was rapidly being solved by advances in communications such as the telegraph, railroads, and steamships.

With the advent of the First Brazilian Republic in 1889, however, paradise became a contradictory trope. The Republic's technocrats, steeped in the positivism that was in vogue at the time, largely derided the romantics' paradise as a subterfuge of the self-satisfied Brazilian Empire. In their minds, self-exoticization had done little to create national civic consciousness among disperse regions and even less to raise Brazil's standing in the modern world order.[12] "Order" and "progress" became the bywords of the Republican regime, as the new flag designed by Comtean disciple Raimundo Teixeira Mendes proclaimed. The mandate to progress extended into every sphere, including nature and its denizens. Such a project required that the idealized national imaginary of Brazil as tropical paradise be discarded in favor of concrete, "positive" analysis of factors that contributed to progress and those that obstructed its advance. Literary naturalism played a key role, as authors from diverse parts of Brazil converged in the labor of rewriting the nation, region by region, in terms of its potential for modern development. Central figures included novelists such as Aluísio Azevedo, Adolfo Caminha, Júlio Ribeiro, and Rodolfo Teófilo; but the most persuasive writing of the period took the form of the essay in authors such as Francisco José de Oliveira Vianna, Alberto Torres, and, perhaps the most iconic of all, Euclides da Cunha.

As much as these authors' works claimed objectivity, however, their theoretical bases often overpowered the evidence they presented. The tropes of racial, social, and even environmental abjection that dominated nineteenth-century European social theories on the colonial subject frequently resurfaced unquestioned in them. In their haste to replace a quasi-religious symbolic system (paradise) with a modern scientific worldview, the ideologues of the Brazilian Republic revived the European Enlightenment debate on the nature of the "New World" and its inhabitants, which almost always ended in negative valuation and the justification of "civilizing" the savages.[13] One must take into account that "paradise" is itself a versatile locus of discourse, rather than a fixed object, and it is ecological in that it embodies the conjunction of harmonious interrelations between humans and the environment, with an eye to optimal habitability. As the negative to uncritical "ufanismo," the system of tropes that coalesced in the debate over development in Brazil at the turn of the twentieth century necessarily took on the same ecological focus on the interrelations between humans and nature, confronting one for one the tropes of paradise: ideal climate, abundant nature, human innocence. Discursive ecologies of abjection congealed, providing totalizing, systematic explanations for the nation's failure to progress satisfactorily, which typically meant on a par with the United States.

In reality, the Brazilian republicans did not invent this counterdiscourse to paradise. It had been present in a much more rudimentary form even before the time of the conquest: latent, from the shadows, lurked the classical cosmology of the uninhabitable nature of the Torrid Zone and medieval prejudices against non–European races, waiting to reemerge and reinvent themselves whenever the colonial project was questioned. From the Enlightenment through the nineteenth century, European philosophers rescued these tropes in justification of the colonial enterprise, reframing them in modern terms of tropical medicine, hygiene, "race science," eugenics, social and political theory, and, simply, "civilization." In the Brazilian context, many of the same sixteenth-century Jesuit missionaries who praised the environment ended up attacking its indigenous residents as immoral, abject figures completely unfit for "civilization" until their culture was "wiped clean."[14] Such views were not limited to the sixteenth century, however: a character in Alberto Rangel's collection of short stories on the Amazon, suggestively entitled *Inferno verde* (1907; *Green Hell*), voices a similar perspective, stating succinctly that "A terra é boa, o homem só é que não presta" (The land is good, its just the people that are worthless).[15] Of course, "paradise," as the origin of history, could have no history itself; nor could the ideal habitat in the European imagination have prior residents with a valid claim to ownership. As the republican ideologues recognized in their criticisms of their romantic predecessors as antimodern, paradise is a natural, not a human utopia; once paradise becomes inhabited it ceases to be paradise and enters history. Therefore, the indigenous either became part of non-human nature, or they too required expulsion from the garden, or at the least infusion with European genes and culture to transform into civilizable, mixed-race *caboclos*.

In any case, many Portuguese colonizers rapidly revised their initial enthusiasm about environmental conditions in Brazil under the onslaught of swarms of biting insects, tropical heat and humidity, and harassment by hostile indigenous groups. Those who strayed from the coast into the interior in particular encountered quite a different scene, as the pleasant *mata atlântica*, or Atlantic subtropical forest, gave way to the arid scrublands of the *sertão*, with all the heat and insects, but little of the abundance or greenery of the coast. Colonial texts by travelers to the region, such as Jesuit priest Fernão Cardim's *Tratados da terra e gente do Brasil* (1585; *Treatises on the Land and People of Brazil*), unveiled the interior as a place of hardship and high mortality due to drought and illness, though they avoided the apocalyptic imagery that became commonplace in more recent literature on the area. Nevertheless, occasional lapses into negativity were typically subsumed to more positive overall assessments supporting the colonial project. A similar trend occurred following independence: it became unpatriotic to question the representations

of the nation as tropical paradise. What I have called ecologies of abjection —
that is, environmental theories depicting uninhabitable geographies characterized by an unbearable climate and hostile nature, including monstrous
and/or parasitical flora and fauna, and physical topographies that defy the
"natural" order and Western aesthetics, which contribute to the evolution of
lazy, immoral, irrational, deformed, and dark-skinned humans who have
undergone pernicious adaptations to the adverse environment — only became
the dominant mode of representation following the proclamation of the
Republic in 1889.

Even then, not all of Brazil was typically depicted as an abject space,
although essayists such as Paulo Prado, in his *Retrato do Brasil* (1931; *Portrait
of Brazil*), came close. According to Prado's assessment of the national psychology (itself a highly suspect premise), a colonial history of selfish egoism,
sexual depravity, racial intermixing, and tropical illness (including gold fever)
led to the formation of a culture characterized by depression and lassitude
that was incompatible with the rational demands of modernity.[16] Though
many intellectuals shared points of contact with Prado, they more commonly
delineated two distinct cultural geographies to capture the contradictions that
they perceived in the formation of the nation: one normative but unstable,
the other aberrational but solid; one simultaneously national and cosmopolitan, the other marginal but essential; one modern and progressive, the other
mired in the past; one paradise, the other a domain of abjection.

I refer, of course, to the construction of concepts of Brazilian nationality as a schizophrenic rift, tragically torn geographically, culturally, and eth-
nically between the more densely populated and developed *litoral*, or Atlantic
coast, and the interior *sertão* regions. Clearly, the geographic division between
coast and interior existed long before the Republic: though they used the
terms much more loosely than today, many of the earliest colonial chronicles
distinguished between the "coastal civilization," where the majority of Europeans settled, and the wild *sertão* inhabited almost exclusively by *indios bra-
bos* ("savage" Indians, to differentiate them from their coastal cousins, the
"domesticated" or *manso* Tupis), tough frontiersmen known as *bandeirantes*,
and their mixed-race descendants. Nevertheless, the Republic's thinkers
endowed the dualism with much greater symbolism than any of their predecessors. As recent studies by authors such as Muniz de Albuquerque, Trindade
Lima, and Vidal e Souza reveal, the *litoral/sertão* dichotomy, which was often
framed in terms of South/North, led to the prevalence in the minds of Brazilian intellectuals at the turn of the twentieth century of the concept of "Os
Dois Brasis," two Brazils, a nation split geographically and culturally, whose
political, economic, and ethnic differences appeared irreconcilable at times.[17]
The discursive divisiveness was exacerbated by the politics of "café com leite"

(coffee with cream) in which Southern politicians from São Paulo and Minas Gerais alternated in the presidency of the Republic, excluding the North and the extreme South almost completely from the equation. This in turn led to a strong reaction of Northeastern "regionalists," who, according to Muniz de Albuquerque, "invented" discursively a distinct region during the 1920s and 1930s as a strategy for challenging Southern political hegemony (19–64).

In any case, the Republic's ideologues and its opponents alike were forced to confront issues that no Brazilian government had ever before faced: the meaning of political citizenship and the realities of democratic participation, concepts that acquired centrality with the abolition of slavery in 1888 and the 1897 Canudos rebellion in the Northeast, which initially appeared to be a monarchist rejection of the new democratic order.[18] Thrust into power not by popular demand, but by military proclamation, the intellectuals who had fought tooth and nail for abolition and the democratic inclusion of all Brazilians in the political process were suddenly forced to address the limits of their definitions of citizenship: were the ex-slaves and mixed-race, backward Northeasterners, who evidently did not believe in democracy, really capable of self-governance?

The dualism *sertão/litoral* was their way of visualizing the problem of national integration: the rather tenuous geographic division symbolized a host of social problems, political divisions, and cultural differences, and its synthesis into a single, united nation was believed to be their resolution.[19] To complicate things, as a reaction against the monarchy's Portuguese roots as well as the rising tide of European immigration to Brazil, many Republican intellectuals discredited the *litoral*'s possibilities for comprising an "organic" nation. These nationalists rejected the colonial model of the "Neo-Europes," believing that an independent nation must be rooted in cultural and even racial autonomy. They turned inward, looking to the isolated *sertões* for the "national essence." Many of them made journeys to the interior in search of preeminent national qualities that would allow for the construction a Brazilian subject free from contamination from external sources. In most cases, however, they got rather more than they bargained for upon coming into contact with environments and cultures that were radically different from the cosmopolitan coastal cities from which they originated.

On the other hand, the interior *sertões* had largely been left to their own devices during the Brazilian Empire, when their semi-feudal economic organization fit smoothly with the patriarchal hierarchy of nobility that dominated the Empire's political scene. Though still largely unmapped and often perceived (somewhat reductively) as beyond the reach of political and judicial institutions, the *sertões* were not yet viewed as problem regions — in fact, the Empire sent several "scientific missions" to reconnoiter their possibilities for development, positing them as important reserves of natural resources for the future. Everything changed at the end of the nineteenth century, however, when three events thrust the *sertões* into the national imagination as zones that were problematic or even dangerous: the massive 1877–1879 drought in the interior of the Northeast, in which as many as 500,000 people succumbed to starvation and epidemics and millions were displaced to the coastal cities; the 1897 War of Canudos, an armed uprising of religious fanatics in the same area; and the rubber boom in the Amazon basin, which led to the rapid, but chaotic settlement of the area as well as border conflicts with the neighboring nations of Bolivia and Peru.[20] All of these events weighed heavily on the minds of those who searched for the meaning of Brazil beyond the coast, and a spate of works were published theorizing these regions' position within the nation, including such landmarks as José do Patrocínio's *Os retirantes* (1879; *The Refugees*), Rodolfo Teófilo's *A fome* (1890; *Hunger*) and *O paroará* (1899; *The Rubber Migrant*), Euclides da Cunha's *Os sertões* (1902; *Rebellion in the Backlands*), Alberto Torres's *O problema nacional brasileiro* (1914; *The Brazilian National Problem*), and Francisco José de Oliveira Vianna's *A evolução do povo brasileiro* (1923; *The Evolution of the Brazilian People*). Tellingly, nearly all these works employ similar tropes, constructing ecologies of abjection that explain in environmental terms the nation's failure to progress materially and to cohere in a uniform national consciousness.

As Trindade Lima points out in her etymology of *sertão*, which likely derives from "desertão" (deserted lands), the term originally referred to any sparsely inhabited interior zone, including parts of Southern states such as Rio Grande do Sul, São Paulo, and Minas Gerais, and it had no environmental specificity: it referred to jungle as much as desert (57–58). Tellingly, she highlights the Portuguese's early use of the word in describing the interior of Africa to unearth the imperial mindset that it embodies: the *sertão* was any area as yet uncolonized, but slated for conquest (57). To a certain degree, it forms an extension of the metropole/colony dichotomy, though with important distinctions. Civilization's other, the *sertão* is uninhabited (and often uninhabitable) as well as unknown to modern man. As Roberto Ventura observes, the *sertão* denotes a space outside of history and geography.[21] It is simultaneously an internal frontier and a nature outside of civilization's bounds, beyond its reach but perennially the object of its gaze. In this sense, *sertão* could also be translated as "wilderness," though not in the control through conservation sense in which the term is used in the United States. The key, as Trindade Lima reveals, lies more in its distance from public power and modernizing projects than its geographic location or lack of human inhabitants — its inhabitants exist, but they don't count: they don't figure as citizens because they have no consciousness of the nation and are not parties to the national social contract, nor do they participate in the national economy (50). Indeed, among many of the intellectuals of the Republic, the *sertão* came to represent a space of national disintegration, a place where the nation fell off the map. Paradoxically, authors such as Fernando de Azevedo postulated that Brazil's enormous size and relatively low population led to the geographical prevalence of these nationless spaces within the nation, thus converting the experiences of isolation and the absence of the State into national commonalities.[22] For this reason, Vidal e Souza finds in these authors a concept of nationhood based on expanding into the *sertão*: Brazil exists only as a future proposition, a "Brazil to be," that acquires form through successive excursions of *bandeirantes* (39–51). Implicit, of course, is the notion that the *sertão* must be constructed (and populated) from the *litoral*.

Following a century of redefinition, *sertão* is now used almost exclusively to designate the arid interior of Northeastern Brazil. This area was institutionalized as the "Polígono das Secas" or "Drought Polygon" by Getúlio Vargas's "provisional" government in 1936, indicating that the entire region has come to be considered a danger zone in the national imagination, a pre-designated disaster area in which drought characterizes every aspect of human and natural life. Partly in order to question this constraining definition of the *sertão*, I wish to return in this essay to the earlier semantic flexibility of the word, studying the modes of representation that Republican writers used to portray two quite different *sertões*: the drought-stricken interior of the Northeast, but also the overly lush, abjectly abundant Amazon basin. I argue that literary assessments of the viability for incorporation into the nation of these regions by authors such as Euclides da Cunha, Francisco José de Oliveira Vianna, and Alberto Rangel created ecologies of abjection that at best represented serious challenges to the concepts and institutions of the modern nation, and at worst threatened its continued existence.

Euclides da Cunha's work is central to my study. As one of the few intellectuals who visited in person both the interior of the Northeast and the Amazon Basin, Cunha provides a unique perspective on nation building that has led many Brazilian scholars to eulogize him, somewhat hyperbolically, as the "father of Brazilian nationality."[23] By establishing a dialogue with these two regions, which represented symbolic poles of absolute otherness from the capital in Rio de Janeiro, he sought to formulate a "unified theory" of Brazilianness that would reconcile environmental, racial, cultural, and geographical differences. His encyclopedic knowledge of his objects of study, garnered through years of researching secondary sources, coupled with the desire to engage all sides of the debate, provides an extraordinary compendium of the threads of thought and points of view that dominated the discussion of these regions' potential for development and integration into the nation. Though it would be an exaggeration to state that Cunha constructed single-handedly the ecologies of abjection that I examine, his relentless drive to synthesize prior discourse did much to tie loose ends into a single "ecology" explaining these regions, and his popularity with his contemporaries made his works an obligatory point of reference for all subsequent discussion, even today.

The Nature of Rebellion: The *Sertões* of Northeastern Brazil

Cunha first became interested in the Northeast when the central government entangled itself in quelling the so-called Canudos Rebellion of 1897. In reality a simple religious tenement founded in 1893 in a forgotten corner of the *sertão* of Bahia by an itinerant preacher, Antonio Vicente Mendes Maciel, nicknamed O Conselheiro (The Counselor), Canudos came to the attention of the federal government due to a dispute with local religious and political authorities and the draw it held for thousands of *sertanejos*, who abandoned their obligations to follow the millenarian religious movement. Its founder preached an apocalyptic message in which sixteenth-century Portuguese king Dom Sebastião would reappear on a cloud to mete out justice, and "o sertão viraria mar" (the land would become sea, or, alternately, the *sertão* would overthrow the *litoral*, as some took his message). By some estimates the second largest city in Bahia at the time, with up to 26,000 inhabitants, Canudos disrupted completely the local economy and oligarchic power structure.[24] Needless to say, the Conselheiro did not recognize the Republic's institutions, and he even rejected the authority of the Catholic Church, which he viewed as corrupt. Convinced of the threat to the nation by local authorities, who greatly exaggerated the organization and political focus of the Conselheiro's movement, the central government ended up sending four military missions to disband the settlement. The first three failed miserably, giving rise to enormous consternation in Rio de Janeiro and dire predictions of the overthrow of the Republic. The fourth succeeded in routing the rebels, razing their city and leaving only a handful of survivors.

Contributing as a journalist to the *Estado de São Paulo* newspaper, Cunha followed closely the events that were unfolding in the Northeast. A firm believer in the Republican ideals, he was as shocked as everyone else by the initial failure of the forces of progress to subdue the barbarous uprising in the backlands, and in 1897 he penned a powerful article entitled "A Nossa Vendeia" ("Our Vendée") comparing the Canudos movement to the 1793–1796 monarchist rebellion that nearly overthrew the newly minted French Republic. Convinced of the precariousness of the situation and desirous of seeing the

Republic at work in its mission to "civilize" and modernize the interior, he jumped at the chance to accompany the fourth military expedition as correspondent of the *Estado de São Paulo*. What he witnessed there transformed his perspective of Brazil and forced him to reconsider drastically his faith in the Republic. Five years later, during which he read exhaustively every available source on the region as well as a smorgasbord of European social and scientific theory, he published his iconic *Os sertões: campanha de Canudos* (1902; *Rebellion in the Backlands*).

The Northeastern *sertões* had already been inscribed as a problem zone in the national imagination two decades earlier, during the Great Drought of 1877–1879, when hundreds of thousands of ragged, starving refugees from the interior overwhelmed regional capitals in search of aid. Newspapers throughout the nation popularized the disaster with sensationalist articles depicting the degradation and suffering of the refugees, and the sudden appearance of literary narratives of the disaster gave rise to what contemporary critic Tristão de Ataíde (a pseudonym used by Alceu Amoroso Lima) called "drought literature," constructing a canon of tropes of abjection and suffering that has dominated representations of the region ever since.[25] Though naturalist drought narratives such as José de Patrocínio's *Os retirantes* (1887) and Rodolfo Teófilo's *A fome* (1890) depicted in painful detail the state of moral and physical degradation in which the refugees found themselves, they did not pay particular attention to the environment beyond describing the disaster's effects on the vegetation. Their criticisms were directed primarily towards the disaster's disruption of the social order and the legendary *sertanejo* moral code.

An ecological view of the disaster only appeared with Cunha's *Os sertões*, whose assessment of the Rebellion of Canudos concluded that the entire ecosystem, characterized by drought and desolation, had given rise to the engrained rebelliousness of the *sertanejos*. As Roberto Ventura has pointed out and I have discussed in greater depth elsewhere, Cunha's work is divided into three sections derived directly from nineteenth-century French social theorist Hippolyte Taine's formulation of environmental determinism: "A Terra" ("The Land," environment or "milieu" in Taine's language); "O Homem" ("Man," or race); and "A Luta" ("The Struggle"), which resonates with Taine's "historical moment," as well as Darwinist social theories such as those of Ludwig Gumplowicz.[26] In Cunha's mind, this triad of factors, which enveloped all others, converged in the evolution of an ungovernable, fanatical, miscegenated sub-race that he terms the *sertanejo*. He had no qualms about positing the Canudos rebels as representative of the whole, and he explicitly frames his view of the Sertão de Canudos as a microcosm of the "sertões do norte."[27]

It is revealing that Cunha's book opens with the section entitled, "The Land": he presents a view in which the landscape dominates despotically its human and non-human inhabitants. He introduces the reader to this landscape gradually, carrying one along with him on a geographic journey beginning in the mountains of Minas Gerais, which rapidly "bury themselves" in the arid plains of the Sertão (33). Verticality assumes a key position in his descriptions: the author's (and his reader's) panoramic view descends from the mountaintops to immerse itself in the hellish nature below. This in turns creates a visual hierarchy in which the Southern traveler (or reader) gains a privileged viewpoint not afforded to the residents of the area. The latter's depth of vision is cut off by the *caatinga*, the dense, spiny scrublands that violently resist even visual intrusion:

> Ao passo que a caatinga o afoga; abrevia-lhe o olhar; agride-o e estonteia-o; enlaça-o na trama espinescente e não o atrai; repulsa-o com as folhas urticantes, com o espinho, com os gravetos estalados em lanças; e desdobra-se-lhe na frente léguas e léguas, imutável no aspecto desolado; árvores sem folhas, de galhos estorcidos e secos, revoltos, entrecruzados, apontando rijamente no espaço ou estirando-se flexuosos pelo solo, lembrando um bracejar imenso, de tortura, da flora agonizante... [70].

> [As the *caatinga* suffocates him, curtailing his vision, attacking him, dazing him, it entraps him in the spiny tangle but it doesn't reel him in; it repulses him with caustic leaves, with spines, with sticks bursting into spears; and it unfolds in front of him for miles and miles, unchanging in its desolate aspect; trees without leaves, of branches shrunken and dried, disorderly, intertwined, pointing harshly into space or slumping flexibly to the ground, reminding one of a huge, torturous spasm of dying vegetation...]

The short-sightedness provoked by the impenetrable labyrinth of spines has devastating effects for the psychological development of the *sertanejo* residents of the area, depriving them of foresight and the ability to perform rational planning, thus making them susceptible to disaster as well as irrational behavior. Clarity of vision is further disrupted by the prevalence of optical illusions: the bases of mountains disappear into the horizon and illusory lakes appear whose false waters reflect blinding sparks of light, making the geography nearly impossible to map (63). In this atmosphere, positive empiricism based on the primacy of vision has no possibility of evolving, and even the observer trained outside of the region finds his finely honed skills of little use.

To make matters worse, all the nature looks the same, fatiguing the observer's eye and disorienting him. Cunha describes how the plant life, viewed together, seems almost of a single species of the same desolate aspect, diverging only in size (70). His insistence on the monotony of the plant life is reminiscent of the colonial trope of the uniformity of races other than European — with all differences subordinated to skin and hair color, "they all look the same." Here the imperial eye is extended to flora: extreme otherness is perceived as indistinguishable uniformity. In the absence of the leaves, fruits, and flowers that naturalists used to distinguish between species in the coastal rainforest, and which led explorers such as Columbus to praise the "mil maneras" (thousands of types) of tropical plant life, the summer deciduous *caatinga* appears an impoverished, abject nature.[28] As Cunha pointedly remarks, its forbidding aspect is such that it led German naturalist Carl Friedrich Philipp von Martius to label it "silva horrida" (horrid vegetation) following a nineteenth-century visit to the region (58). Its sole redeeming quality is its ability to survive in hostile conditions (70).

Overall, the vision of the *sertão* that Cunha constructs is that of a nature that traumatizes its viewer (50). He describes a geography of stone composed of gneiss and granite, in which plant life holds on only tenuously in the fissures, resulting in the "strange nakedness of the land" (48). The vegetation is agonistic, seared, tortured by the stony landscape and the caustic sun, and it is nearly uninhabited by humans, whose presence is only betrayed by ghost towns of abandoned structures (43–44). Drawing on social theories that posit human population growth as the basis of material progress, he reiterates frequently the trope of the depopulation of the *sertão*, an image that he extends to the landscape: he speaks of mountains that lie in ruins and fallen blocks of stone that remind him of dead cities, creating the sensation of walking on the rubble left by successive earthquakes (293). The land and its inhabitants are equally martyred by the elements and the "unbreathable air" (493). For Cunha, the *sertão* is a traumatized landscape forged by disaster, and it is nearly uninhabitable, especially by modern man.

Though much, much more can be said about Cunha's representation of the *sertão*'s nature, due to space constraints I wish only to emphasize two additional, related key tropes: the concept that the *sertão* is an unstable, degraded space and the idea that it is a land outside of history. Throughout the text, Cunha describes the *sertão* as a geography in flux that is destabilized by the climate. This is in part due to extreme oscillations in the air temperature, which fluctuates in an "intermitir ináturavel" (unnaturalizable intermittence) between burning days and freezing nights (59). However, the physical geography itself is also unstable and chaotic: eroded ridges crisscross haphazardly, creating intermittent streams that occasionally even flow uphill or against each other (52–53). He theorizes that this geographical instability of the region is due to a relatively youthful geological history. Influenced by socio-geological theories postulating that the most developed civilizations had sprung up where nature itself was more ancient, and thus more amenable to human life, he writes that: "Acredita-se que a região incipiente ainda está preparando-se para a vida: o líquen ainda ataca a pedra, fecundando a terra"

[It leads one to believe that the incipient region is still preparing itself for life: lichen is still attacking the stone, fertilizing the earth] (50). He thus attributes the poverty of vegetable life to the incompletion of nature's project to prepare itself for human habitation. Tellingly, the descriptions of a youthful *sertão* are never characterized by the exuberance that European explorers associated with "New World" environments; instead they live side by side with descriptions of premature decadence. Given the emphasis placed by nineteenth-century naturalism on steady-state evolutionary forms achieved through protracted historical progression, a concept that extended even to theories of race and nationalism, Cunha found the unstable, shifting geography of the *sertão* particularly troublesome, for how could one hope to construct a solid national edifice on such a mutable, unfinished landscape?

Not surprisingly, considering his adhesion to the principles of environmental determinism, Cunha extends his view of the *sertão* environment to the *sertanejos* themselves in the section dedicated to "Man." I have already touched upon the way in which he believed that the labyrinthic *caatinga*, with its impenetrable tangle of spines, literally disrupted the line of sight of the *sertão*'s inhabitants, making it impossible for them to develop the foresight and objectivism necessary for rational thought. He argues furthermore that the inclement environment forced a physiological "de-evolution" or evolutionary regression that ruptured the equilibrium between cerebral and muscular development (88). He praises repeatedly the *sertanejos'* physical fortitude and tenacity for survival, giving rise to the most cited line from his book: "O sertanejo é, antes de tudo, um forte" [More than anything, the *sertanejo* is strong] (146). Unfortunately, the prevalence of physical strength implies the decline of rational as well as "moral" function, as his next lines make clear. Like the *sertanejo* flora, the sole admirable quality of the *sertanejo* people is their ability to survive in the hellish conditions. And ultimately, the unstable environment gives rise to the mental imbalances that allow widespread, unorthodox religious fanaticism to take root (172).

The effects of the local environment on the human body and mind are not the only elements that Cunha takes into account in his examination of the causality behind the Canudos rebellion. He also dedicates a large portion of his essay to the topic of race, which presents a deep quandary to his thought. Citing European theorists such as Foville and Spencer, Cunha postulates that the *sertanejo*, as the product of miscegenation between "conquerors" and "the conquered," is racially unbalanced — "um desequilibrado" constantly oscillating between the antagonistic, "pure" races that formed it (133–141). This interiorization of racial opposites leads to the formation of a "hysterical," schizophrenic being, who is, naturally, predisposed to religious fanaticism and against rational thought. These "inescapable natural laws" of human evolution rub Cunha the wrong way, however. Basing himself on European postulations of ethnic unity as the foundation of shared citizenship, he, like many of his contemporaries, entertains the notion that the *curiboca*, or mixture of indigenous Tupi and Portuguese phenotypes, represents the future of Brazilian nationality. In fact, he arrives at the point of declaring that the *sertanejos*, whom he considers the purest *curibocas* due to their relative isolation from the coastal populations of black slaves and European immigrants, have the potential to form the "rocha viva," or bedrock, of Brazilian nationality (133, 605). Unfortunately, they don't seem to have arrived at the racial steady state that would make this possible: their irrational fanaticism and stubborn servitude to outdated traditions strikes a serious blow against their possibilities for representing the national subject. Instead, he predicts that they will go extinct, as their miscegenated racial makeup and overly specialized adaptations to the environment of the *sertão* cause them to straggle further and further behind in the "universal," evolutionary march of progress (17–19).

In this way, Cunha weaves a perspective of the Canudos conflict in which the *sertão* and its residents alike are completely at odds with modernity. In fact, he states in one moment that due to the radical environmental and cultural differences that they confronted in the *sertão*, the Republic's troops felt as if they were fighting a war on foreign soil (515).[29] Tellingly, the *sertão* environment itself becomes the accomplice of the *sertanejos* in their war against progress, attacking the Republican troops and protecting their opponents. As Cunha declares at one point, describing the logistical problems that plagued the military: "O que era preciso combater a todo o transe, e vencer, não era o jagunço, era o deserto" [What was necessary to combat and defeat the entire way was not the *jagunço*, it was the desert] (504).[30] The *sertão* and the *sertanejos* together form a single rebellious, antagonistic ecology, and in order to defeat and reform the *sertanejo* people, the hellish environment must first be overcome.

This "rehabilitation" will come through what Cunha and many of his contemporaries referred to as the "saneamento da terra" (the healing, or alternately sanitization, of the land): the technological modification of the environment to make it more amenable to human habitation, specifically through irrigation, the implementation of industrialized agriculture, and modern hygiene and tropical medicine. As he points out repeatedly, the potential is present, for during the rainy season the *sertão* reverts to the green abundance that fits in more clearly with the national imaginary of Brazil as tropical paradise: the "tropical flora re-emerges triumphantly," suddenly converting the *sertão* into a bucolic paradise that contrasts starkly with his earlier descriptions of the area (79–82). In this way, he frames the social disaster of drought, the *sertanejo* failure to progress intellectually and materially, and the rebellion of Canudos as direct consequences of a lack of water. The implication, which he develops more explicitly in *Contrastes e confrontos* (1907; *Contrasts and Confrontations*), is that technical modernization will solve all the region's problems, transforming its abject nature into a reflection of the national imaginary of abundance and incorporating the rebellious *sertanejos* into the national market and political structure.[31] Of course, his solution signifies the end of the *sertão* and the *sertanejo* as autonomous entities: with their environmental and cultural differences erased, their quintessential *brasilidade* (Brazilian-ness) will be free to shine through.

Opulent Chaos and Flawed Grandeur: the Amazon Basin

Cunha's *Os sertões* became a bestseller almost immediately following its publication in 1902. The Brazilian reading public rushed to buy his book in unprecedented numbers, desirous of knowing the lurid details of what had really happened in Canudos and enchanted by Cunha's eloquent style and nuanced interpretation of events.[32] He became one of Brazil's most recognized celebrities overnight. His sudden rise to fame culminated in his election to the Brazilian Acadêmia de Letras in 1903, a mere year after the publication of his book. Surprisingly, the speech that he gave upon accepting his chair in the Acadêmia in 1906 did not even allude to *Os sertões*, focusing instead on his recent journey to the Amazon.[33]

In 1904, Cunha's close friend, historian Manuel de Oliveira Lima, introduced him to then Minister of Foreign Relations, José Maria da Silva Paranhos Júnior, the Baron of Rio Branco. The Baron had achieved national fame for negotiating shrewdly boundary disputes with Brazil's neighbors, and most recently for resolving the conflict with Bolivia over the Amazonian territory of Acre, which Bolivia ceded to Brazil in the Treaty of Petrópolis (1903). In 1904, Brazil found itself immersed in yet another tussle over land in the Amazon, this time with Peru over the Upper Purus river basin. Rio Branco invited Cunha to head up the Brazilian contingent of a bilateral expedition to map the course of the Purus and fix the national boundaries. Cunha accepted without hesitation, avid to experience in person the fabled nature that so many of the European naturalists he admired had exalted in their works. He arrived in the Amazon in 1905, at the height of the rubber boom, spending nine months mapping the territory as well as studying its nature and the rubber economy. Upon returning to Rio de Janeiro, he published a rather dry official report on his expedition in 1906, and several more suggestive essays that he wrote detailing his experience appeared posthumously under the title *À margem da História* (1909; *On the Margin of History*). A more definitive text, compiling all of his work and correspondence relating to his experiences in the Amazon, was published in 1976 as *Um paraíso perdido* (*A Paradise Lost*), a title suggested by a letter in which he stated that he was working on the Amazonian equivalent of *Os sertões*. Unfortunately, this project was cut tragically short by his untimely death in a duel in 1909.

Somewhat surprisingly, given the vast differences between the two ecosystems, Cunha's writings on the Amazon repeat variations on many of the tropes found in *Os sertões*. As in his first contact with the arid interior of the Northeast, Cunha found himself unpleasantly disillusioned with the nature of the Amazon when his ship pulled into the mouth of the river. Having repeated the pattern of performing extensive textual research before visiting the region, his theoretical formation once again came into conflict with visual observation, creating a crushing tension between the literary sublimation of his sources on the Amazon and personal experience. In his acceptance speech to the Academia, he described the spectacular disappointment that he experienced when he perceived that the famed "rio-mar" (river-sea) was, in reality, merely a vast swamp in which land and river were indistinguishable, an uninspiring, "shipwrecked" landscape that was but a muddy imitation of the sea without its mysteries or attractions.[34] The Amazonian environment mirrored the lack of definition of the *caatinga* in the Northeastern *sertão*, and the instability that he attributed to the *sertão* as an environment still in development was exacerbated in the Amazon. Here, the geography was literally mutable, inverting the "natural" geological order as the river dominated and molded the land instead of the other way around.

As Cunha's statement to the Academia makes evident, his work on the Amazon endows visual observation with a similar primacy to that given it in *Os sertões*, and he encounters similar frustrations to those he experienced in the *caatinga*. Reflecting on his ascension of the Purus River, he notes that after traveling hundreds of miles, the observer has the impression of being trapped in a circular trajectory in which all the geological features repeat themselves interminably (99). With no vertical variation, the observer's eyes become fatigued and, as in the *caatinga*, he feels that "o seu olhar, inexplicavelmente, se abrevia nos sem-fins daqueles horizontes vazios e indefinidos como os dos mares" [His gaze is inexplicably curtailed in the endlessness of those horizons, empty and undefined like those of the ocean] (99). And once again, limited sight translates into a lack of moral and political vision for the region's inhabitants.

On the other hand, the stationary observer is alarmed by sudden transformations of nature directly before his eyes, leading Cunha to the conclusion that in the Amazon, movement is not spatial but temporal (99). Given the centrality of linear movement in the Enlightenment concept of progress, with its emphasis on spatial expansion and bridging distances, its frustration here forces Cunha to reconsider once again his premises regarding the construction of Brazilian nationality in the Western model of modernity. In fact, he is only able to "see" the Amazon following a visit to the Museum of Pará in the company of two local naturalists: only the museum's mediation allows what formerly seemed a void, featureless landscape ("an excess of skies over an excess of waters") to transform before his very eyes into a still incomplete "contemporary and unpublished page of Genesis" (84). He must read the Amazon through the museum's logical reordering of its chaotic nature, which forces him to the realization that in order to perceive it with any kind of objectivity, he must reeducate his eyes and learn a new way of seeing, which he describes as a "microscopic" perspective. As a lover of grand, panoramic vistas, he is unable to adapt completely, leaving to others the labor of unraveling the mysteries of the Amazon. In fact, he postulated in his foreword to Rangel's *Inferno verde* that in order for modern man to comprehend completely the Amazon, an evolutionary transformation in consciousness must occur, for perceiving the Amazon is akin to perceiving infinity.[35]

The Amazonian landscape is transitory; islands form and disappear in mere months, and the topography of the river banks is constantly shifting as the rivers form and undo loops and folds, or collapse in on themselves in the dreaded "terras caídas" (fallen lands), sometimes carrying human settlements with them, as is the case in Rangel's story of the same name in *Inferno verde*.[36] The Amazon River itself confounds geographical logic, periodically reversing its flow and becoming a "tributary of its own tributaries" (106). Likewise, the plant life is anything but harmonious, cannibalizing itself in an endless "vast, noiseless battle" (105). The Amazonian ecosystem represents nature at war with itself. In such a disordered environment, evolution itself becomes a chaotic process, giving rise to "singular and monstrous fauna": "animais que existem imperfeitamente, como tipos abstratos ou simples elos da escala evolutiva" [animals that exist imperfectly, as abstract types or mere links in the evolutionary chain] (100). Summarizing, Cunha muses that "Tal é o rio; tal a sua história: revolta, desordenada, incompleta" [Thus is the river; thus is its history: agitated, disordered, incomplete] (106). This chaotic environmental instability in turn reflects on the human social landscape, giving rise to a predominantly nomadic society that lacks the permanent ties to the land that he considers the basis of civilization. As the moral of Rangel's "Terra caída" makes clear, constructing a local economy, much less a modern nation, on such treacherous soil is a Sisyphean exercise in failure.

In fact, the Amazon, like the Northeastern *sertões*, becomes a point of national disintegration. In one particularly engaging passage, Cunha laments that the Amazon does not have a proper delta, which would normally expand a nation's territory by depositing silt at the river's mouth (104). Here, the opposite is true: the Amazon grinds down the national soil and dumps it unceremoniously into the Atlantic, where it is swept away on currents to the U.S. states of Georgia and South Carolina. He waxes poetic, remarking that the Brazilian who disembarks on those shores experiences the paradoxical feeling of standing on Brazilian land outside of Brazil, thus creating a strange twist on the extraterritoriality associated with exile: the "landless nation" becomes a "nationless land" in a kind of "telluric emigration," in which the land "abandons man" (104). Concluding this meditation on the unfaithfulness of the Amazon, he highlights the irony that "O rio que sobre todos desafia o nosso lirismo patriótico, é o menos brasileiro dos rios. É um estranho adversário, entregue dia e noite à faina de solapar a sua própria terra" [The river that more than any other provokes our patriotic lyricism is the least Brazilian of all rivers. It's a strange adversary, dedicated day and night to the labor of undermining its own land] (104). And a few pages onward, he dialogues transparently with his comment in Os sertões that the soldiers involved in the Canudos conflict felt "outside the nation": he compares the Southern bureaucrat assigned to the region to an exile, who feels "quarantined from human culture," dislocated in time and space to a "dark waiting room of history" (126).

Though Cunha repeats the tropes of distance and depopulation that were central in Os sertões, he diverges significantly on two other counts, which signifies a shift away from environmental determinism towards a more positive assessment of the possibilities for integration of marginal environments and their inhabitants into Brazilian nationality. Conspicuously absent from his writings on the Amazon are the meditations on race that soured the outlook for national unity in Os sertões. Once again, he largely ignores the indigenous populations, who are viewed alternately as mere functions of the landscape or as precursors of the caboclo, to which he now gives full credence as the national phenotype. Likewise, he pays little attention to the local or Amazonian caboclos. In contrast, he repeatedly voices his admiration for the Northeastern sertanejo migrants to the area, who have transformed drastically from their representation in Os sertões as abject drought victims and ungovernable jagunços into modern day bandeirantes, who persevere in the labor of forging the nation. Though still portrayed as victims of the rubber economy, the sertanejo rubber workers, or seringueiros, have been completely rehabilitated through their patriotic expansion of the nation during the conflict with Bolivia over Acre. Without any material or medical support from the nation, the sertanejos succeeded in colonizing the tropics in only twenty years, a feat that bested even the British and French colonial projects with their vast resources and schools of tropical medicine. The *sertanejos'* elevation to the status of intrepid national founders doesn't modify entirely Cunha's views on the region's inhabitants, however; what he chalked up to racial abjection in *Os sertões* is substituted for by moral degradation, which is now caused not by miscegenation, but the execrable exploitation of *seringueiros* in an abject economy approaching slavery.

Likewise, Cunha reformulates his views on the tropical climate. In *Os sertões*, he had postulated that the climate of the Amazon forced an evolutionary regression as human organs adapted in negative ways to the climate — adaptations that would be transmitted to future generations through Lamarckian use inheritance, inducing further regressions until the modified sub-race eventually went extinct (112–13). He contradicts his former point of view in letters detailing his personal "adaptation" to the climate and a section in *Terra sem história* entitled "A clima calumniada" ("A Maligned Climate"). Though he concedes that the Amazonian climate is wholly habitable, and in fact quite pleasant due to the moderating influence of the surrounding forest (he even goes so far as to compare it to that of the Mediterranean), he does not completely abandon his Darwinist leanings (229). Instead, he develops a theory of "telluric selection," in which the Amazonian environment weeds out the weaklings. In fact, this concept lies at the heart of his "rehabilitation" of the *sertanejo*— only a few hardy settlers survived the hardships of life in the Amazon, the rest having succumbed to hunger and sickness, particularly since they were already weakened from suffering drought and moral degradation. The remaining survivors form a new class of "fortes," who will form the base of the Brazilian nationality.

For Cunha, the *sertanejo* migrants to the Amazon turned a new leaf in tropical medicine: by adapting to and harnessing the hostile environment, they initiated the process of "healing" the pathological region. And like the *sertões* of the Northeast, the transformation of the abject environment through modernization, urbanization (in Manaus and Pará), and hygiene will make possible its incorporation into the national economy. The colonization of the region by the national phenotype, the *caboclo*, will continue the labor of ethnic consolidation that will eventually give birth to the true Brazilian citizen. Cunha's ecologies of abjection are thus not purely derogatory; national integration is within reach, it simply requires the annulment of difference. Still at issue, however, was the potential for these groups to participate in democratic governance, particularly given the desire of the newly constituted Acreans to establish political autonomy as a recognized Brazilian state, a movement that evoked violent reactions from Southern politicians and thinkers such as Francisco José de Oliveira Vianna.[37]

The Natural Nation

Euclides da Cunha and his contemporaries developed powerful foundational narratives based on the incorporation of the *sertões* into the nation, which they saw as still under construction. Confronted with radical environmental and cultural differences in their travels in the interior, nation building translated for these Southern intellectuals into the extension of the *litoral* into the *sertão*, contingent on the annulment or at least attenuation of the latter's differences. This is not to say that they saw the South as a perfect model; on the contrary, nearly all of their writings reveal increasing disillusionment with the Republic and what Cunha in one moment criticized as the coastal "civilização de copistas" (civilization of copiers) of European models. Oliveira Vianna in particular became fiercely critical of "legal Brazil," whose paper democracy patterned on the Constitutions of the U.S. and Western Europe did not correspond in the least to Brazilian social and political reality (144–46). In any case, most Southern intellectuals were willing to make at least some concessions in search of a common denominator of national unity, and Cunha himself ended up positing the *sertanejo* as the most authentic example of *brasilidade*, or Brazilian-ness.[38] Nevertheless, their representations of the *sertões* reveal that as much as they may have wished, they were never completely successful in freeing themselves from a concept of the nation based on the South. Nowhere does this become clearer than in the literary construction of the *sertões* as ecologies of abjection that required drastic transformations through technological modifications of the environment, hygiene, civic education, and even, for some, eugenics, in order to conform to their notions of Brazilian territoriality.

Depictions of these regions as the "negative" or "other" of modern Brazil reveals continued adhesion to the foundational narrative of a national ecology, if no longer a perfect paradise, still based on the coastal climate, flora, and economy. The *mata atlântica*, the subtropical coastal ecosystem in which once abounded the *pau-brasil* (Brazilwood), the tree whose wood formed the foundation of the early colonial economy and for which Brazil was named, continued to be the model by which all other ecosystems were measured, thus constituting a kind of national nature in the Brazilian imagination. Tellingly, despite the prevalence of naturalism in the literature of the Republic, the tropes of paradise never disappeared completely: Roberto Ventura reveals their persistence in the "tropical style" that turn-of-the-twentieth-century literary critic Capistrano Abreu proposed as a national aesthetics (17–19). Furthermore, Murilo Carvalho details how many of the same Republican authors that attacked uncritical "ufanismo" in erudite essays addressed to their colleagues paradoxically employed those same tropes in the textbooks that they wrote for schoolchildren, actively propagating this view among future generations (114). In this way, the tropes of a national paradise based on the coastal ecosystem lived on side by side with more critical views, and they even complemented each other, solidifying the notion that the rest of Brazil should somehow come to resemble the South, a view that retains much of its strength even today.

Despite the powerful dominance in the national imagination of the subtropical coastal ecosystem as "national nature," to the exclusion of all others, there were dissenters among intellectuals hailing from the *sertões*, many of whom wrote equally eloquent replies attacking the "geographic fatalism" of their detractors. In 1923, José Américo de Almeida published a voluminous essay entitled *A Paraíba e seus problemas (Paraíba and its Problems)* that refuted one for one the deterministic, often racist arguments that portrayed the local environment and inhabitants as unfit for modernity. Similarly, Araújo Lima defended the *Amazônia: a terra e o homem (Amazonia: The Land and its Men*; 1932), blaming the negative depiction of the region on out-of-touch theories formulated by Europeans who had never visited the region. Though he concedes that the Amazon is a difficult environment, he argues that the lack of hygiene and education are the only factors holding back its development. Strangely, neither of these authors refutes Southern claims of embodiment of the national nature: in fact, they acknowledge transparently their regions' social and environmental marginality. Perhaps recognizing the futility of struggling against the dominant discourse, they prefer to work from within it, limiting differences and emphasizing compatibilities with the national model. In other words, they rewrite their regions in terms of the national paradise.

Nevertheless, regionalist challenges to paradise's exclusivity and inroads in modernization in the *sertões* forced the amendment of its tropes, leading eventually to the relative abandonment of their restriction to the coastal South. In the second half of the twentieth century, abstract nationalist discourses of *mestiçagem* and *brasilidade* that proclaimed Brazil a homogenous, perfectly blended racial and cultural utopia came into vogue, displacing the primacy of the discourse of paradise as a uniform, national nature. Of course, this reformulation of Brazil as a social paradise reflected the notions of Brazilian nationality as a project still under construction: the social utopia was a paradise to be, a promise not yet fully come to fruition. As in Columbus's days, paradise was still just around the corner. And, unavoidably, the discursive construction of a social paradise, with its emphasis on national homogeneity, brought with it its own problems in the continued marginalization of those who did not fit its schema.

NOTES

1. All translations are my own unless otherwise noted.

2. See Sérgio Buarque de Holanda's *Visão do paraíso* for a detailed examination of the European debate on the location of the Garden of Eden.

3. *Ibid.*, 272.

4. *Ibid.*, 254.

5. *Ibid.*, 164.

6. Murilo de Carvalho, "The Edenic Motif in the Brazilian Social Imaginary," 112.

7. See Crosby, *Ecological Imperialism: The Biological Expansion of Europe, 900–1900*.

8. Carvalho, "Edenic Motif," 112.

9. Holanda, *Visão do paraíso*, 15–16; Carvalho, "Edenic Motif," 112.

10. Carvalho, "Edenic Motif," 113.

11. See the introduction to Elaine Freedgood's *Victorian Writing about Risk*.

12. In *A formação da literatura brasileira: momentos decisivos*, Antonio Candido postulates that the Brazilian romantics' adhesion to European models forced them to view themselves through foreign eyes, thus resulting in the sense of the exotic self that their works impart (II, 324).

13. See the first chapter of Roberto Ventura's *Estilo tropical: história cultural e polêmicas literárias no Brasil, 1870–1914*.

14. Holanda, *Visão do paraíso*, 344–45.

15. Rangel, *Inferno verde: cenas e cenários do Amazonas*, 62.

16. Prado, *Retrato do Brasil: ensaio sobre a tristeza brasileira*.

17. See Durval Muniz de Albuquerque, Jr., *A invenção do nordeste e outras artes*; Nísia Trindade Lima, *Um sertão chamado Brasil: intelectuais e representação geográfica da identidade nacional*; and Candice Vidal e Souza, *A pátria geográfica: sertão e litoral no pensamento social brasileiro*.

18. See the third chapter of Thomas Skidmore's *Black into White: Race and Nationality in Brazilian Thought*.

19. See the second chapter of Trindade Lima's *Um sertão chamado Brasil*.

20. The statistics I cite on drought come from Marco Antonio Villa's *Vida e morte no sertão: história das secas no nordeste nos séculos XIX e XX*, 83.

21. Ventura, "Visões do deserto: selva e sertão em Euclides da Cunha," 137.

22. Azevedo, *A cultura brasileira*, 75.

23. Exemplary are Paulo Dantas's comments in *Os sertões de Euclides e outros sertões*, in which he calls Cunha the "proto-thinker," the "designer of the master plan of our nationality," 10.

24. Nogueira Galvão, *Gatos de outro saco: ensaios críticos*, 83.

25. For an early genealogy of this "drought literature," see the second part of Tristão de Ataide's *Afonso Arinos*.

26. Ventura, "Visões do deserto," 138; Anderson, "From Natural to National Disasters: Drought and the Brazilian Subject in Euclides da Cunha's *Os sertões*," 549.

27. Cunha, *Os sertões (campanha de Canudos)*, ed. and introd. Adelino Brandão. (São Paolo: Martin Claret, 2005), 64.

28. Hyperbolic descriptions of "New World" natural abundance are a key trope in foundational texts of the discourse of paradise such as the "Carta de Colón anunciando el descubrimiento del Nuevo Mundo" ("Columbus's Letter Announcing the Discovery of the New World"; 1493).

29. Maria Zilda Ferreira Curry comments that at root of this sense of exile lay the fact that the *sertão* did not conform to the imaginary of Brazil as tropical paradise in "*Os sertões*, de Euclides da Cunha: Espaços," 73.

30. Cunha uses *jagunço* to designate the *sertanejo* guerrilla warriors that fought against

the government in the War of Canudos. As Nogueira Galvão notes, the term has negative connotations of banditry, living outside the law, and working as hired guns for local *coronéis*, or politicking landowners (74–75).

31. Cunha, *Contrastes e confrontos* (São Paulo: Cultrix, 1975).

32. For a recounting of the commercial success of Cunha's book, refer to Regina Abreu's *O enigma de Os sertões*.

33. See Cunha, "Falando aos acadêmicos" in *Um paraíso perdido*.

34. *Ibid.*, 83.

35. This foreword is included in *Um paraíso perdido*, 287.

36. These descriptions appear on page 106 of Cunha's *Um paraíso perdido*.

37. See Oliveira Vianna's 1921 "O erro da autonomia acreana," which cites Cunha's early postulations that the *sertanejos* were historically and evolutionarily incapable of understanding the political abstractions necessary for democratic citizenship.

38. As is often pointed out, Cunha's work gives contradictory representations of the *sertanejo* simultaneously as an abject sub-race slated for extinction and as an admirably resistant phenotype that may contain the seeds of Brazil's only hope for a nationality based on the racial homogeneity postulated by European theorists as the basis of national commonality. Clearly, these paradoxes reveal contested spaces or fissures in Cunha's discourse in which theory and practice enter into conflict. In the most lucid reading of this problem to date, Nogueira Galvão associates these tensions with Cunha's development of a method that uses aesthetics to synthesize opposing strains of thought and impose coherence on irreconcilable ideological stances (81, 94).

WORKS CITED

Abreu, Regina. *O enigma de Os sertões*. Rio de Janeiro: Funarte/Rocco, 1998.

Almeida, José Américo de. *A Paraiba e seus problemas*. 1923. João Pessoa: Estado da Paraíba, Secretaria da Educação e Cultura, Diretoria Geral de Cultura, 1980.

Anderson, Mark. "From Natural to National Disasters: Drought and the Brazilian Subject in Euclides da Cunha's Os sertões." *Hispania* 91.3 (2008): 547–57.

Araújo Lima, José Francisco de. *Amazônia: a terra e o homem*. 1932. São Paulo: Editora Nacional, 1937.

Ataíde, Tristão de. *Afonso Arinos*. Rio de Janeiro: Anuário do Brasil, 1922.

Azevedo, Fernando de. *A cultura brasileira: introdução ao estudo da cultura no Brasil*. São Paulo: Melhoramentos, 1958.

Buarque de Holanda, Sérgio. *Visão do paraíso: os motivos edênicos no descobrimento e colonização do Brasil*. Rio de Janeiro: José Olympio, 1959.

Candido, Antonio. *Formação da literatura brasileira: momentos decisivos*. 2 vols. Belo Horizonte: Itatiaia; São Paulo: Universidade de São Paulo, 1975.

Cardim, Fernão. *Tratados da terra e a gente do Brasil*. São Paulo: Editora Nacional, 1939.

Crosby, Alfred. *Ecological Imperialism: The Biological Expansion of Europe, 900–1900*. Cambridge: Cambridge University Press, 2004.

Cunha, Euclides da. *Contrastes e confrontos*. São Paulo: Cultrix, 1975.

———. *Um paraíso perdido: reunião dos ensaios amazônicos*. Edited by Hildon Rocha. Petrópolis: Vozes, 1976.

———. *Os sertões (campanha de canudos)*. Edited with an introduction by Adelino Brandão. São Paolo: Martin Claret, 2005.

Dantas, Paulo. *Os sertões de Euclides e outros sertões*. São Paulo: Conselho Estadual de Cultura, Comissão de Literatura, 1969.

Ferreira Curry, Maria Zilda. "*Os sertões*, de Euclides da Cunha: espaços." *Luso-Brazilian Review* 41.1 (2004): 71–79.

Freedgood, Elaine. *Victorian Writing about Risk: Imagining a Safe England in a Dangerous World*. Cambridge: Cambridge University Press, 2000.

Holanda, Sérgio Buarque de. *Visão do paraíso: os motivos edênicos no descobrimento e colonização do Brasil*. Rio de Janeiro: José Olympio, 1959.

Lima, Nísia Trinidade. *Um sertão chamado Brasil: intelectuais e representação geográfica da identidade nacional*. Rio de Janeiro: Revan; Universidade Candido Mendes, 1998.

Muniz de Albuquerque, Durval Jr. *A invenção do nordeste e outras artes*. Recife: Fundação Joaquim Nabuco, Massangana; São Paulo: Cortez, 1999.

Murilo de Carvalho, José. "The Edenic Motif in the Brazilian Social Imaginary." *Brazilian Review of Social Sciences* Special issue 1 (2000): 111–28.

Nogueira Galvão, Walnice. *Gatos de outro saco: ensaios críticos*. São Paulo: Brasiliense, 1981.

Oliveira Vianna, Francisco José de. "O erro da autonomia sertaneja." *Pequenos estudos de psicologia social*. São Paulo: Editora Nacional, 1942. 143–56.

Prado, Paulo. *Retrato do Brasil: ensaio sobre a tristeza brasileira*. Rio de Janeiro: José Olympio, 1962.

Rangel, Alberto. *Inferno verde: cenas e cenários do Amazonas*. Manaus: Valer, 2001.

Skidmore, Thomas. *Black into White: Race and Nationality in Brazilian Thought*. New York: Oxford University Press, 1974.

Trindade Lima, Nísia. *Um sertão chamado Brasil: intelectuais e representação geográfica da identidade nacional*. Rio de Janeiro: Revan; Universidade Candido Mendes, Instituto Universitário de Pesquisas do Rio de Janeiro, 1999.

Ventura, Roberto. *Estilo tropical: história cultural e polêmicas literárias no Brasil, 1870–1914*. São Paulo: Companhia das Letras, 1991.

_____. "Visões do deserto: selva e sertão em Euclides da Cunha." *História, ciências, saúde: Manguinhos* 5 (1998): 133–47.

Vidal e Souza, Candice. *A pátria geográfica: sertão e litoral no pensamento social brasileiro*. Goiâna: Universidade Federal de Goiâna, 1997.

Villa, Marco Antonio. *Vida e morte no sertão: história das secas no nordeste nos séculos XIX e XX*. São Paulo: Ática, 2000.

Epilogue:
"Beyond the Telluric Novel"

Adrian Taylor Kane

The ecocritical analyses in the preceding essays make a convincing argument that environmental criticism offers a more profound understanding of Latin American and Latina/o literatures and cultures. If it is true, as Lawrence Buell has suggested, that "environmental criticism is in the tense but enviable position of being a wide-open movement still sorting out its premises and its powers," the horizon of opportunity for this form of criticism in Latin American and Latina/o studies is even broader, as there is an enormous amount of terrain that has yet to be explored.[1] In this sense, the current volume is a scratch in the surface of the vast quantity of cultural production that merits ecocritical analysis. As evidenced in this anthology and other ecocritical scholarship, environmental criticism in Latin American and Latina/o studies promises the opportunity for innovative re-readings of canonical texts, scrutiny of contemporary and environmentally oriented writing, and rediscovery of previously overlooked works.

In the conclusion of "Nature and the Discourse of Modernity in Spanish American Avant-Garde Fiction," I have suggested that the role of the Latin American intellectual in the twenty-first century will be to continue to redefine modernity to include a paradigm for sustainable living. In Spanish American fiction, such a critique of modernity has already begun to play out aesthetically in the emergence of a new body of novels dedicated to environmental issues. Laura Barbas Rhoden, in her study of Gioconda Belli's novel *Waslala* (1996) and Anacristina Rossi's *La loca de Gandoca* (1992), signals a greening of Central American literature.[2] The analyses in the present volume of Mempo Giardinelli's *Final de novela en Patagonia* (2000; End of Novel in Patagonia), Edgardo Rodríguez Juliá's *San Juan, ciudad soñada* (2005; *San Juan: Memoir of a City*) and Mayra Montero's *Tú, la oscuridad* (1995; *In the Palm of Darkness*) indicate that the greening trend that Barbas Rhoden observes in Central American fiction can be extended to other regions of Spanish America as well.

As the scope of this anthology has not been limited to environmental writing, there are several novels not analyzed here that also point toward a heightened ecological consciousness in contemporary Spanish American fiction in recent decades. Among these works are Guatemalan author Rodrigo Rey Rosa's *Lo que soñó Sebastián* (1994; What Sebastian Dreamt), Mexican novelist Leonardo da Jandra's *Huatulqueños* (1991; The People from Huatulco), his compatriot Héctor Aguilar Camín's *El resplandor de la madera* (2001; The Brilliance of Wood), and Ecuadorian Demetrio Aguilera-Malta's *Canal Zone* (1977). *Lo que soñó Sebastián* presents one man's resistance to poachers in the Petén jungle. *Huatulqueños* captures the struggle between indigenous citizens and the federal government over the use of natural resources in Oaxaca. *El resplandor de la madera* portrays the mahogany forests of a mythical Caribbean town as casualties in the capitalist battle for accumulation, and *Canal Zone* includes discussion of the ecological impact of the Panama Canal.[3] As Jonathan Tittler has suggested in "Ecological Criticism and Spanish American Fiction," other contemporary Spanish American authors interested in environmental themes are the Chilean novelists Luis Sepúlveda and Fernando Castellanos Raga, and the Mexican Homero Aridjis. Sepúlveda's *Mundo del fin del mundo* (1991; The World at the End of the World) is the story of illegal whaling and destruction of other forms of marine life in the waters of Patagonia. Castellanos Raga's 2005 science-fiction novel *Los hijos de Gaia* (The Children of Gaia) explores the relationship between environmental thought and political systems. And Aridjis's novels *Playa nudista* (1982; Nude Beach), *La leyenda de los soles* (1993; The Legend of the Suns), *¿En quién piensas cuando haces el amor?* (1996; Who Do You Think of When You Make Love) share a common apocalyptic impulse.[4] Jorge Marcone and Priscilla Solís Ybarra also point to Vicente Leñero's *La gota de agua* (1984; A Drop of Water) and Carlos Fuentes's *Cristóbal Nonato* (1987; Christopher Unborn) as examples of Mexican novels related to urban environmental disasters.[5] The emergence of this corpus of novels suggests that it is now possible to speak of the environmental novel as a bona fide subgenre of Latin American fiction, which undoubtedly merits careful analysis itself. As Greg Garrard states, "environmental problems require analysis in cultural as well as scientific terms, because they are the outcome of an interaction between ecological knowledge of nature and its cultural inflection."[6] If the analysis of the environment in Spanish American fiction was once primarily limited to the study of the regional novels of the 1920s and 30s, it is clear that ecocriticism has begun to open the discussion beyond the confines of the telluric novel.

Other topics only briefly touched upon in the current volume that deserve a central place in future ecocritical scholarship on Latin America include the representation of nature in indigenous cultural production, intersections between environmentalism and popular culture, the effect of natural disasters on culture, and the roles of race and class in environmental issues. Social justice has long been a central theme of Latin American literature, and ecocriticism provides an important method of inquiry into links between social and environmental justice. For, as Elizabeth M. DeLoughrey, Renée K. Gosson, and George B. Handley argue "threats to ecology cannot be separated from their social causes."[7]

Similar to what Marisa Pereyra has shown in her analysis of *Waslala*, Barbas Rhoden asserts that "an ecocritical approach to Latin American literature will expose prejudicial power structures and also point to alternatives to these structures, conceived from different sources within society."[8] Ecocritical analysis of Latin American culture also offers insight into the unique perspectives of Latin American societies whose ecosystems are constantly affected by the consumption habits and business decisions of the world's economic powers. As Ursula K. Heise asserts, "the environmentalist ambition is to think globally, but doing so in terms of a single language is inconceivable — even and especially when that language is a hegemonic one."[9] In this sense, ecocritics cannot afford to ignore Latin American cultural production. Its cultural narratives, environmental and political rhetoric, and counter-hegemonic discourses constitute an indispensable contribution to the global discussion of environmentalism.

As Buell has observed, "second-wave ecocriticism has so far concentrated strongly [...] on locating vestiges of nature within cities and/or exposing crimes of eco-injustice against society's marginal groups."[10] Increased attention to Latin America could expand the focus of this second wave to include international crimes of environmental injustice by multinational corporations and industrialized nations against lesser developed countries. Moreover, Dora Ramírez-Dhoore's essay "Dissecting Environmental Racism" is evidence that criticism focused on eco-injustice is also particularly pertinent to U.S. Latina/o literature. Marcone and Solís Ybarra assert that Chicana/o writing, in particular, "firmly plants environmental concerns in a colonial context, past and present."[11] To be sure, ecocritical studies of these often culturally hybridized texts in the context of both Latin American and U.S. cultural and literary traditions will continue to prove fruitful.

According to Patrick Murphy, ecocriticism "remain[s] very much at the beginning. Not being a fad, but a fundamental orientation toward the world and the literature produced by beings in the world."[12] The potential for ecocriticism in Latin American studies is enormous, and given today's pressing environmental concerns, the moment is propitious. Studies focusing on cultural representations of specific bio-regions and their inhabitants (such as Candace Slater's 2002 *Entangled Edens: Visions of the Amazon*), historical peri-

ods, genres or subgenres, cultural discourses, environmental issues, or theoretical variants of ecocriticism would all be worthy projects in contributing
to further understanding of the relationship between human beings and their
environments. If this volume helps advance ecocritical discussions of Latin
American and Latina/o literatures and cultures in any such way, it will have
achieved its goal.

NOTES

1. Buell, *The Future of Environmental Criticism*, 28.
2. Barbas Rhoden, "Greening Central American Literature," 1–17. Joel Thomas
Postema examines the relation between indigenous identity and ecological awareness in
Central American authors Manlio Argueta, Arturo Arias, Miguel Ángel Asturias in addition to Belli and Rossi in his dissertation "Ecological Awareness and Cultural Identity in
Twentieth-Century Central American Narrative."
3. See Rojas Pérez, *La ecocrítica hoy*, 84–93 for analysis of *Canal Zone*.
4. See Binns, *¿Callejón sin salida?: La crisis ecológica en la poesía hispanoamericana*, 144–48.
5. Marcone and Solís Ybarra, "Mexican and Chicana/o Environmental Writing," 102.
6. Garrard, *Ecocriticism*, 14.
7. DeLoughrey, Gosson, and Handley, *Caribbean Literature and the Environment*, 27.
8. Barbas Rhoden, "Greening Central American Literature," 3.
9. Heise, "The Hitchhiker's Guide to Ecocriticism," 513.
10. Buell, *The Future of Environmental Criticism*, 24.
11. Marcone and Solís Ybarra, "Mexican and Chicana/o Environmental Writing," 109.
12. Murphy, foreword to *The ISLE Reader*, xix.

WORKS CITED

Barbas Rhoden, Laura. "Greening Central American Literature." *Interdisciplinary Studies
in Literature and Environment* 12.1 (2005): 1–17.
Binns, Niall. *¿Callejón sin salida?: La crisis ecológica en la poesía hispanoamericana*. Zaragoza:
Prensas Universitarias de Zaragoza, 2004.
Buell, Lawrence. *The Future of Environmental Criticism: Environmental Crisis and Liter-
ary Imagination*. Blackwell Manifestos. Oxford: Blackwell, 2005.
DeLoughrey, Elizabeth M., Gosson, Renée K., and George B. Handley, eds. *Caribbean
Literature and the Environment: Between Nature and Culture*. New World Studies. Char-
lottesville: University Press of Virginia, 2005.
Garrard, Greg. *Ecocriticism*. The New Critical Idiom. London: Routledge, 2004.
Heise, Ursula K. "The Hitchhiker's Guide to Ecocriticism." *PMLA* 121.2 (March 2006):
503–16.
Marcone, Jorge, and Priscilla Solis Ybarra. "Mexican and Chicana/o Environmental Writ-
ing: Unearthing and Inhabiting." In Laird Christensen, Mark C. Long, and Fred Waage,
eds., *Teaching North American Environmental Literature*, 93–111. Options for Teaching.
New York: Modern Language Assoc. of America, 2008.
Murphy, Patrick. Foreword to *The ISLE Reader: Ecocriticism: 1993–2003*, vii–ix. Edited
by Michael P. Branch and Scott Slovic. Athens: University of Georgia Press, 2003.
Postema, Joel Thomas. "Ecological Awareness and Cultural Identity in Twentieth-Century Central American Narrative." Diss. Washington University, 2005.
Rojas Pérez, Walter. *La ecocrítica hoy*. San José, Costa Rica: Aire Moderno, 2004.

About the Contributors

Mark D. Anderson is an assistant professor of Spanish at the University of Georgia, where he teaches Latin American and Trans-Atlantic/Spanish Peninsular literature and culture. His areas of research are Mexican and Brazilian literature and culture, the modern Latin American novel, and contemporary Latin American literature and culture. His articles have been published in journals including *Symposium*, *Hispania*, *Bulletin of Spanish Studies*, and *Revista de Estudios Hispánicos*. In 2008 he received a John W. Kluge Fellowship to carry out research at the Library of Congress for his forthcoming study of narratives of natural disasters in Latin America.

Martín Camps is an assistant professor of Spanish and Latin American literature at the University of the Pacific in Stockton, California. His areas of research are Mexican literature and culture, fiction of the U.S./Mexican border region, and narrative from the Southern Cone. His articles have appeared in journals such as *Con-Textos*, *Ciberletras: Journal of Literary Criticism and Culture*, and *Revista de Literatura Mexicana Contemporánea*. He is the author of *Cruces fronterizos: hacia una narrativa del desierto* (2007) and co-editor of *Acercamientos a la narrativa de Luis Arturo Ramos* (2005). He has also published several books of poetry. He is currently preparing a manuscript on travel narrative and landscape in Argentina and Chile.

Adrian Taylor Kane is an assistant professor of Spanish at Boise State University, where he teaches courses on Hispanic and Latin American literature. His areas of research include the Central American and Mexican narrative, as well as Spanish American avant-garde and postmodern fiction. His publications include articles in *Bulletin of Spanish Studies* and *Istmo: Revista virtual de estudios literarios y culturales centroamericanos*. He is currently researching a book on the Spanish American environmental novel.

Gustavo Llarull is a teaching associate and M.F.A. candidate at the University of Massachusetts, Amherst, where he teaches composition and literature courses. He earned his Ph.D. from the Philosophy Department at the University of California–Riverside, where he also completed graduate work in Hispanic studies. His dissertation, "Narrative Self-Conception, Ethics, and Literature," explores the moral psychology of literary reading, with an emphasis on modern and contemporary Latin American fiction. His current research expands on topics and themes discussed in his dissertation, including the moral-political import of the writings of disappeared writer Rodolfo Walsh, as well as the McOndo and post–McOndo generations (e.g., Héctor Abad FacFacilince, Rodrigo Fresán, David Toscana).

Lizabeth Paravisini-Gebert is a Randolph Distinguished Professor and chair of the Department of Hispanic Studies at Vassar College, where she is a participating faculty member in the Africana studies and Latin American studies programs. She is the author or editor of 20 books, anthologies and critical editions on Latin American and Caribbean literatures and cultures including *The Literature of the Caribbean* (2008) and *Women at Sea: Travel Writing and the Margins of Caribbean Discourse* (2000). Her article "'He of the Trees': Nature, Environment, and Creole Religiosities in Caribbean Literature" appeared in the 2005 anthology *Caribbean Literature and the Environment*, and her book *Endangered Species: Ecology and the Discourse of the Caribbean Nation* is forthcoming.

Marisa Pereyra is an assistant professor and chair of the Foreign Languages and Literatures Department at Immaculata University in Pennsylvania. She teaches Spanish composition, Spanish conversation, as well as Latin American literature and Latin American civilization and culture. She has published several essays about utopian discourses in the narrative of contemporary women writers of the Southern Cone. Her essays have been published in *Confluencia, Hispanic Journal, Chasqui, Latin American Essays — Maclas, and Ciberletras.*

Dora Ramírez-Dhoore, associate chair of the English Department and assistant professor of ethnic American literature at Boise State University, earned her Ph.D. in ethnic literature from the University of Nebraska–Lincoln in 2003. Her work incorporates ideas of nation-building while examining the internalization of socio-political global affects within the Latina/o population. Dora is the author of "The Cyberborderland: Surfing the Web for Xicanidad" (*Chicana/Latina Studies*, 2005) and "Discovering a 'Proper Pedagogy': The Geography of Writing at UTPA" (*Teaching Writing with Latino/a Students*, eds. Cristina Kirklighter et al., 2007).

Traci Roberts-Camps is an assistant professor of Spanish at the University of the Pacific in Stockton, California. Her teaching and research areas are twentieth-century Latin American literature, contemporary Mexican literature, Mexican women novelists, Latin American women film directors, feminist literary criticism, and Chicana literature. She has also taught an interdisciplinary course on ecology in Latin America. She is the author of *Gendered Self-Consciousness in Mexican and Chicana Women Writers*. Her articles have appeared in *Con-textos, Revista de Literatura Mexicana Contemporánea*, and *Literature and Its Times*.

Jonathan Tittler is a professor of Hispanic studies at Rutgers University, Camden, where he has taught courses on ecological criticism and Hispanic eco-fiction at both the undergraduate and graduate levels. He has lectured on literature and the environment at such diverse places as the University of Auckland (New Zealand), the University of East London, Cornell University, Southwest Indiana State University, the Universidade Federal de Minas Gerais (Belo Horizonte, Brazil), and the Universidad Central del Valle (Tuluá, Valle, Colombia). His publications on related topics include articles in *Tabula Rasa, Ixquic*, and *Actas del XV Congreso de la Asociación de Colombianistas*. He is a member of the Sociedad Latinoamericana y Caribeña de Historia Ambiental.

Raymond L. Williams is a professor of Hispanic studies at the University of California, Riverside. He has written 15 books and published numerous articles on modern Latin American fiction. His teaching and research have focused on issues related to modernity, the postmodern, Colombian society and literature, Gabriel García Márquez, Carlos Fuentes, Mario Vargas Llosa, women's writing, ecocritical approaches to Latin American literature, and Mexican fiction. Recent books are *The Columbia Guide to the Latin American Novel* (2007) and *The Twentieth-Century Spanish American Novel* (2003). He is currently researching a book on loss and trauma in modern Latin American narrative.

Index